CONTENTS

T0386092

Focus 1 Workbook walkthrough

UNITS (pp. 4–107)

UNIT 0

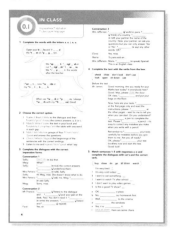

UNITS 1–8

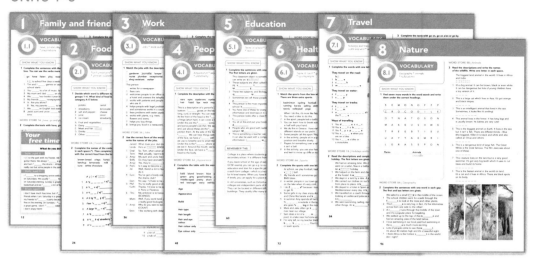

BACK OF THE BOOK (pp. 108–143)

> The VOCABULARY BANK is a topic-based word list including vocabulary from all units. It is followed by exercises which provide more vocabulary practice.

> The GRAMMAR: Train and Try Again section provides more grammar activities for self-study. Students can check their answers in the answer key at the end of the Workbook.

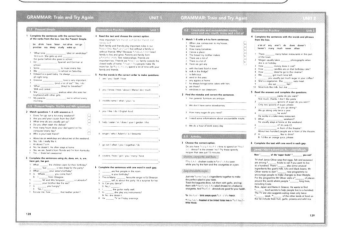

> The WRITING BANK provides a list of the useful phrases from the WRITING FOCUS boxes in the Student's Book.

> The answer keys to the SELF-CHECK and GRAMMAR: Train and Try Again sections support self-study and promote student autonomy.

DON'T MISS

The SHOW WHAT YOU KNOW tasks in the Vocabulary and Grammar lessons serve as a warm-up and revise vocabulary or grammar students should already know.

1 **Decide which word is different to the others in groups 1–4. What kind of food is it? Find the right category A–E below.**

potato	carrot	(salmon)
1 strawberry	lemonade	apple
2 salt and pepper	cheese	milk
3 juice	onion	tea
4 ice cream	strawberry	apple

A Fruit and vegetables: _____
B Dairy: _____
C Meat and fish: _salmon_
D Drinks: _____
E Other: _____

The SHOW WHAT YOU'VE LEARNT tasks in the Vocabulary and Grammar lessons help students to check their progress and be aware of their own learning.

7 **Choose the correct option.**

1 I work _from / on / in_ home, so I don't need to dress smartly.
2 My mum works _with / on / in_ a supermarket but not on a checkout.
3 Kate is an _actor / acting / actress_. Her dream is to go to Hollywood.
4 I love working _with / for / from_ animals. That's why I work at our local zoo.
5 I don't want a badly- _pay / money / paid_ job. I want to be rich!
6 Do you always work _long / hard / team_?
7 My dad is a _lawyer / plumber / mechanic_. People often phone up in the middle of the night because there is water on their kitchen floor.
8 I work eight hours _in / the / a_ day. I start at 7 a.m. and finish at 3 p.m.
9 Do you want a full-time or _part- / short / half-_ time job?
10 I don't want to work outside, so I don't want to be _an accountant / a gardener / a secretary_.

/10

The SHOW THAT YOU'VE CHECKED section in the Writing lessons is a useful checklist that accompanies the final writing task.

Finished? Always check your writing. Can you tick √ everything on this list?

In my email:

- I have started the email with an appropriate greeting, e.g. _Greg, Hi Monica_, etc. ☐
- I have explained the situation. ☐
- I have listed all my requests in a clear and kind way. ☐
- I have mentioned my expectations. ☐
- I have apologised for the whole situation and expressed my thanks for helping me. ☐
- I have used contractions (e.g. _I'm / aren't / that's_). ☐
- I have checked my spelling. ☐
- My text is neat and clear. ☐

The REMEMBER BETTER boxes provide tips on learning, remembering and enriching vocabulary.

To remember the names of containers in which certain products are sold, learn them as chunks (a container and a sample product together), e.g. ~~I've got some chocolate.~~ _I've got a bar of chocolate._

Look in your fridge at home. Complete the sentences about the food you can see in the fridge. Check any new words in a dictionary.

In my fridge, there is: | In my fridge, there are:
1 _a carton of milk_ | 3 _____
2 _____ | 4 _____

The REMEMBER THIS boxes focus on useful language nuances.

College is a place where students go to study after secondary school. It is different from university.

If you leave school at the age of sixteen (after GCSE exams), you can go e.g. to a _college of further education_ and train for a specific job, or you can go to a _sixth-form college_ – which is a two-year preparation for A-level exams. When you have the right number of A levels, you can apply for a place at a university.

In old universities, such as Oxford and Cambridge, colleges are independent parts of the university. They can be located in different (often historic) buildings. They usually offer many different subjects.

The star coding system shows the different levels of difficulty of the activities in the Grammar lessons.

2 ★ **Complete the dialogue with the correct comparative form of the adjectives in brackets.**

Emily: Two boys want to go to the end of school dance with me.
Kirsten: Who?
Emily: Wayne and Theo.
Kirsten: Well, go with Wayne. He's _better-looking_ (good-looking) than Theo. He's ¹_____ (thin) too.
Emily: Well, Theo isn't fat! Anyway, Wayne is ²_____ (boring) than Theo. Theo is ³_____ (funny) than Wayne and he's ⁴_____ (clever).
Kirsten: … so, go with Theo.
Emily: Well … Wayne has a lot of friends. He's ⁵_____ (sociable) than Theo. Theo is ⁶_____ (shy). Maybe it's better to go to the dance with Wayne, but it's a difficult decision.
Kirsten: Yes, but it's less difficult than deciding what to wear. That's impossible!

3 ★ ★ **Complete the sentences with the correct forms of the adjectives in capitals.**

My mum is _older_ than my dad but the _oldest_ person in our family is my dad's grandmother. She's 98. **OLD**

1 Harry isn't shy at all – he's the _____ boy in our class. In fact, he's _____ than our teachers! **CONFIDENT**
2 I'm not _____ than my mum. She's the _____ person in the house. **SHORT**
3 Who is the _____ person in my family? My baby sister. My brother Tom is _____ than me – he's ten and I'm twelve years old. **YOUNG**
4 I'd like to be _____ than I am but I'll never be the _____ person in my class. Seven people play sports for school teams. **FIT**
5 Ela's got _____ hair than me. She's got the _____ hair in our class. Some of the boys call her 'Rapunzel' but she doesn't mind. **LONG**

The SPEAKING BANK lists the key phrases from the lesson.

Ordering food

Are you ready to order? _____

I'd like a/an/some … / Can I have a/an/some … _____

What would you like to drink? _____

Large or small? _____

Anything else? _____

No, thanks. That's it. _____

How much is it? _____

It's … (+ _price_) _____

Here you are. _____

Enjoy your meal. _____

Speaking tasks in the exam format help students prepare for their exams.

IN CLASS

0.1

Imperatives • alphabet
• classroom language

1 Complete the words with the letters a, e, i, o, u.

Open your b_o_ _o_ks and ¹r __ __ d the ²t __ xt on ³p __ g __ ten.

We ⁴sp __ __ k ⁵__ ngl __ sh in our ⁶__ ngl __ sh ⁷l __ ss __ ns. We ⁸r __ p __ __ t the words after the teacher.

I ⁹wr __ t __ new ¹⁰w __ rds in my ¹¹n __ t __ b __ __ k.

When we ¹²w __ rk in ¹³p __ __ rs, I always ¹⁴w __ rk with my ¹⁵fr __ __ nd, David.

2 Choose the correct option.

1 ᵃ*Listen / Read / Write* to the dialogue and then ᵇ*match / put / choose* the correct answers: a, b or c.

2 ᵃ*Read / Write / Listen* the text in your book and ᵇ*underline / complete / tick* the table with one word in each gap.

3 ᵃ*Ask / Tell / Work* in groups of four. ᵇ*Think / Ask / Speak* and answer the questions.

4 *Check / Match / Repeat* the beginnings of the sentences with the correct endings.

5 Listen to me and *repeat / tick / speak* what I say.

3 Complete the dialogues with the correct imperative forms.

Conversation 1
Sally: *Don't do* (✗ do) that.
Meg: What?
Sally: ¹_____ (✗ tick) the correct answers. ²_____ (✓ underline) them.
Mrs Peters: ³_____ (✗ talk), Sally.
Sally: It's Meg, miss. She doesn't know what to do.
Mrs Peters: ⁴_____ (✓ ask) me, Meg. ⁵_____ (✗ ask) Sally.
Meg: Sorry, miss.

Conversation 2
Mr Francis: ¹_____ (✓ listen) to the dialogue and … ²_____ (✓ put) your pen on the desk, Paul. You don't need it. ³_____ (✗ write) the answers. ⁴_____ (✓ listen) and ⁵_____ (✓ repeat).
Paul: Yes, sir.

Conversation 3
Mrs Jefferson: ¹_____ (✓ work) in pairs. ²_____ (✓ think) of a country. ³_____ (✗ tell) your partner the name of the country. Now, your partner can ask you questions but you can only answer 'Yes' or 'No'. ⁴_____ (✗ say) any other words. OK?
Class: Yes, miss.
Maria: *Tu pais está en …*
Mrs Jefferson: Maria, ⁵_____ (✗ speak) Spanish. This is an English class.

4 Complete the text with the verbs from the box.

check ~~close~~ don't look don't use
look open sit down use

Before the test …
Mr Jones: Good morning. Are you ready for your Maths test today? Is everybody here? Good. Max, please *close* the door. OK class, ¹_____ and put your bags on the floor.

Now, here are your tests. ²_____ at the first page only and read the instructions, please. ³_____ at the other pages – wait for me to tell you when you can start. Do you understand? ⁴_____ a pen to complete the test. Please ⁵_____ a pencil – it's easy to correct any mistakes you make when you write with a pencil.

Remember to ⁶_____ your tests carefully for mistakes before you give them to me. Are you all ready? OK, please ⁷_____ your test booklets now and start the test. Good luck!

5 Match sentences 1–5 with responses a–e and complete the dialogues with *Let's* and the correct verb.

buy close do go ~~sit down~~ watch

I'm very tired. _f_
1 It's very cold today! __
2 I want to eat something. __
3 I want to watch TV after school. __
4 I don't want to play video games. __
5 Is this a good TV show? __

a OK. _____ a pizza.
b No, _____ our homework first.
c Well, _____ to the cinema.
d _____ the windows.
e Yes, it is. _____ it.
f *Let's sit down*. Here are some chairs.

I'M FROM ...

0.2

To be • subject pronouns • numbers • countries and nationalities • age

1 Complete the email. Write the countries or nationalities.

Hi Emma,

I'm in Amsterdam. It's great here. I'm with eight other people. Lucia is *Brazilian* (Brazil), Aslan is ¹_____ (Turkey), Sebastian is ²_____ (France), Elof is from ³_____ (Swedish), Thu is ⁴_____ (Vietnam), Kostas is from ⁵_____ (Greek), Gabor is ⁶_____ (Hungary) and Hiroko is ⁷_____ (Japan). And, of course, I'm ⁸_____ (Ireland)! We're a really multicultural group.

More later,
Caitlin

2 Complete the email. Write the numbers in words.

Attachment: jpeg picture, Mr and Mrs De Jong

Hi Emma,

Thanks for the email. The people here are all from *fifteen* (15) to ¹_____ (18) years old. There are three teachers with us. One is a student teacher. He's ²_____ (22) and two other teachers are older: Mr Blake is ³_____ (38) – I think – and Mrs Kirk is ⁴_____ (51). She's great! Mr Blake is here with his two children. They are ⁵_____ (12) and ⁶_____ (5). They're nice. Finally, the hotel managers are a man and a woman, Mr and Mrs De Jong. He's ⁷_____ (73) and she is ⁸_____ (69). They're lovely. They give us food and drink all the time! ☺

See you soon,
Lindsey

3 Use the prompts to write dialogues.

Conversation 1

Adrian: That boy's name is Andrew.
Helen: How old / he? *How old is he?*
Adrian: He / sixteen. ª_____
Helen: Where / from? ᵇ_____
Adrian: He / the USA ᶜ_____

Conversation 2

Sue: Henri and Claudia / French teachers. ª_____
Leo: How old / they? ᵇ_____
Sue: I don't know!
Leo: they / from Paris? ᶜ_____
Sue: No / not. ᵈ_____ from / Lille ᵉ_____

Conversation 3

Francesca: Carla and I / from Spain. ª_____
Simon: Really? you / from Madrid? ᵇ_____
Francesca: No / not. ᶜ_____ from / Barcelona ᵈ_____
Simon: How old / you? ᵉ_____
Francesca: I / eighteen and Carla / seventeen. ᶠ_____

4 Complete the crossword with the nationalities.

Across
2 Spain
4 Greece
6 Australia
9 Switzerland
10 France

Down
1 Portugal
3 Poland
4 Germany
5 Jamaica
7 Italy
8 The Czech Republic

5 Complete the sentences about the famous sportspeople with the nationalities from the crossword in Exercise 4.

Nick Kyrgios is *Australian*.
1 Robert Lewandowski is _____ .
2 Roger Federer is _____ .
3 Usain Bolt is _____ .
4 Garbiñe Muguruza is _____ .
5 Cristiano Ronaldo is _____ .
6 Stefanos Tsitsipas is _____ .
7 Zinédine Zidane is _____ .
8 Sebastian Vettel is _____ .
9 Gianluigi Buffon is _____ .
10 Petra Kvitová is _____ .

FAVOURITES

0.3

Demonstrative pronouns
• plural nouns • colours
• adjectives • objects

1 Correct the sentences. Write the opposites of the underlined adjectives. The first letters are given.

My brother is very old. He's only nine years old. **y**_oung_

1 Those new houses are really <u>beautiful</u>. I don't like them. **u**_____
2 My computer is very <u>fast</u>. I need a different one. **s**_____
3 These headphones are <u>fantastic</u>. I can't hear the music at all. **t**_____
4 Our school is quite <u>big</u>. There are only 120 students. **s**_____
5 This is my <u>old</u> watch. I think it's beautiful. **n**_____

2 Complete the names of the colours. The first letters are given.

b_lue_ sky
1 **o**_____ carrot
2 **p**_____ or **r**_____ roses
3 **b**_____ chocolate
4 **b**_____ sky at night

5 **y**_____ banana
6 **w**_____ snow
7 **g**_____ hair when you get old!
8 **g**_____ or **p**_____ grapes

3 Complete the sentences with the words from the box.

beanbag ~~comic~~ headphones photos skateboard sunglasses T-shirt watch

I love this _comic_. There are some great stories in it.
1 Look at these _____ . You're in some of them.
2 I don't know which _____ is good for the concert tonight. I like this black one but it's a bit small.
3 You can sit here on this big _____ .
4 I use _____ when I watch TV. My parents talk very loudly all the time and I can't hear what people say.
5 This is my _____ . It's really fast. It's my favourite sports piece of equipment.
6 You don't look cool with those _____ on at night. You look stupid and you can't see!
7 That's strange. My _____ says 08.50 but my computer says it's 09.20.

4 Choose the correct words a–f. Write plural forms of the words in brackets.

Conversation 1

Emily: Who are ª _that / those_ _children_ (child)?
Amanda: Where?
Emily: Over there.
Amanda: I think they're from St Paul's School. And
ᵇ _that / those_ four ¹_____ (man) and
²_____ (woman) with them are their
teachers.

Conversation 2

Andy: Come in. ᶜ _This / That_ is my bedroom.
Frank: Cool. I like ᵈ _this / these_ three
³_____ (poster). Oh, wow! And all ᵉ _these / this_ ⁴_____ (comic) and ⁵_____ (photo). And what is ᶠ _that / those_?
Andy: It's a beanbag. Sit down!

Conversation 3

Tom: What's the time?
Melissa: I'm not sure. My two ⁶_____ (watch) and my phone all say different times!

5 Look at the picture and complete the text with the words from the box. There are four extra words.

big comics fantastic it's new photo posters
that that's these they're ~~this~~ those young

Hi. My name's Jake. I'm a university student and _this_ is my room. ¹_____ a very nice room. ²_____ are my books over there. ³_____ for all my subjects. My computer is on the desk. The computer isn't ⁴_____ – it's six years old, but it's a ⁵_____ computer! My pens and ⁶_____ notebooks are on the desk, and some great ⁷_____ are on the wall. Look outside the window – ⁸_____ my bike. Oh, and ⁹_____ are my headphones!

MY FAMILY

0.4

Possessive adjectives
• possessive 's • family

1 Look at the underlined words. Write the correct family members. One underlined word is correct.

My family

My <u>mum</u>'s name is John. He's thirty-eight. He's got one ¹<u>brother</u>. Her name is Lisa. She's got one child – a ²<u>son</u> called Julia. Julia is three years old. She's very funny. Lisa's ³<u>wife's</u> name is Tony. He's forty-two years old. I like him. He's my favourite ⁴<u>aunt</u> and Julia is my favourite ⁵<u>cousin</u>.

I've got one ⁶<u>sister</u>. His name is Luke. He's sixteen. That's my family. Oh … wait a minute! My mum's mum – my ⁷<u>grandfather</u>. Her name is Emily. She's eighty-three years old. She makes great chocolate muffins.

<u>dad</u>

1 _____   4 _____
2 _____   5 _____
3 _____   6 _____
                  7 _____

2 Choose the correct option in the dialogue between Walter and Sonia.

W: Hi. ¹*I'm / My* name's Walter. Where are ²*you / your* from?
S: Hi. ³*I'm / My* Sonia. I'm from Canada.
W: Great. Are ⁴*you / your* parents Canadian?
S: No, ⁵*they / their* aren't. My dad is Polish. ⁶*He's / His* name is Radek. My mum is Brazilian. ⁷*She's / Her* name is Carla.
W: Wow. So ⁸*your / you're* half Brazilian and half Polish!
S: Well, not exactly. My dad's parents are Polish. ⁹*They're / Their* from Warsaw. My mum's dad is Brazilian but my mum's mum isn't. ¹⁰*She's / Her* from Chile! But, ¹¹*we're / our* very Canadian now. ¹²*We / Our* like hockey and ¹³*we're / our* favourite food is pancakes with maple syrup!

3 Complete gaps *a* with the correct question words.

A: ª<u>*What*</u> is your ᵇ<u>*dad's*</u> (dad) name?
B: It's James.
1 A: ª_____ is your ᵇ_____ (mum) phone?
   B: I think it's in the car.
2 A: ª_____ are those ᵇ_____ (boys) names?
   B: William and Neil.
3 A: ª_____ is your ᵇ_____ (sister) favourite singer?
   B: I don't know. She likes lots of terrible singers!
4 A: ª_____ are your ᵇ_____ (parents) photos?
   B: They're in this box. Do you want to look at them?
5 A: ª_____ is ᵇ_____ (Steve) new friend?
   B: A girl called Debbie. She doesn't go to our school.

4 Complete gaps *b* in Exercise 3. Use the correct possessive form of the words in brackets.

5 Think of the members of your family you like the most. Write their names, ages and relationship to you. Then complete the sentences.

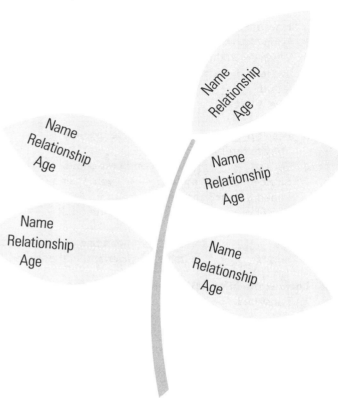

Name
Relationship
Age

Name
Relationship
Age

Name
Relationship
Age

Name
Relationship
Age

Name
Relationship
Age

I'm _____ and these are the members of my family.
_____ is _____ old.
He/She is my _____ .
_____ is _____ old.
He/She is my _____ .
_____ is _____ old.
He/She is my _____ .
_____ is _____ old.
He/She is my _____ .
_____ is _____ old.
He/She is my _____ .
I love them a lot.

6 Put the words in the correct order to make questions. Then write answers that are true for you.

name / your / is / mum's / what
What is your mum's name? Her name's Ewa.
1 names / are / cousins' / what / your
  _____
2 is / best friend / who / your
  _____
3 your / band / what / favourite / is
  _____
4 what / favourite / your / is / sport
  _____
5 colour / your / are / what / dad's eyes
  _____

7

ABILITIES

0.5

Can/can't • common verbs

1 Complete the sentences with the correct verbs. The first letters are given.

How many languages do you **s**_peak_?

1 I don't know how to **u**_____ my new phone.

2 When I'm in the shower, I always **s**_____ old songs.

3 We're in a disco. The music is great. Come on, let's **d**_____ .

4 I want to **c**_____ Chinese food for dinner but I don't know how.

5 I can't **p**_____ . Look at these pictures. They're terrible.

6 Let's **p**_____ my new computer game.

7 Sit down and let me **d**_____ you. Wait a minute. I need a pencil and paper.

8 The film starts in five minutes. Come on. **R**_____ ! I don't want to be late.

9 I **ᵃs**_____ in the Mediterranean Sea in the summer and **ᵇs**_____ in Italy or Switzerland in the winter.

2 Look at the information and complete the questions and answers.

	paint	cook	dance
You	√	✗	✗
Your sister	✗	✗	√
Your parents	✗	√	√

you / paint? *Can you paint* ?
           Yes, I can.

1 you / cook? ᵃ_____?
           ᵇ_____.

2 What / your sister / do? ᵃ_____?
  She / dance ᵇ_____.

3 your sister / cook? ᵃ_____?
           ᵇ_____.

4 your parents / cook? ᵃ_____?
           ᵇ_____.

5 your parents / paint? ᵃ_____?
           ᵇ_____.

3 Use information from Exercise 2 and make full sentences. Use *can* or *can't* and the linkers *and* or *but*.

you / paint / you / cook.
You can paint but you can't cook.

1 Your sister / dance / she / cook.
_____

2 Your parents / cook / they / dance.
_____

3 Your parents / cook / they / paint.
_____

4 Your parents / dance / you / dance.
_____

5 Your parents and your sister / dance / they / paint.
_____

6 Your sister / paint / she / cook
_____

4 Choose the correct option.

Grandpa Paolo is 90, but he *can / can't* do a lot of things! He **¹***can / can't* use a mobile phone – look at the messages I have from him! His legs are strong and he **²***can / can't* run, but he **³***can / can't* run Wings for Life. He can draw **⁴***and / but* he can paint – he's a very good artist! He **⁵***can / can't* speak Italian, French and German, but he **⁶***can / can't* speak English, so he **⁷***can / can't* help me with my English homework ☹ He's old, **⁸***and / but* he still feels young! ☺

5 Match the verbs with the actions. Then write the questions and the answers that are true for you. Use *can* or *can't*.

(cook   dance   play   sing   speak   swim)

(across the Atlantic   Adele's songs   Cyberpunk
  Esperanto   spaghetti   the waltz)

Can you cook spaghetti ?
Yes, I can.

1 _____?
  _____.

2 _____?
  _____.

3 _____?
  _____.

4 _____?
  _____.

5 _____?
  _____.

0.6

Prepositions • *there is/there are*
• *rooms and furniture*

1 Complete the words with one letter in each space.

- You sit on these: **c**h a i r, ¹a _ _ _ _ _ _ _ r, ²s _ _ a
- You wash (things) in these: ³b _ _ h, ⁴s _ _ k,
  ⁵d _ _ _ _ _ _ _ _ r
- Food goes in here: ⁶f _ _ _ _ e, ⁷c _ _ _ _ r
- This gives light or lets light into the room: ⁸l _ _ p,
  ⁹w _ _ _ _ w
- You walk on this: ¹⁰c _ _ _ _ t
- You put things on or in these: ¹¹d _ _ k, ¹²t _ _ _ e,
  ¹³w _ _ _ _ _ _ _ e
- You sleep on this: ¹⁴b _ d
- There are four of these in a room: ¹⁵w _ _ _ s
- You put these up and look at them: ¹⁶p _ _ _ _ _ _ s

2 Look at the picture and choose the correct prepositions.

1 The window is *in front of / between / opposite*
   two posters.
2 There are some photos *above / under / behind*
   the window.
3 There is a desk *above / behind / in front of* the window.
4 The computer is *on / above / in* the desk.
5 There's a bin *next to / behind / under* the desk.
6 There's a lamp *between / next to / opposite* the computer.
7 There is some paper *on / in / under* the bin.
8 The window is *opposite / next to / between* the door.

3 Complete the dialogue between Sally and Kirsty with *there is, there are, is there, are there, there isn't* **or** *there aren't.*

S: It's a nice flat. Only £80 a week.
K: I'm not sure. *Is there* a bath?
S: Yes, ¹_____ and ²_____ a shower.
K: What about the living room? ³_____
   an armchair or a sofa?
S: Yes. ⁴_____ two nice armchairs and a big sofa.
K: OK, what about the kitchen. ⁵_____
   a dishwasher?
S: No, ⁶_____ , I'm afraid, but ⁷_____
   a table. It's a big room.
K: ⁸_____ any chairs?
S: No, ⁹_____ , but we can ask the owner
   to give us two or three.
K: Can I think about it?
S: OK. Phone me anytime.

4 Look at the picture of the upside-down house below and choose the correct prepositions in the text.

Look! He's ¹*in / on* a house and it's upside down! A carpet
is ²*opposite / on* the floor. A table is ³*between / in front of*
the sofa. The window is ⁴*behind / above* the sofa.
⁵*In front of / Next to* the window is a lamp. I can see
another table and two chairs. The table is ⁶*in / between* the
chairs. The black chair is ⁷*opposite / behind* the white chair.
The man is ⁸*under / behind* one of the chairs. The chair is
⁹*between / above* him. It's crazy!

5 Look at the picture again and write the questions and answers.

armchair → *Is there an armchair* ? *No, there isn't* .
1 fridge → _____ ? _____ .
2 sink → _____ ? _____ .
3 beds → _____ ? _____ .
4 tables → _____ ? _____ .
5 lamp → _____ ? _____ .
6 woman → _____ ? _____ .

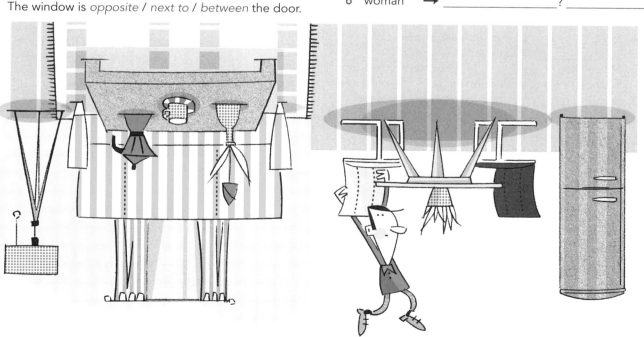

GADGETS

0.7

Have got • gadgets

1 Complete the table with the words from the box or with –. Two words are used in both lists.

(camera   console   phone   player   reader   stick)

Gadgets I've got and gadgets I want!

Have got		Want	
a digital *camera*		a laptop	–
1 a CD		5 a games	
2 an e-book		6 an MP3	
3 a memory	(lots!)	7 a tablet	
4 a mobile	(old)	8 a smart	

2 Complete the dialogue between Graham and Jason with the correct form of *have got*.

G: Hi, Jason. What's this? A gadget dream list?

J: Hi, Graham. Yes.

G: What kind of phone *have you got* (you/have) at the moment?

J: Er … I'm not sure. It's old. That's why I want a smartphone.

G: ¹_____ (My sister/have) one. She loves it.

J: ²_____ (you/have) a smartphone?

G: ³_____ (✗). I hate mobile phones.
⁴_____ (I/have) a games console. It's cool. And an MP3 player for music. How about your e-book reader? How many books ⁵_____ (you/have)?

J: Hundreds but ⁶_____ (it/have) a lot on it when you buy it. It's good for holidays.

G: Yes, ⁷_____ (my dad/have) one. He takes it everywhere.

J: ⁸_____ (your mum/have) one?

G: ⁹_____ (✗). She likes real books.

J: Me too but ¹⁰_____ (I/not/have) space for books and my camera when I travel.

G: Yes, ¹¹_____ (you/have) a great camera.
¹²_____ (you/have) a photo website?

J: ¹³_____ (✓). Do you want to see it?

G: Not now. ¹⁴_____ (I/not/have) time. Later.

J: OK. See you.

3 Find these gadgets in the wordsearch box. The words can be in any direction.

(CD player   digital camera   e-book reader
games console   laptop   memory stick
mobile phone   MP3 player   smart phone   tablet)

A	E	L	O	S	N	O	C	S	E	M	A	G	M
T	R	V	C	V	F	F	C	K	U	R	Y	E	M
Y	C	E	D	X	E	G	M	E	N	M	R	O
L	I	U	M	C	P	R	D	D	A	O	T	E	B
E	Q	O	F	A	Y	L	A	A	R	I	A	Y	I
M	N	W	H	Q	C	E	A	Y	J	X	B	A	L
F	A	O	Y	H	R	L	S	Y	D	H	L	L	E
G	B	Z	H	K	K	T	A	D	E	X	E	P	P
T	H	H	O	P	I	K	X	T	I	R	T	3	H
G	H	O	R	C	T	R	A	G	I	G	V	P	O
W	B	O	K	R	N	R	P	A	M	G	X	M	N
E	P	O	T	P	A	L	A	L	G	Q	I	J	E
Z	I	V	V	V	L	Q	E	M	U	X	N	D	B
P	Z	X	I	V	R	C	C	S	S	R	J	O	P

4 Look at the picture below and complete the dialogue with the words from the box.

(can   can't   have got   hasn't got   haven't got
that   there are   ~~there is~~   these   this   those)

Tonight there is a party at Stan's house …

Mel: Hi, Stan. Happy birthday!

Stan: Thanks, Mel. Hey, everyone, ¹_____ is Mel.

Mel: Er, hi.

Stan: ²_____ is Max over there with the games console and ³_____ are my games. He loves video games.

Mel: Oh, I see. And who are ⁴_____ people on the sofa?

Stan: Oh, they're my cousins – Jeff and Tina. They ⁵_____ new smartphones.

Mel: And who is the girl with the digital camera?

Stan: That's Amanda. She likes photography, but she ⁶_____ a camera. It's my camera.

Mel: And what about the girl with the tablet?

Stan: That's my friend Carly. She ⁷_____ take videos on the tablet.

Mel: Cool. … Well, it's nice to see you Stan, but I ⁸_____ stay.

Stan: Oh, please stay! ⁹_____ nice snacks in the kitchen.

Mel: Sorry, I ¹⁰_____ time. See you later.

1 Write the days of the week.

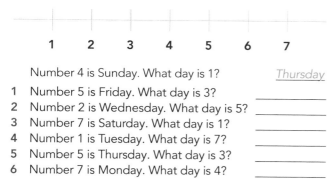

	1	2	3	4	5	6	7

Number 4 is Sunday. What day is 1?   *Thursday*

1 Number 5 is Friday. What day is 3? _____
2 Number 2 is Wednesday. What day is 5? _____
3 Number 7 is Saturday. What day is 1? _____
4 Number 1 is Tuesday. What day is 7? _____
5 Number 5 is Thursday. What day is 3? _____
6 Number 7 is Monday. What day is 4? _____

2 Write the times and dates in words.

7.30 4/12
It's half past seven on the fourth of December.
9.15 5/3
1 It's ᵃ_____ on the ᵇ_____ of ᶜ_____ .
11.45 7/7
2 It's ᵃ_____ on the ᵇ_____ of ᶜ_____ .
10.25 15/11
3 It's ᵃ_____ on the ᵇ_____ of ᶜ_____ .
8.35 21/6
4 It's ᵃ_____ on the ᵇ_____ of ᶜ_____ .
6.10 30/1
5 It's ᵃ_____ on the ᵇ_____ of ᶜ_____ .
4.50 22/4
6 It's ᵃ_____ on the ᵇ_____ of ᶜ_____ .

3 Complete the dialogue between Juan and Klaudia with one word in each gap. The first letters are given.

J: When's your birthday?
K: In August.
J: August? Is that the **t**_enth_ (10th) month? The one after
   ¹**S**_____ ?
K: No, it's the ²**e**_____ (8th) month. It's in the
   ³**s**_____ holidays.
J: Oh yes. I always make that mistake. So, what is the tenth month?
K: ⁴**O**_____ . It's a great month. I love the
   ⁵**a**_____ when the trees are brown and orange.
J: Yes, but after that it is the ⁶**w**_____ when it is cold and dark.
K: There are lots of nice days at that time of year.
   Christmas Day on the ⁷**t**_____-**f**_____ (25th)
   of ⁸**D**_____ , New Year's Eve on the
   ⁹**t**_____-**f**_____ (31st). Then we get a holiday
   in ¹⁰**F**_____ , the ¹¹**s**_____ (2th) month, and we
   can go skiing.
J: My favourite time of year is the ¹²**s**_____ when it
   isn't very hot but the sun comes out and everything
   wakes up after the cold weather. And my birthday is
   on the ¹³**s**_____ (6th) of May!
K: Really? My birthday is in May too. On the
   ¹⁴**t**_____ (12th). We're both Taurus – the bull.
   That's why we've got similar personalities.

4 Complete the sentences with the names of the months and the seasons.

Germany and New Zealand have opposite seasons.
In *December, January and February* when it is *summer*
in New Zealand, it is winter in Germany.
¹_____ , ²_____ and ³_____
are the ⁴_____ months in New Zealand, but it's
time for spring in Germany then.
June, July and August are the months for ⁵_____
holidays in Germany, but it's very cold then in New
Zealand because it's ⁶_____ – there is snow
and people can ski in the mountains!
After a cold winter, New Zealand is ready for
⁷_____ in the months of ⁸_____ ,
⁹_____ and ¹⁰_____ – but German
students say 'hello' to the autumn and a new school year
then!

5 Write the date of the special days.

20/3 International Day of Happiness
      the twentieth of March
1 21/4 British National Tea Day
        _____
2 24/6 International Fairy Day
        _____
3 7/7   World Chocolate Day
        _____
4 8/8   World Cat Day
        _____
5 25/10 World Pasta Day
        _____
6 10/12 International Human Rights Day
        _____

6 Write the years in words.

1990 *nineteen ninety*
1 1999 _____
2 2000 _____
3 2002 _____
4 2019 _____
5 2021 _____

INTERNATIONAL DAY OF HAPPINESS

HAPPY

20th MARCH

Family and friends

VOCABULARY

1.1

have, go and *play* • collocations
• prepositions

SHOW WHAT YOU KNOW

1 Complete the sentences with the verbs from the box. You can use the verbs more than once.

(go   have   listen   play   read   watch)

I *go* to school five days a week.
1 Tim and I _____ games on our phones before school starts.
2 You _____ to a lot of music. Is this a good CD?
3 My mum and dad _____ an old film every Friday.
4 We _____ four books a year in English.
5 My friends _____ newspapers on their computers.
6 **A:** Are you alone?
   B: Yes, my parents _____ to work on Saturdays.
7 We _____ an English test every Monday morning.
8 Jack's aunt and uncle _____ to the radio all the time.

WORD STORE 1A | *have, go* and *play*

2 Complete the texts with *have*, *go* or *play*.

Your free time

What do you do?

Nikki, aged 16

I *go* to the park with my friends. We ¹_____ the guitar there. We always ²_____ a good time. Mick and Sam ³_____ the drums – African drums. They're really cool but some people in the park don't like them!

Molly, aged 16

I ⁴_____ to a shopping centre with my friends on Saturdays. We usually ⁵_____ to the cinema on Saturday evening. Sunday is great! We ⁶_____ basketball and we ⁷_____ a lot of fun together!

Bruce, aged 17

I don't have much free time, but I ⁸_____ out with friends when I can. Saturday is a good day for one of my friends to ⁹_____ a party because I'm usually free in the evening. On Sundays, I ¹⁰_____ chess. It's a great game. I don't ¹¹_____ video games because I don't enjoy them!

3 Complete the sentences with the correct form of *have*, *go* or *play* and the words from the box.

(chess   cinema   drums   fun   good time   ~~guitar~~
out   party   piano   shopping centre   sports
video games)

I love rock music and I want to be in a band, but I can't ᵃ*play* the ᵇ*guitar* because I'm a bad musician!
1 My friends and I always ᵃ_____ ᵇ_____ when we go out together.
2 I ᵃ_____ a ᵇ_____ with my family when we visit another country.
3 My brother wants to ᵃ_____ ᵇ_____ like football with me and my friends, but he's only 5 years old and we're 14!
4 Do you remember who ᵃ_____ the ᵇ_____ in the Rolling Stones? Is it Keith Richards?
5 Mick loves classical music. He can ᵃ_____ the ᵇ_____ really well because he goes to lessons at the local music school.
6 I sometimes ᵃ_____ ᵇ_____ with my grandfather but I never win. He always takes my queen quickly!
7 I always ᵃ_____ to a ᵇ_____ on Saturday. I love to look at the latest fashions even if I don't buy anything.
8 It's my friend's birthday on Saturday but I can't ᵃ_____ to her ᵇ_____ because it's my mum's birthday on the same day.
9 Lisa and Mark ᵃ_____ to the ᵇ_____ every Friday. They love watching films together.
10 Where do you usually meet when you ᵃ_____ ᵇ_____ with your friends?
11 My brothers ᵃ_____ ᵇ_____ every evening. They sit in front of the computer for hours!
12 Alice has just finished university and she wants to ᵃ_____ a ᵇ_____ to celebrate.

WORD STORE 1B | Collocations

4 Choose the correct verb.

Free time survey

How do you spend your free time?

1	read / watch / visit **books**	a lot
2	spend / visit / write **friends**	a lot
3	read / watch / write **films**	sometimes
4	watch / write / read **magazines**	sometimes
5	read / spend / watch **TV / the telly**	a lot
6	visit / spend / watch **time alone**	sometimes
7	watch / write / visit **videos**	never
8	spend / watch / read **things on the Internet**	a lot

To remember verb-noun collocations better, think of more examples from your own life.

Complete the collocations and write sentences that are true for you.

I read   *books*.
          things on the Internet.
          _____
          _____

I watch   *videos*.
          Quentin Tarantino films.
          _____
          _____

I go to   *the park*.
          the cinema.
          _____
          _____

I have   *fun with my friends*.
          a party on Saturday.
          _____
          _____

WORD STORE 1C | Prepositions

5 Choose the correct option.

Fehmi: Hi Jean. Thanks for agreeing to answer my questions for my English project. So, tell me about your free time.

Jean: Well, after school, I spend time **¹**at / in / on my room. I do my homework and listen **²**at / with / to music. Then I eat something and watch TV.

Fehmi: And at the weekend?

Jean: On Saturdays, I spend time **³**for / with / at my friends. We do lots of different things together. Sometimes we go **⁴**about / at / for a walk in the park – the park in our town is very nice. Or we go to a café and we talk **⁵**about / on / for films or sport. I never spend time **⁶**in / to / at home on Saturdays! On Sundays, I spend my time **⁷**in / at / with my grandparents. Oh, and I study English! That's it, I think.

Fehmi: OK. Thanks.

We sometimes follow *go to* with *a*, sometimes with *the* and sometimes with no article. That's why it is a good idea to remember phrases and chunks of language rather than single words, e.g.

	a	party/café/restaurant
go to	**the**	cinema/theatre/gym/zoo
	Ø	school/work/bed

6 Read REMEMBER THIS. Complete the text with *a*, *the* or Ø.

My week

I'm 17 and from Monday to Friday I go to Ø school. After school, I spend time at **¹**___ home because I have homework. On Fridays, I'm free! Sometimes, I go to **²**___ party, sometimes my friends and I go to **³**___ cinema. We always have **⁴**___ fun on Fridays! On Saturdays, I do lots of different things. Sometimes, I go for **⁵**___ walk with my friends. We go to **⁶**___ park or we go to a café for **⁷**___ coffee. We talk about **⁸**___ sport, films and books. On Sundays, I meet my best friend at his house. We play **⁹**___ video games. He has a guitar and drums. He plays **¹⁰**___ guitar and I play **¹¹**___ drums. It's great! And noisy! We have **¹²**___ really good time together!

7 Choose the correct answers A–C.

1 My sister and I __ films together every weekend.
   A play   B watch   C have

2 My brother and his friends __ party every week.
   A go to a   B go to the   C go to

3 My mum and dad always go to __ on Sunday morning.
   A shopping   B the park   C out

4 See you later. Have a __ .
   A fun   B party   C good time

5 Can you play the __ ?
   A piano   B chess   C sports

6 I go out __ my friends a lot.
   A for   B to   C with

7 We often talk __ books when we meet.
   A about   B with   C to

8 It's Saturday! We can have __ .
   A party   B fun   C good time

9 You can't __ out this evening. You have homework to do.
   A have   B go   C play

10 Steve isn't here. He and his girlfriend always go __ a walk on Saturday afternoon.
   A for   B to   C in

/10

13

GRAMMAR

1.2

Present Simple

SHOW WHAT YOU KNOW

1 Complete the sentences with the verbs from the box. There are three extra verbs.

> drink   go   have   listen   lives
> loves   plays   reads   ~~watch~~   writes

I _watch_ a lot of films. I love them.
1 My parents don't _____ coffee. They don't like it.
2 My friends and I _____ to the park on Saturdays.
3 Kelly _____ a blog every day. It's always very interesting.
4 My dad _____ a newspaper every day. He loves politics.
5 Andy _____ the guitar. He wants to be in a band.
6 My mum _____ cats. She thinks they are beautiful.

2 ★ Complete Text B with the correct form of the verbs in Text A.

> **A**
> ... Finally, write a short paragraph about yourself so other members of the site can find out a little about you.
>
> My name is Carole. I live in Newcastle. I have a cat and a dog. I go to Bridge Street School. In my free time, I play sports and I watch films. I like books and I read a lot. Sometimes, I listen to music but I don't play video games. I don't like video games – but I love playing chess!
>
> 11:23

> **B**
> ### OUR NEW MEMBERS
>
>
>
> **This is Carole.**
> Her name is Carole. She _lives_ in Newcastle. She ¹_____ a cat and a dog. She ²_____ to Bridge Street School. In her free time, she ³_____ sports and she ⁴_____ films.
> She ⁵_____ books and she ⁶_____ a lot. Sometimes, she ⁷_____ to music but she ⁸_____ video games. She ⁹_____ video games – but she ¹⁰_____ playing chess!
>
> Click here to send a message to Carole.

3 ★ ★ Complete the dialogues with the correct positive (+) or negative (–) form of the verb in capitals.

PLAY

Heather: There's Mark. He's in a band. He _plays_ (+) the guitar.
Lin: He _doesn't play_ (–) the guitar. He _plays_ (+) the drums.
Heather: Oh, yes. That's right.

Conversation 1   LISTEN

Sian: I love music. Not pop music. I ¹_____ (–) to pop music. I hate it. I ²_____ (+) to Mozart or Beethoven.
Kelly: My mum ³_____ (+) to Mozart when she wants to relax. I think that kind of music is boring.

Conversation 2   WATCH

Donna: My brother ¹_____ (+) television all the time. He ²_____ (+) sport. Football, volleyball, tennis. Every kind of sport.
Simon: And you?
Donna: I ³_____ (–) sport. Never. I hate sport. I ⁴_____ (+) music videos on YouTube.

Conversation 3   LIKE

Sally: My mum ¹_____ (+) cats. My dad doesn't. He ²_____ (+) dogs but my mum ³_____ (–) them.
Jake: What about you?
Sally: I ⁴_____ (–) cats or dogs – but I love spiders! I've got a tarantula at home!

4 ★ ★ ★ Put the words in the correct order and the verbs in the correct form.

Fridays / not go / usually / I / the park / to / on
I don't usually go to the park on Fridays.
at home / always / after school / Sam / be
Sam is always at home after school.
1 often / go / Mark / to / on / a party / Fridays
_____
2 read / I / day / things / every / on the Internet
_____
3 sister / a / my / not play / instrument / musical
_____
4 dad / shopping / my / not like
_____
5 grandparents / visit / at / I / my / often / the weekend
_____
6 go / Sunday / Susan / on / always / to / park / the
_____
7 to / usually / Louise / Saturdays / the cinema / go / on
_____
8 Saturday / shopping / my / go / mum / every
_____

SHOW WHAT YOU'VE LEARNT

5 Put the words in brackets in the correct form and order. Use short forms if possible.

I _often play_ (play / often) chess with my brother.
1 Jo _____ (always / watch) TV in the afternoon.
2 Lisa _____ (not / do) sports, but she likes watching sports on TV.
3 My parents _____ (often / be) hungry in the evening. They don't eat at work.
4 Chen _____ (be / never) at home when I want to visit him.
5 Lu _____ (go / often) for a walk on Sundays.
6 Noah _____ (not / like) video games.

/6

GRAMMAR: Train and Try Again page 128

14

■ **Complete gaps 1–3 with the phrases from the box. There are three extra phrases.**

> can you describe your   can you do
> ~~I want to know~~   what are you   what do you
> what does your   what's your

Extract from Student's Book recording 🔊 **1.29**

Reporter: It's Friday afternoon and *I want to know* what people do at the weekend. Hello. ¹_____ name?

Simon: Hi, I'm Simon.

Reporter: ²_____ typical weekend for our listeners?

Simon: Sure. My weekends are usually busy with football. I ᵃ*run / walk* a football club for children in my area. I ᵇ*bus / coach* the kids on Saturdays. It's really nice to watch them – they have a lot of fun and the exercise is good for them. Then on Sunday mornings, I play with my local team. It's the football season, so I also watch football on TV or on the Internet. I really love my weekends.

***

Lena: My name's Lena.

Reporter: Hello Lena. ³_____ do at the weekend?

Lena: Well, every weekend, I go to a different part of the city and ᶜ*take / make* hundreds of photos. I photograph people, places and situations – anything that looks interesting or unusual. In the evening, I ᵈ*look at / watch* the pictures on my computer and ᵉ*send / post* the best ones on Facebook. A lot of people ᶠ*discuss / comment* on the photos. It's really interesting. You can see them there.

2 **Choose the correct verbs a–f in Exercise 1.**

3 **Complete the dialogue with the verbs in italics from Exercise 1.**

Paul: I *work* in a restaurant, but in my free time, I ¹_____ a photography club.

Stuart: Really?

Paul: Yes. I ²_____ a lot of photos of sports events. Do you want to ³_____ them?

Stuart: OK. Where are they?

Paul: On the Internet. I ⁴_____ the photos on my website. Here they are.

Stuart: Very nice. Do people ⁵_____ on them?

Paul: No, they can't. Not on my website but there are some in the local newspaper.

Stuart: Hey. I ⁶_____ young children to play tennis. Can you put some photos of us in the newspaper?

Paul: Of course. What time are the lessons?

REMEMBER THIS

Some words have more than one meaning.

Run

A to move very fast, by moving your legs faster than when you walk, e.g. *run a marathon, run to school*

B to organise or be in charge of an activity, business, organisation, or country, e.g. *run a company*

Post

A to send a letter, package, etc. by post, e.g. *post a birthday card to your aunt*

B to put a message or computer document on the Internet so that other people can see it, e.g. *post a comment on Facebook*

4 **Read REMEMBER THIS. Decide if the underlined word has meaning A or B.**

1 Can you <u>post</u> this letter for me, please? ____
2 My teacher wants me to <u>run</u> the school chess club. ____
3 I <u>run</u> two kilometres every day before school. ____
4 Can you show me how to <u>post</u> a video on YouTube? ____

WORD STORE 1D | Prepositions and nouns

5 **Complete the dialogue with the correct prepositions *in*, *on* or *at*.**

Ray: Hi Emily, do you want to go for a coffee?

Emily: No, thanks. It's Saturday. I play sports *on* Saturday.

Ray: Do you do a lot of exercise?

Emily: Well, ¹_____ a typical weekday, I run before I go to school.

Ray: Even ²_____ Monday mornings?

Emily: Yes, every day. ³_____ the weekend, I play tennis ⁴_____ the afternoon.

Ray: I know why you don't run ⁵_____ Saturday or Sunday morning. You're the same as me. You sleep a lot and eat breakfast ⁶_____ noon ⁷_____ the weekend.

Emily: No, I eat breakfast at 8 o'clock ⁸_____ the morning but I go for a walk after that.

Ray: Oh wow! Do you run ⁹_____ night too?

Emily: Not often! I sometimes run ¹⁰_____ the evening but only in the summer when it's light and warm. What about you? Do you run?

Ray: Sometimes ¹¹_____ midnight when Mum and Dad phone me and say 'It's late! Come home, now!' I don't really like sport. I like making videos. I post them ¹²_____ the Internet. You know. ¹³_____ video sharing sites.

Emily: I know. I don't watch videos online but I know some people like them. I sometimes watch films ¹⁴_____ TV but not often. I just prefer doing exercise. It's great. Run with me later.

Ray: Let's run now, to the pizza restaurant.

READING

1.4

Working away from home
• phrasal verbs and collocations
• daily routine

1 **Read the text quickly and choose the best title.**

A I love my long holidays at home

B Life is difficult when my husband comes home

C This is not the right job for me

Arthur lives in Portsmouth with his wife and three children. He has a good job but he isn't happy. Arthur is the captain of a large tanker. He loves ships and the sea and is good at his job. He earns a lot of money and has a lot of free time at work to study languages and write. So what's the problem?

Arthur has a 'three months on – two months off' contract, which means that he goes to sea for three months and then has two months' holiday. This means that some years he isn't at home for Christmas, some years he is away during the summer holidays and every year he misses someone's birthday, school shows and other special days. His children are twelve, ten and six and they grow quickly at that age.

When Arthur comes home, the children spend a day or two just looking at him and trying to think of what to say. The last week of his leave is filled with tears. There are also good times. The family have parties to celebrate any birthdays missed and they sometimes have Christmas dinner in November or January but there is always a feeling of sadness that they can't happen at the right time.

Life is also difficult for his wife, Theresa. She is a teacher and, for three months, has no husband to help her with shopping, cooking, cleaning and checking homework. She is very strict, so the children help with the housework, go to bed at nine o'clock and get up for school without any problems. Theresa prepares dinners in advance and makes the most of every hour of the day. Then, Arthur comes home. He ignores the normal bedtimes because he wants to tell his children stories and play with them. The children stop doing housework and, because they go to bed late, they are tired when they get up in the morning. Of course, Theresa understands and is pleased to see her family so happy, but it takes a week or more to get life back to normal when Arthur goes back to sea.

Now, Arthur wants to find a job on land but he knows it isn't easy. What can a ship's captain do when he isn't on a ship? Arthur's dream is to be a writer of children's books and work from home. This dream cheers him up when he is on the other side of the world and still has two months before he sees his family again.

GLOSSARY

tanker (n) – a large ship that carries oil

leave (n) – time that you are allowed to spend away from your work

strict (adj) – expecting people to obey rules or to do what you say

2 Read the text and choose the correct answers A–C.

1 Arthur doesn't like
   A working on a boat.
   B spending time away from his children.
   C the captain on his ship.

2 Arthur gets two months' holiday
   A after working for three months.
   B once a year.
   C at the same time each year.

3 Arthur never
   A spends Christmas at home.
   B celebrates his children's birthdays.
   C has a year when he is at home for all the special days.

4 Arthur's wife
   A doesn't do all the housework when Arthur is away.
   B doesn't go out to work.
   C isn't very well organised.

5 When Arthur is at home, his wife
   A is angry with him for changing the children's bedtime.
   B is tired for the first week because of the changes.
   C is happy to see how her husband spends time with their children.

6 In the future, Arthur wants to
   A work on ships that don't sail long distances.
   B write about his life at sea.
   C stay at home and write stories for children.

3 Look at the underlined phrases in the text. Complete the sentences with one word in each gap. The first letters are given.

My sister's son is fifteen. He's a bit difficult. I think a lot of children are, at that a*ge*.

1 It's a very sad film. My eyes are always filled with t_____ when I watch it.
2 Don't wait for the day of the concert to buy tickets. We can buy them in a_____ on the Internet.
3 This is the last day of our holiday. Don't spend the time at your computer. Make the m_____ of the day. Go swimming, go for a walk, have some local food.
4 My dad works three days on, three days o_____, so he often works at the weekend.
5 My mum works f_____ home, so she is always there when we get back from school.
6 We're in Australia! I can't believe it. We're on the other s_____ of the world!

REMEMBER THIS

Expressions with 'of'

The genitive form in English is often written with 'of', e.g.

the captain of a ship
a feeling of sadness
the last week of his leave
a writer of children's books

---

4 Read REMEMBER THIS. Put the words in the correct order.

is / a / Lucy / English / of / teacher
Lucy is a teacher of English.

1 children / Elizabeth / a / three / of / is / mother
   _____

2 the / is / of / last / school / this / week
   _____

3 week / my / the / Saturday / favourite / is / day / of
   _____

4 my / of / skateboard / this / the / dreams / is
   _____

VOCABULARY PRACTICE | Phrasal verbs and collocations

5 Look at the vocabulary in lesson 1.4 in the Student's Book. Choose the correct word.

Our lives

We are all different and here is your chance to tell other people about your typical day.

Joanna, aged 17

My mum gets up ¹*last / late / first*, but I also get up early – at 7 o'clock every morning. Then I ²*take / wake / get* up my brothers. They don't like getting ³*off / up / on* early, that's why I 'help' them ☺. We ⁴*get / go / make* dressed and have our breakfast. We ⁵*have / take / wash* the dishes and go to school.

School finishes at half past three. At home, I look ⁶*for / after / up* my two brothers. My parents finish work at five o'clock. At seven o'clock we eat together and then I do my homework. I usually take the dog ⁷*out / on / up* for a walk. I love our dog Maxy and I always enjoy our walks. I ⁸*go / fall / get* asleep at ten o'clock! It's a busy life, but at the weekend, I am free! And I can get up ⁹*early / late / first* at last!

Comments (1)   *Wednesday 18th April, 23.14*

Are you sure you go to bed at 10? Look at the time of your post!

WORD STORE 1E | Daily routine

6 Complete the sentences with the words from the box.

at   for (x2)   on (x2)   out of   to (x3)

I don't want to stay *at* home on Saturdays.
1 They like to go _____ museums and look at the beautiful things there.
2 Our cat often sits _____ the sofa with us.
3 Aylin goes _____ a run in the park every day.
4 Sometimes it's difficult to get _____ bed in the winter when it's so dark outside.
5 At the weekend, we go _____ a swim at the beach.
6 Boris usually lies _____ the sofa all weekend and watches TV!
7 My grandparents never go _____ bed late.
8 My brother often goes _____ the gym with his friends.

17

GRAMMAR

1.5

Present Simple;
Yes/No and *Wh-* questions

---

1 Complete the questions with the words from the box.

> Are   How   Is   ~~What~~   When   Where   Who

What is your name?
My name's Joe.

1 _____ you American?
Yes, I am.

2 _____ are you from in the USA?
I'm from Seattle, in Washington State.

3 _____ that your car?
No, it isn't. I can't drive.

4 _____ is that girl?
That's my sister, Clara.

5 _____ old are you?
I'm 17.

6 _____ is your birthday?
In May. On the seventeenth.

2 ★ Complete the dialogue with *do* or *does*.

Cheryl: Hi, I'm Cheryl. *Do* you work here?

Harry: Yes, I ¹_____ . Are you here for a job?

Cheryl: Yes, but Mr Parkin isn't here. What time ²_____ he usually arrive?

Harry: At about 10 o'clock. ³_____ you want a cup of coffee?

Cheryl: Yes, please. Thanks. What ⁴_____ you do here?

Harry: I clean the kitchen and the tables in the restaurant.

Cheryl: ⁵_____ you like your job?

Harry: It's OK. I like the money.

Cheryl: ⁶_____ lots of people come here to eat?

Harry: Yes, they ⁷_____ . From about 12 o'clock until 3. Then we can relax.

Cheryl: What time ⁸_____ the restaurant close?

Harry: At 5, but we work until 6. Here's Mr Parkin now. ⁹_____ you want me to tell him you're here?

Cheryl: Just let me finish my coffee! Right. I'm ready. ¹⁰_____ I look OK?

3 ★ ★ Use the words in brackets to complete the questions and short answers.

Conversation 1

Neil: *Does Jenny like* (Jenny/like) music?

Will: ¹_____ (yes/do). We listen to my CDs all the time.

Neil: ²_____ (what/she/do) at the weekend?

Will: I play football and she watches. She loves football.

Neil: ³_____ (she/go) shopping?

Will: ⁴_____ (she/not). That's lucky because I hate shopping.

Conversation 2

Sally: ¹_____ (you and Will/like) the same kind of music?

Jenny: ²_____ (no/we/not). He plays his CDs all the time. They're awful!

Sally: ³_____ (what/you/do) at the weekend?

Jenny: I watch Will play football, but it's really boring.

Sally: ⁴_____ (you/like) shopping?

Jenny: ⁵_____ (yes/do). I love it but Will hates shopping, so I never go with him.

4 ★ ★ ★ Look at the underlined words in the answers and complete the questions.

Where do you go in the evening?
I go to <u>the cinema</u>.

1 _____ is your favourite sport?
<u>Volleyball</u> is my favourite sport.

2 _____ friends do you have at school?
I have <u>many</u> friends at school.

3 _____ do you wake up in the morning?
I wake up at <u>seven o'clock</u>.

4 _____ do you do at the weekend?
I <u>spend time</u> with my friends.

5 _____ of music do you listen to?
I listen to <u>rock and pop music</u>.

6 _____ video games?
No, I <u>don't</u> play video games – I don't like them!

7 _____ plays the guitar?
<u>Jason</u> plays the guitar.

---

5 Complete the sentences with the correct form of the words from the box. There are two extra sets of words.

> Amy / speak   Ellen and Sonia / go   Jake / live
> Jason / spend   Karl / have   ~~you / do~~
> your parents / read   you / watch   your mum / like

What *do you do* in your free time?

1 _____ in Windsor or Winchester?

2 How often_____ DVDs?

3 How many languages_____ ?

4 _____ lunch at school?

5 What kind of music_____ ?

6 Where_____ after school?

/6

GRAMMAR: Train and Try Again page 128

1.6 SPEAKING

Expressing preferences

1 Translate the phrases into your own language.

SPEAKING BANK

Preferences

Do you like (films/ reading)? _____

What kind of (music/ books/films) do you like? _____ _____

Who's your favourite (singer/writer)? _____ _____ _____

What's your favourite (sport)? _____ _____

What do you think of ...? _____

What about you? _____

I (really) like/love ... _____

I like ... a lot. _____

My favourite (actor/ writer) is ... _____ _____

(I think) He/She/It is good/great/awesome/ brilliant. _____ _____ _____

I don't like ... (very much). _____

I hate/can't stand ... _____

(I think) He/She/It's terrible/awful/rubbish. _____ _____

He/She/It's OK, but I prefer ... _____ _____

2 Match questions 1–3 with answers a–f. There are three extra answers.

1 Which of these two activities do you like best? ☐
2 What's your favourite free time activity? ☐
3 Do you like playing computer games? ☐

a No, I don't. I like looking at YouTube videos but I don't play games on the computer.
b I love swimming. I go swimming three times a week.
c Yes, I do. I love walking with my friends.
d I don't like spending my free time alone.
e I prefer the first one. I prefer walking with friends, not sitting alone with a computer game.
f I prefer films, not books.

3 Complete the dialogue with the answers from the box.

> I always go on Saturday afternoon
> I don't like them very much   I don't know it
> I like comedies – films that make me laugh
> I love Ben Stiller   Yes, I do
> The one I like best is called *The Royal Tenenbaums*

Greg: Do you like films?
Selma: *Yes, I do*.
Greg: When do you usually go to the cinema?
Selma: ¹_____.
Greg: What kind of films do you like?
Selma: ²_____.
Greg: Who's your favourite actor?
Selma: ³_____ . He's brilliant.
Greg: What's your favourite film?
Selma: ⁴_____ . I think it's awesome. My friends don't agree!
Greg: What do you think of fantasy films?
Selma: ⁵_____ . I can't stand the *Twilight Saga* films and I don't really like *Harry Potter*.
Greg: What about *The Lord of the Rings*?
Selma: ⁶_____ . My friend's got it on DVD but I always choose something else to watch. What about you?
Greg: Oh, I love fantasy films. My favourite is *The Hobbit*.

4 Complete the text with one word in each gap. The first letters are given.

Dave: Do you **l**ike sports?
Amelia: Well, I like some.
Dave: What ¹**k**_____ of sports do you like?
Amelia: I like sports that I can do alone. I like walking and running. I like swimming a ²**l**_____ , too. I don't like football very ³**m**_____ and I ⁴**h**_____ Formula 1 – it's awful.
Dave: ⁵**W**_____'s your favourite sportsperson?
Amelia: I don't know. I guess I like Ryoyu Kobayashi. He's awesome.
Dave: What do you ⁶**t**_____ of Cristiano Ronaldo?
Amelia: I can't ⁷**s**_____ footballers with all their ⁸**t**_____ ...
Dave: He doesn't have any tattoos.
Amelia: Well, that's good but I ⁹**p**_____ people who love their sport but don't do it for the money. People like Ola Taistra. She's a climber. She's ¹⁰**b**_____ , and a nice person too, I think.

WRITING

1.7

An informal email

1 Which of these expressions should <u>not</u> be used when:

starting an email:
1 A Dear Dave   B Hi Dave   C I'm Dave

finishing an email:
2 A Write soon   B Thanks for your email
   C Say hello to your parents
3 A All the best   B Nice to see you   C Bye for now
4 See you …
   A best   B soon   C in June
5 Have a
   A good time   B good trip   C fun
6 A Regards, Tom   B Love, Tom   C You're Tom

2 Change the underlined words to contractions.

Hi Sofia,

Thanks for your email. <u>I'm</u> / <u>I am</u> glad you want to write
to me. I ¹_____ / <u>do not</u> speak Spanish, so ²_____ /
<u>it is</u> lucky that your English is so good.
What are you interested in? I love travelling and
photography. ³_____ / <u>I have</u> got a blog with photos of
my holidays on it. <u>Click here.</u> Do you like them?
I ⁴_____ / <u>do not</u> think they are very good but they are
my photos! My next holiday (next week!) is in Greece!
⁵_____ / <u>It is</u> great that you can come to England. My
mum is very excited but ⁶_____ / <u>she is</u> worried. She
⁷_____ / <u>does not</u> know how to cook Spanish food.
She wants to know what you like so she can find it on the
Internet! Say hello to your family. See you in July.

Bye for now,
Ruby

3 Complete the email with one word in each gap.
The last letters are given.

Hi Ruby,

<u>Thank</u>s for your email. I love your photos! I can teach you
some Spanish if you like and then you can come to Spain,
take lots of photos and try our food!
I'm ¹_____d in travel too. I sometimes go to
Morocco – it isn't far from my town! I love the food there
and the people. They are very friendly. I like Moroccan
music too. Do you like ²_____t? What kind of
music are you interested ³_____n? Please say
thank you to your mum but I want to eat real English
food when I am in England. ⁴_____y hello to your
parents. See you ⁵_____n. I hope you like Greece.
⁶_____e a good trip!
⁷_____l the best,

Sofia

SHOW WHAT YOU'VE LEARNT

4 You want to write to someone from a different
country. You see this message on a website and
decide to write an email to Marysa.
- Start and finish the email appropriately.
- Tell Marysa about yourself (age, town, family).
- Ask questions about her life and hobbies.
- Tell her about your interests and how you spend
  your free time.

Hi!
My name is Marysa. I'm a Dutch girl
from a small town near Amsterdam.
I am 18 years old. I speak Dutch, English
and German. I want to find friends from
all over Europe.
Please write to me at marysa17@poli.nl

SHOW THAT YOU'VE CHECKED

Finished? Always check your writing.
Can you tick ✓ everything on this list?

In my email invitation:
- I have started the email correctly, e.g. *Hi Marysa.* ☐
- I have given personal information about myself – my town, family, age, etc. ☐
- I have asked Marysa about herself. ☐
- I have talked about my interests. ☐
- I have talked about my free time activities. ☐
- I have asked Marysa about her interests and free time. ☐
- I have used the Present Simple correctly. ☐
- I have checked my spelling. ☐
- My text is neat and clear. ☐

20

1 **In pairs, ask and answer the questions.**

PART 1

Talk about your family.
1 How big is your family?
2 Have you got any brothers or sisters?
3 What are your parents' names?
4 How many rooms are there in your house or flat?
5 What furniture have you got in your room?

PART 2

Talk about your day.
1 What things do you do every morning?
2 Who wakes you up in the morning?
3 How do you get to school?
4 What do you do after school?
5 What time do you fall asleep?

2 **Look at the photos that show free time activities.**

PART 1

Which of these activities do you do? Discuss in pairs.

PART 2

In pairs, ask and answer the questions.
1 Do you think listening to music is fun? Why?/Why not?
2 Do you like reading? Why?/Why not?
3 Do you like spending time with friends? Why?/Why not?
4 Do you enjoy playing sports? Why?/Why not?
5 Do you prefer listening to music or playing music? Why?
6 Do you prefer playing sports or playing video games? Why?
7 Which of these free time activities do you like best? Why?

3 **Read the instructions on your card. In pairs, take turns to role-play the conversation.**

Student A
This is your survey about films. Ask Student B the questions.   • Say hello.   • Ask if he/she likes watching films.   • Ask what sort of films he/she likes.   • Ask who his/her favourite actor is.   • Ask what his/her favourite film is.   • Ask how often he/she goes to the cinema.   • Say thank you and end the conversation.

Student B
Answer Student A's questions for a survey about films.   • Say if you like watching films.   • Say what kind of films you like.   • Say who your favourite actor is.   • Say what your favourite film is.   • Say how often you go to the cinema.

VOCABULARY AND GRAMMAR

1 Match beginnings 1–5 with the correct endings a–i.
There are three extra endings.

We don't often visit ... `i`
1 We can go for ...
2 Sam and his friends always talk ...
3 It's nice to go ...
4 Mandy always has ...
5 I never go to the ...

a cinema but I watch a lot of films on TV.
b for a walk in the park on a sunny day.
b blog every day.
b about sports and video games.
e the guitar with my friends.
f lunch to the cafeteria.
g time with our friends.
h fun at parties.
i my aunt and uncle.

/5

2 Complete the text with *in*, *on* or *at* in each gap.

Holiday time!

8th *July*

No school for two months, so I don't get up early *in* the morning. ¹___ a typical day, I have breakfast ²___ noon! Then I read emails and funny stories ³___ the Internet and, late ⁴___ the afternoon, I go out with friends. We usually go to a café. I often get home ⁵___ midnight and then I watch a video and go to bed at about 2 a.m.
I love the holidays!

/5

3 Complete the text with a verb in each gap.
The first letters are given.

Holiday time! – 2

12th *July*

My parents don't like the way I **s**pend my time on holiday. Now, I ¹**g**_____ up at eight o'clock. When my parents go to work, I ²**l**_____ after my ten-year-old sister. After breakfast, we ³**g**_____ to the park or the shopping centre. I can go out with my friends in the evening and I ⁴**h**_____ a good time with them at parties or the cinema, but I am home at 11 p.m. I ⁵**g**_____ to bed before midnight.

The holidays are still cool!

/5

4 There is a mistake in each sentence. Rewrite them correctly.

My dad play basketball every Saturday with friends from his work.
My dad plays basketball every Saturday with friends from his work.

1 We always are tired after school.
_____

2 My brother don't like reading books – he prefers video games.
_____

3 Mike has never lunch at school, so he is always hungry by 3.30 p.m.
_____

4 Erin doesn't watches television very often because she thinks it's boring.
_____

5 What kind of music you listen to when you want to relax?
_____

/5

5 Use the words in brackets to make full questions.

What kind of books / read? (your parents)
What kind of books do your parents read?

1 What sports / play? (your best friend)
_____

2 What / favourite film? (your cousin's)
_____

3 What / eat for breakfast? (your father)
_____

4 What time / get up on Saturdays? (your sisters)
_____

5 How often / go to discos? (you)
_____

/5

6 Choose the correct answers A–C.

I never get up ___ 6 o'clock on Sunday.
A in   B on   Ⓒ at

1 What do you usually do ___ Sunday afternoons?
A in   B on   C at

2 Come and work at the café with me. It's great.
We always ___ a good time.
A have   B play   C do

3 Do you want to ___ shopping with me on Saturday?
I need to buy some things for university.
A go to   B go   C go for a

4 Tim ___ often stay at home at the weekend.
He goes out with his friends all the time.
A doesn't   B isn't   C don't

5 **Claire:** Matt's got a new guitar.
Annette: Really? What music ___ ?
A he plays   B he does play   C does he play

/5

Total /30

7 Choose the correct answers A–C.

He ___ football.
A don't play
B⃝ doesn't play
C doesn't plays

1 ___ magazines?
A Do you read
B Read you
C You read

2 I ___ on Saturday night.
A go usually out
B go out usually
C usually go out

3 How many hours ___ at school every day?
A spend they
B they spend
C do they spend

4 'What kind of films ___ ?'
'She prefers funny films.'
A do Tina like
B does Tina like
C Tina likes

5 Tom and his cat ___ in front of the TV.
A doesn't fall asleep
B never fall asleep
C always falls asleep

/5

8 Complete each pair of sentences with the same word A–C.

Do you ___ video games?
Tom and Harry ___ the drums – they're very good.
A watch   B have   C⃝ play

1 Do you get ___ early every morning?
It's ten o'clock. Wake ___ , Dan!
A out   B on   C up

2 They sometimes ___ for a walk in the park.
We can ___ to the cinema in the town.
A go   B have   C meet

3 I want to take the dog ___ for a walk.
Do you often go ___ in the evening?
A up   B out   C to

4 Do you want to ___ a party for your birthday?
They always ___ fun with their cousins.
A do   B have   C get

5 Why does he lie ___ the sofa all day?
What do you usually do ___ Saturdays?
A in   B at   C on

/5

9 Put the words in the correct order to make sentences or questions.

Leo: What do you think of Sia?
Jenny: She's great! all her / listen / I / music / to
I listen to all her music.

1 Tom: kind of / like / what / you / books / do
_____?
Anne: I really like books about famous people.

2 Lisa: What do you do on Sundays?
Bart: with / spend / I / time / my family
_____

3 Pam: I love country music!
Ben: Really? it / stand / can't / I
_____! I think it's terrible.

4 John: today / don't / up / I / get / want to
_____
Mary: Why? Are you still sleepy?

5 Bob: Does Cara visit her friends at the weekend?
Lily: No, never. stays / TV / at home / she / and / watches
_____

/5

10 Complete the second sentence so that it has a similar meaning to the first. Use between two and five words, including the word in capitals.

Jack does exercises at the gym every day. **GOES**
Jack *goes to the gym* every day.

1 I always enjoy parties. **GOOD**
I always _____ at parties.

2 Come with me – we can run together. **GO**
Let's _____ together.

3 Sandy is fifteen and her brother is only seven – so she helps him. **AFTER**
Sandy is fifteen and her brother is only seven – so she _____ him.

4 It's time for school, here are your clothes. **DRESSED**
It's time for school, please _____ now.

5 Colin is always asleep before 11 p.m. **GOES**
Colin always _____ before 11 p.m.

/5

Total   /20

23

2 Food

VOCABULARY

2.1
Food containers • food products
• phrases related to food

SHOW WHAT YOU KNOW

1 Decide which word is different to the others in groups 1–4. What kind of food is it? Find the right category A–E below.

potato	carrot	(salmon)
1 strawberry	lemonade	apple
2 salt and pepper	cheese	milk
3 juice	onion	tea
4 ice cream	strawberry	apple

A Fruit and vegetables: _____
B Dairy: _____
C Meat and fish: _salmon_
D Drinks: _____
E Other: _____

WORD STORE 2A | Food containers

2 Complete the names of the containers with one letter in each space (ᵃ). Then complete the shopping list with the correct food from the box (ᵇ).

> brown bread   crisps   ~~honey~~   ice cream
> ketchup   lemonade   milk   potatoes
> tuna   white chocolate

A j <u>a</u> r of <u>honey</u>.

1 A ᵃp _ _ _ _ t of ᵇ_____

2 A ᵃt _ n of ᵇ_____

3 A ᵃl _ _ f of ᵇ_____

4 A 5 kg ᵃb _ g of ᵇ_____

5 Four ᵃc _ _ s of ᵇ_____

6 A large ᵃb _ r of ᵇ_____

7 A ᵃb _ _ _ _ e of ᵇ_____

8 A ᵃt _ b of strawberry ᵇ_____

9 A ᵃc _ _ _ _ n of ᵇ_____

REMEMBER BETTER

To remember the names of containers in which certain products are sold, learn them as chunks (a container and a sample product together), e.g. ~~I've got some chocolate.~~ *I've got a bar of chocolate.*

Look in your fridge at home. Complete the sentences about the food you can see in the fridge. Check any new words in a dictionary.

In my fridge, there is:
1 _a carton of milk_
2 _____

In my fridge, there are:
3 _____
4 _____

---

3 **Choose the correct option.**

Lisa: This healthy food camp is a great idea but it's a long walk to get there. Have you got a drink?

Chris: Yes. I've got some cola.

Lisa: Cola! That isn't healthy. I've got two small ¹*cartons / boxes / packets* of juice.

Ten minutes later …

Chris: Oh, great, a shop. Wait a minute.

Lisa: What do you want to buy?

Chris: A small ²*tub / bottle / jar* of ketchup. Cheese sandwiches are boring without ketchup.

Lisa: You could buy a tomato and some lettuce to make it nicer. Not ketchup.

Half an hour later …

Lisa: We've still got five kilometres to go. Let's stop and eat. Have you got something for lunch?

Chris: Yes. My cheese sandwiches, two ³*bars / tubs / tins* of chocolate, two ⁴*tins / jars / cans* of cola and a ⁵*box / packet / jar* of crisps.

Lisa: You really need this healthy food camp, Chris.

The next morning …

Lisa: Morning, Chris. Time for breakfast.

Chris: We haven't got any bread!

Lisa: That's OK. All we need for breakfast is a ⁶*packet / tin / carton* of milk and some cornflakes.

Chris: But I've got a jar of chocolate spread in my bag!

Lisa: Chris, why exactly are you on this camp???

WORD STORE 2B | Food products

4 **Look at Word Stores 2A and 2B in the Student's Book. Complete the expressions.**

1 a bag of _potatoes_ / _____ / _____
2 a bar of _____
3 a bottle of _____ / _____
4 a can of _____ / _____
5 a carton of _____ / _____ / _____
6 a jar of _____ / _____ / _____
7 a loaf of _____
8 a packet of _____ / _____ / _____ / _____ / _____
9 a tin of _____ / _____
10 a tub of _____

---

5 Complete the text with the words from the box.

bag   bars   bottle   ~~dish~~   jar   packet (x2)
tin   tub

BLOG

Pasta Primavera

My favourite *dish* is Pasta Primavera. It's delicious!
It's a great vegetarian dish – you only need
vegetables. I'm at the supermarket now because
I want to make it tonight. I need a ¹_____
of spaghetti of course – it's an Italian dish!
I also want a ²_____ of oil, but I only need
to use a quarter of a cup. I want a ³_____
of onions, but I only need to use one. I also need
a ⁴_____ of peas, three carrots, two red
peppers, half a kilo of small tomatoes, salt and
pepper. Some people prefer to use a ⁵_____
of tomato sauce, but I like fresh tomatoes for
this recipe. Oh, I also need a ⁶_____ of
Parmesan cheese! It's very easy to make. You
can find the recipe here on the Internet.

For something sweet after the pasta, get a
⁷_____ of vanilla ice cream or some
⁸_____ of chocolate for your friends or family.

WORD STORE 2C | Phrases related to food

6 Complete the dialogue with the expressions
from the box. There is one extra word.

food   have them for dessert
get a takeaway   ingredients   ~~make a snack~~

Amy: I'm hungry.
Liz: What do you do when you're hungry? Do you
        make a snack?
Amy: Yes, sometimes, when I have the
        ¹_____ that I need, but today I want
        to ²_____ .
Liz: Great! Indian or Chinese?
Amy: Indian. I love Indian food.
Liz: We can go to my house. There's a good film on
        this evening.
Amy: OK. I've got some strawberries.
        We can ³_____ .
Liz: Not ice cream?
Amy: No. Not after a big Indian dinner.

SHOW WHAT YOU'VE LEARNT

7 Choose the word that is wrong.

1   I don't eat a lot of meat but I often use vegetables
    like __ to make very nice meals.
    A onions   B eggs   C carrots
2   If you're going to the shops, could you get me
    a carton of __ , please?
    A orange juice   B milk   C crisps
3   This packet of __ is nearly empty. How can I cook
    dinner now?
    A tuna   B rice   C pasta
4   I can't eat dairy food, so I never have __ . Well,
    I have it if it is made from soya.
    A cheese   B juice   C milk

8 Complete the dialogue with the words from the box.
There are three extra words.

~~bag~~   bar   bottle   cans   cartons
jar   loaf   packet   tins   tub

In a supermarket …

Mr Jenkins: Well, here we are at the supermarket.
              What do we need to buy today?
Mrs Jenkins: Let me see. Ah yes, I want a 10 kg *bag*
              of potatoes, onions, tomatoes, five
              ¹_____ of milk, a ²_____ of
              spaghetti, water and two ³_____ of
              tuna. OK. You get the vegetables, and I'll
              get the rest.
Mr Jenkins: OK, OK …

Five minutes later …

Mr Jenkins: … I've got everything.
              Can we pay and go now?
Mrs Jenkins: No, I forgot to get a ⁴_____ of
              bread. Is there anything you want?
Mr Jenkins: Well, I'd really like a ⁵_____ of
              chocolate and a ⁶_____ of ice
              cream!
Mrs Jenkins: Oh, Harry …
Mr Jenkins: For dessert!

/10

GRAMMAR

2.2

Countable and
uncountable nouns

SHOW WHAT YOU KNOW

1 Write the plural forms of the nouns in brackets.

When we go on walks, we always take lots
of _carrots_ (carrot) to eat.

1 Do you want _____ (potato) with your
chicken or do you prefer rice?
2 I love June. _____ (Strawberry) are so cheap.
3 For a real Spanish omelette, you need five or
six _____ (egg).
4 When I cut _____ (onion), I always cry.
5 These _____ (orange) are very juicy. You
only need two of them to make a glass of juice.

**2 ★ Find nine more food items in the word search.
Decide if they are countable or uncountable.**

C	O	L	I	V	E	O	I	L
H	R	E	G	G	A	N	Y	T
E	A	G	F	R	U	I	T	F
E	N	B	O	R	I	O	A	L
S	G	R	E	T	H	N	H	O
E	E	E	N	P	O	F	R	U
M	N	A	P	P	L	E	Y	R
S	O	D	H	O	T	D	O	G

Countable	Uncountable
egg	

3 ★ ★ Choose the correct option.

Peter: I think we're ready to start dinner. There ¹_is some /
are some / is any_ cheese in the fridge.
Sian: Great! Er ...²_Is there any / Is there some /
Are there any_ mushrooms? I can't see them.
Peter: Mushrooms. Oh, no. I forgot.
Sian: And there ³_isn't some / aren't some / isn't any_
spaghetti.
Peter: Oh.
Sian: So, no spaghetti bolognese for us today. What
can we eat?
Peter: ⁴_Is there any / Are there some / Are there any_
bread?
Sian: Bread? I don't want a sandwich. I want dinner!
Peter: Well, there ⁵_is some / are some / are any_
potatoes. We can have fried eggs and potatoes.
Sian: Er …, Peter.
Peter: Yes?
Sian: There ⁶_isn't any / aren't some / aren't any_ eggs.
Peter: Oh.

4 ★ ★ Complete the questions and short answers.

Woman: Can you make a shopping list and go shopping
for me?
Man: OK. What do you want?
Woman: I don't know. That's why I want you to make a list.
Man: Right. _Is there any fruit_ (fruit)?
Woman: _Yes, there is_ (✓). There are apples and oranges.
Man: Good. ¹_____ (eggs)?
Woman: ²_____ (✓).
Man: Great. ³_____ (ketchup)?
Woman: ⁴_____ (✗).
Man: Oh, right. Ketchup. ⁵_____
(honey)?
Woman: ⁶_____ (✓). We've got four
jars. Don't buy any honey.
Man: ⁷_____ (vegetables)?
Woman: ⁸_____ (✗).
Man: Oh, is there any …
Woman: Please, just go to the kitchen and look.

**5 ★ ★ ★ Complete the questions and answers with
one word in each gap.**

Maggie: _How much_ fruit do you eat, Alex?
Alex: Oh, I eat a ¹_____ of fruit. I love apples.
Maggie: So, ²_____ _____ apples do you eat in
a week?
Alex: I eat about two a day, so fourteen.
Maggie: Wow. That's ³_____ lot. What about other
food? ⁴_____ _____ eggs do you eat?
Alex: ⁵_____ _____ . One or two a month.
Maggie: And ⁶_____ _____ cheese do you eat?
Alex: ⁷_____ _____ . Just a little bit on
a Saturday evening.
Maggie: OK. Last question. ⁸_____ _____ hot
dogs do you eat a week?
Alex: Hot dogs? Yuk. I don't eat ⁹_____ hot dogs
or hamburgers. I hate fast food.

SHOW WHAT YOU'VE LEARNT

6 Complete the dialogue with one word in each gap.

Tanya: The party starts in an hour. Are you ready?
Brett: I think so. Are there _any_ crisps here?
Tanya: Yes, there ¹_____ . There are a ²_____
of packets in the kitchen. About twenty, I think.
Brett: Twenty! Wow. And have we got any cola?
Tanya: Yes. Not ³_____ . One or two bottles.
Brett: Oh. Why not more?
Tanya: Well, there is ⁴_____ lot of juice and
⁵_____ many of our guests drink cola.
Brett: OK, you know best. Oh, here's the phone
number of the pizza restaurant. We can order
some for nine o'clock.
Tanya: Good idea. How ⁶_____ do you want?
Brett: I think eight is enough.
Tanya: One for you and seven for the rest of us!

/6

GRAMMAR: Train and Try Again page 129

1 Put the words in the correct order to make questions 1–4. Then complete the conversation with the questions in the correct places A–D.

How / it / make / you / do
How do you make it?

1 need / many / you / do / How / eggs
_____

2 you / a healthy recipe / got / for / pancakes / Have
_____

3 do / What / need / you
_____

4 so / you / the pancakes / make / do / OK, / how
_____

Extract from Student's Book recording 🔊 **1.46**

Part 2

KG: For the first recipe you just need eggs, potatoes and olive oil. It's called a Spanish omelette.

P: *How do you make it?*

KG: There are many different ways. But this is how you make a healthy Spanish omelette. First, slice four potatoes. Then boil the potatoes in some water. After that, put the potatoes in a bowl, add some eggs and mix together.

P: OK, so you mix all the ingredients. **A** _____ ?

KG: You need six eggs for four people. So, mix the eggs with the potatoes. Then put some olive (*N*) ¹oil (___) into a pan. Fry the omelette on both sides. And that's it – your ²Spanish (___) ³omelette (___) is ready! Eat it with some salad for a really healthy meal.

Extract from Student's Book recording 🔊 **1.48**

Part 3

P: And what about dessert, Kate? My favourite dessert is pancakes. **B** _____ ?

KG: Yes, I've got a very easy recipe for ⁴fruit (___) ⁵pancakes (___).

P: Cool. **C** _____ ?

KG: Some fruit, for example some bananas and strawberries. Then you need one cup of flour, one cup of milk and one egg. Plus some oil.

P: OK, so bananas, strawberries, flour, milk, an egg and oil. What do you do?

KG: First you chop the fruit and then you make the pancakes.

P: **D** _____ ?

KG: You mix the flour, milk and the egg together. Then you put some oil into a pan. When it is hot, you put some of the mixture into the pan and make a pancake. You fry it on both sides. Take it out of the pan and put the fruit on top.

REMEMBER THIS

In English food names often consist of two words: adjective + noun or two nouns (compound noun), e.g. *a Spanish omelette* (adj + n), *a chocolate cake* (n + n).

2 Read REMEMBER THIS. Look at the underlined words 1–5 in the text in Exercise 1 and decide whether the words are adjectives (A) or nouns (N).

3 Match the words 1–6 and a–g to make food names. Then complete the sentences with the correct food names.

fruit
1 birthday   a sandwiches
2 hot   b oil
3 olive   c flakes
4 tomato   d dog
5 cheese and tomato   e sauce
6 corn   f cake
                  g pancakes

I love *fruit pancakes*. My favourites are with strawberries. What are your favourite kinds?

1 When you have a _____ , do you put mustard or ketchup on it?

2 In Italy, they often put _____ on bread. I know it's unhealthy, but I prefer butter. Which do you prefer on your bread?

3 Some people always call _____ ketchup. Do you put ketchup on a lot of food?

4 For lunch, I often have two _____ . Sometimes, I have ham.

5 I always have _____ with lots of milk on them for breakfast.

6 **Jenny:** This is a lovely _____ . Thank you.
   Mum: Well, it's a special day. You're eighteen. An adult.

WORD STORE 2D | Cooking verbs

4 Choose the correct option.

1 *Fry / Slice* the omelette for one minute on each side.

2 *Mix / Chop* the fruit into small pieces and put them into a bowl.

3 *Boil / Fry* the potatoes in some water for about 25 minutes.

4 *Slice / Mix* the eggs with the potatoes, then add salt and pepper.

5 *Chop / Fry* the meat for about 5 minutes. Be careful not to let it burn.

6 *Slice / Boil* the cheese thinly and put it on the bread.

Eat out for less

'How much is it?' In some restaurants, the answer is: 'What you want to pay.' Here are some of the 'Pay-what-you-want' restaurants around the world.

A Der Wiener Deewan, Vienna, Austria

This is a Pakistani restaurant but it is in Vienna. You go down some stairs to a small room with seats for about fifty people. There are no menus and no waiters. The food is in large, hot, containers on a table and you take what you want. The meal then costs

what you want to pay. The traditional, Pakistani food is delicious, but be careful, some of it is very spicy! Try the **Methi Gajar** — spicy but sweet vegetables — and, of course, some Pakistani **rice**. The restaurant isn't only a 'pay-what-you-want' restaurant but also a 'play what you want' restaurant. In the evenings, you can take a djembe, an African drum, and play music with others. It's a really cool place to spend some time.

B Soul Kitchen – Red Bank, New Jersey, USA

Soul Kitchen is a great place to go for lunch. The menu has choices of **starters** — my favourite is the **mixed green salad, main course** — fish, meat or vegetarian, and **dessert**. But, it doesn't have any prices. That's because you can pay what you want. The restaurant asks for $10 or more, but people who haven't got $10 can eat there and work for an hour to pay for their meal. The food is healthy and local. The restaurant even has a garden and grows a lot of the **vegetables** that they use in their meals.

C Lentil As Anything, Melbourne, Australia

This is a vegetarian restaurant in Australia's second city. In fact, there are four Lentil As Anything restaurants in the city. Nine hundred people eat in the restaurant in the Abbotsford district of the city every day. The restaurants are open all day and you can eat **breakfast, lunch** and **dinner** there. They are friendly places where you can chat to other customers, listen to good music and, when you leave, you put some money in a box. The food is healthy and delicious. They don't serve meat but you can find great food with other ingredients like **pumpkin**. Their **pumpkin curry** is amazing.

GLOSSARY

drum (n) – a musical instrument played by hitting it with your hand or a stick
grow (v) – to make plants develop and produce fruit or flowers or become big enough to eat
district (n) – an area of a town

chat (v) – talk in a friendly, informal way
customer (n) – someone who buys goods or services from a shop, restaurant, etc.
pumpkin (n) – a large, orange vegetable that is popular at Halloween

1 Read the text and decide which restaurant A–C is best for customers 1–4. One customer doesn't have a suitable restaurant.

1 'I love hot food from China and India. I'd like to try food from a different country in Asia.' ☐

2 'I don't eat meat. I think it is wrong to kill animals for food. I don't even like seeing other people eat meat.' ☐

3 'I love traditional English breakfasts with sausages, bacon and fried eggs.' ☐

4 'I haven't got a job. I have a lot of time in the middle of the day but I haven't got money for food.' ☐

2 Read the text again. Match questions 1–9 with the restaurants. Write DWD (Der Weiner Deewan), SK (Soul Kitchen) or LAA (Lentil As Anything).

Where …

1 do they grow some of the food they serve? _____
2 do they use recipes from different countries? _____
3 can you pay for your food or work? _____
4 can you choose from four restaurants with the same name? _____
5 can you play music? _____
6 can you eat at any time of the day? _____
7 can you get a three-course meal? _____
8 can you put the food you want on your plate? _____
9 can't you eat meat? _____

3 Look at the underlined verbs + prepositions in the text. Then complete the sentences with the verbs from the box.

(chat   ~~eat~~   go (×2)   listen   pay   play)

You can *eat* in a café or restaurant.

1 You can _____ for your meal with cash or a credit card.
2 People _____ to music on MP3 players and CDs.
3 There is a café and a restaurant in the building. You _____ up some stairs to the café and down some other stairs to the restaurant.
4 I often _____ to my friends on my computer. We use Skype.
5 After school, I sometimes _____ for a pizza or a hot dog with my friends.
6 My brother is in a band and sometimes he lets me _____ the guitar with them.

4 Complete the sentences with the correct verbs and prepositions from Exercise 3. Use the correct form of the verbs.

When I'm on holiday, I always *eat in* small, local restaurants.

1 I've got the chance to _____ the guitar _____ some really good musicians.
2 Where do you want to _____ _____ dinner?
3 My dad always _____ _____ the meal when we go out to a restaurant with the whole family.
4 To get to the toilet, _____ _____ the stairs and turn left.
5 The tables in the restaurant are very big, so you can meet other people and _____ _____ them.
6 Jan likes it when she can _____ _____ Spanish music in real Spanish restaurants.

REMEMBER THIS

The word *meal* means everything we eat, e.g. for breakfast or dinner. Some meals, e.g. dinner, consist of *courses*, e.g. *soup, meat and vegetables, dessert*. The word *ingredients* means the food items a particular *dish* is made from, e.g. to make *spaghetti bolognese* or *Yorkshire pudding* (a dish) we need *cheese* and *tomatoes*, or *flour, milk* and *eggs* (ingredients).

5 Read REMEMBER THIS. Put the words in bold from the text on page 28 under the correct heading.

Meals of the day	Courses	Dishes	Ingredients
breakfast	_____	_____	_____
_____	_____	_____	_____
_____	_____	_____	_____

WORD STORE 2E | Food adjectives

6 Complete the sentences with one word in each gap. The first letters are given.

I love this restaurant. The waiters are polite and the food is **d**_elicious._

1 This bread is very **f**_____ . It's still warm.
2 I don't eat meat. What **v**_____ dishes do you serve?
3 Can I have a glass of water, please? This curry is very **s**_____ !
4 I'm sorry, we don't have rice. We only serve **l**_____ food and we don't grow rice in this country.
5 I hope you like this. It's a **t**_____ meal from my country. My grandmother always cooks it when I go home to visit.
6 I don't like fried food, especially meat. I prefer it **g**_____ – it's healthier.

VOCABULARY PRACTICE | Food

7 Look at the vocabulary in lesson 2.4 in the Student's Book. Complete the sentences with one word in each gap. The first letters are given.

There are some strange foods that people eat. Are they **t**_asty_? Read on to find out.
There are some very unusual **d**_____ in countries around the world. In Iceland, for example, a famous **s**_____ is hákarl. Hákarl is shark meat that is dried. It smells terrible! But it tastes much better than it smells, they say.
In Cambodia – a country in Southeast Asia – a very popular **s**_____ **f**_____ is spiders. I've heard they taste like chicken. Would you like to eat hákarl or fried spiders for your **m**_____ ?

Hákarl

SHOW WHAT YOU KNOW

1 Write *a* or *an* before the nouns.

   an apple   5 ____ jar
1 ____ egg   6 ____ bag
2 ____ potato   7 ____ onion
3 ____ orange   8 ____ pizza
4 ____ carrot   9 ____ ingredient

2 ★ Choose the correct word.

Nopal is ¹*a / the* cactus. There are a lot of nopal plants in Mexico and many Mexicans use nopal as ²*an / a* ingredient in their meals. The Festival del Nopal is a festival of nopal cooking but it happens in ³*the / Ø* Santa Cruz, California. ⁴*A / The* festival is very popular and you can eat different food made with nopal. It is great with tomatoes and onions, with cheese, or you can make ⁵*a / the* dessert with ⁶*Ø / the* fruit from the nopal plant. ⁷*A / The* festival happens in ⁸*Ø / the* July. It's a great way to find out about this delicious plant.

3 ★ ★ Complete the text with *a*, *an*, *the* or *Ø* in each gap.

My aunt lives in *a* big city. It is called ¹____ Bristol. My aunt's house is in ²____ city centre. Bristol is ³____ exciting city. There are ⁴____ lot of restaurants and we always eat in one when we stay with my aunt. Near her house, there is ⁵____ Chinese restaurant, ⁶____ Indian restaurant, ⁷____ two Italian restaurants and ⁸____ Moroccan restaurant. ⁹____ Moroccan restaurant is my favourite. ¹⁰____ food there is amazing. I love ¹¹____ Moroccan food.

4 ★ ★ ★ Each sentence has one mistake. Find the mistake and correct it.

I don't eat ~~the~~ meat but I eat a lot of vegetables. __—__
1 The shops in this town don't sell an ingredients I need. ____
2 I live in the town in southern England. ____
3 We've got a pizza for lunch but the pizza has got mushrooms on it and I don't like the mushrooms. ____
4 We stay in a small town in the Italy every August. ____

5 ★ ★ ★ Add two articles to each sentence. Rewrite the sentences with the articles in the correct places.

Do you like food that they sell at café in Market Street?
Do you like the food that they sell at the café in Market Street?
1 I need onion for this dinner but I haven't got any and shops near here aren't open.

   _____
   _____

2 There is food festival in main square of our town in June.

   _____
   _____

3 I'm good cook but recipes in this book are very difficult.

   _____
   _____

4 I like pizzas but I don't like pizzas from restaurant near our school.

   _____
   _____

SHOW WHAT YOU'VE LEARNT

6 Complete the dialogue with *the* (x1), *a* (x2) and *Ø* (x3).

Melanie: This is <u>a</u> good photo. Where is it?
Jason: That's me in ¹____ Spain. We go there every year in ²____ August.
Melanie: Are you in ³____ restaurant in this photo?
Jason: It's a café. ⁴____ cakes there are delicious. We always go there on the way back to the hotel from the beach.
Melanie: So what are those things on your plate?
Jason: They are churros. They are Spanish cakes.
Melanie: So, you like ⁵____ Spanish cakes, eh?
Jason: I love all cakes, from England, Spain, Germany – everywhere.
Melanie: Well, I've got ⁶____ cake here. It's a carrot cake.
Jason: Carrot cake? A cake with carrots in it?? Maybe there are some cakes that I don't like.

                              /6

GRAMMAR: Train and Try Again page 129

1 Translate the phrases into your own language.

SPEAKING BANK

Ordering food

Are you ready to order? _____

_____

I'd like a/an/some … / _____
Can I have a/an/some … _____

_____

What would you like to _____
drink? _____

_____

Large or small? _____

Anything else? _____

No, thanks. That's it. _____

How much is it? _____

It's … (+ *price*) _____

Here you are. _____

_____

Enjoy your meal. _____

2 Complete the sentences with the prices in words. Use the verb *be* in the correct form.

Menu

| Burger | £2.79 |
| Tuna sandwich | £3.89 |

Menu

| Tea | 99p |
| Apple | 45p |

Menu

| Hot dog | €3.00 |
| Cheese sandwich | €3.50 |

A burger *is two pounds seventy-nine*.
1 A hot dog _____.
2 Tuna sandwiches _____.
3 Cheese sandwiches _____.
4 Tea _____.
5 An apple _____.

3 Put the words in the correct order.

are / Hi, / order / ready / to / you
Hi, are you ready to order? ☐W

1 OK. / to / What / you / drink / like / would
_____ ? ☐

2 that's / No / it. / thanks / much / it / How / is
_____ . ☐
_____ ?

3 your / meal / Enjoy
_____ . ☐

4 pounds / It's / seventy-five / two
_____ . ☐

5 have / please / I / juice, / Can / orange / an
_____ ? ☐

6 Yes, / a / like / hot dog / I'd
_____ . ☐

7 you / Here / are
_____ . ☐

8 else / Anything
_____ ? ☐

4 Look at the sentences in Exercise 3. Decide who says them: the customer (C) or the waiter (W).

5 Put the conversation in Exercise 3 in the correct order.

Waiter: *Hi, are you ready to order*?
Customer: 1_____
Waiter: 2_____
Customer: 3_____
Waiter: 4_____
Customer: 5_____
Waiter: 6_____
Customer: 7_____
Waiter: 8_____
Customer: Thanks.

6 Complete the dialogue with one word in each gap.

Waiter: Are you ready to *order*?
Customer: Yes, please. I'd ¹_____ a hot dog.
Waiter: What ²_____ you like to ³_____ ?
Customer: A mineral water, please.
Waiter: ⁴_____ or small?
Customer: A small one, please.
Waiter: ⁵_____ else?
Customer: No, thanks, ⁶_____ 's it. How ⁷_____
           is it?
Waiter: It's two pounds ninety-five.
Customer: ⁸_____ you are.
Waiter: ⁹_____ your meal.
Customer: Thanks.

WRITING

An email of invitation

1 Complete the sentences related to parties with the words from the box.

> clothes   everyone   ~~everyone~~   people
> presents   spicy   the holidays

1 *Everyone* makes some Indian food.

2 ᵃ_____ usually bring ᵇ_____ .

3 My friend's curries are really _____ .

4 We always talk about _____ – not school work!

5 ᵃ_____ wears strange ᵇ_____ .

2 Match the sentences from Exercise 1 with the parties. Two sentences match the same party.

A a fancy dress party
B a bring-your-own-curry party
C a birthday party
D an after-exams party

3 Choose the correct answers A–C.

> ¹___Tom!
> ²___ are you? I'm fine. It's my birthday next week.
> ³___ you like to come to my party? It's ⁴___ Friday at my house. ⁵___ you come?
> Write soon.
>
> Jessica

1	A Hi	B Bye	C High
2	A Who	B How	C What
3	A Do	B Are	C Would
4	A at	B in	C on
5	A Do	B Can	C Are

4 Complete the email with the words from the box. There are two extra words.

> at   delicious   hope   let   love   party
> text   ~~things~~   want   wishes   would

> Hi Mary,
> How are *things*?
> Do you ¹_____ to come to our ²_____ ? It's on Saturday ³_____ 4 p.m. at the pizza restaurant in Turner Road. The pizzas there are ⁴_____ . It's an after-exams party – no-one talks about school or exams!
> I ⁵_____ you can come. Email or ⁶_____ me and ⁷_____ me know.
> Best ⁸_____ .
>
> Adam

5 You are organising a party and you want to invite your friend. Write an email to him/her.

- Use appropriate expressions to start and finish it.
- Invite your friend to your party.
- Include the details about the party (occasion, place, date, time, etc.).
- Ask your friend to confirm that he/she will come and – if yes – tell him/her what to bring to the party.

Finished? Always check your writing. Can you tick √ everything on this list?

In my email invitation:

- I have started with an appropriate greeting, e.g. *Hi, Martha.* ☐
- I have asked how my friend is. ☐
- I have invited my friend to my party. ☐
- I have given the details about the party. ☐
- I have finished the email appropriately. ☐
- I have used an appropriate ending, e.g. *Love, Best wishes*, etc. ☐
- I have used contractions (e.g. *I'm / aren't / that's*). ☐
- I have used emoticons ☺ and/or acronyms (*info / CU / gr8*), but not too many. ☐
- I have checked my spelling. ☐
- My text is neat and clear. ☐

1 In pairs, ask and answer the questions.

PART 1

Talk about your free time.
1 What do you like doing at the weekend?
2 Do you prefer staying at home or going out? Why?
3 What do you like doing with your friends in your free time?
4 Do you play a musical instrument?
5 Do you enjoy going for a run? Why?/Why not?

PART 2

Talk about food.
1 Do you like eating healthy food? Why?/Why not?
2 Do you prefer hamburgers or pizza? Why?
3 What do you usually eat for dessert?
4 Do you often get a takeaway? Why?/Why not?
5 What's your favourite local food? Why?

2 Look at the photos that show types of food.

PART 1

Which of these types of food do you eat? Discuss in pairs.

PART 2

In pairs, ask and answer the questions.
1 How do you make pancakes?
2 How often do you eat vegetarian food?
3 Do you prefer eating vegetables or meat? Why?

4 What's your favourite type of street food? Why?
5 Is it healthy to eat a lot of fast food? Why?/Why not?
6 Do you like eating spicy food? Why?/Why not?
7 Which of these types of food do you like best? Why?

3 Read the instructions on your card. In pairs, take turns to role-play the conversation.

Student A

**You are the waiter in a restaurant.
Ask Student B the questions.**

• Say hello and ask Student B if he/she is ready to order.
• Ask what he/she would like to eat.
• Ask what he/she would like to drink.
• Ask if he/she wants a large or a small drink.
• Say that the large drink is $2.
• Ask if he/she wants anything else.
• End the conversation.

Student B

You're in a restaurant and Student A is the waiter. You want to order the grilled salmon and potatoes and some orange juice. Answer Student A's questions.

• Say that you are ready to order.
• Answer the question about the food.
• Answer the question about the drink.
• Ask about the price of the large drink.
• Say that you would like the large size.

VOCABULARY AND GRAMMAR

1 **Choose the correct option.**

	Mum:	Dan, can you buy a *bar / jar /* (*loaf*) of bread on the way back from school?
	Dan:	Sure, no problem.
1	Mum:	What do you want to drink?
	Colin:	A *bar / can / tub* of lemonade, please.
2	Debbie:	Do you want me to buy anything from the shop?
	Mum:	Just a *loaf / bar / packet* of flour.
3	Dad:	Do you need any vegetables?
	Mum:	Er … yes. Get half a kilo of *strawberries / eggs / onions*.
4	Celina:	Do you eat a lot of dairy food?
	Donna:	Yes. I have *cheese / tuna / onions* with everything.
5	Sara:	Oh, no. I shouldn't.
	Fiona:	Go on. It's only a small *tub / bar / can* of chocolate.

/5

2 **Complete the note with one word in each gap. The first letters are given.**

Jack,

Please go to the supermarket and get these things for me.
I need a c<u>*an*</u> *of soup,*
a ¹b_____ of sugar,
a ²b_____ of oil,
a ³c_____ of orange juice,
a ⁴j_____ of mayonnaise and
a ⁵p_____ of cocoa.

Mum

/5

3 **Complete the sentences with one word in each gap. The first letters are given.**

This is a **t**<u>*raditional*</u> meal from the south of Spain.
1 Ali: This curry is very **s**_____ .
  Noah: Good, I love hot food.
2 I can't **f**_____ the eggs. There isn't any oil.
3 The food here is all **l**_____ , from farms in the area.
4 Can you **s**_____ the onions into thin pieces before you cook them, please?
5 Shane: Is your dinner OK?
  Janine: Yes, it's **d**_____ .

/5

4 **Complete the sentences with one word in each gap.**
Conversation 1
Paul: There's no orange juice. <u>*How*</u> <u>*much*</u> do you drink every day?
Cathy: Not much. One glass, at breakfast time. Oh, and a glass when I get home. And before I go to bed. Actually, I drink quite _____ _____.

Conversation 2
Jack: ª_____ _____ _____ potatoes?
Tia: No, but ᵇ_____ _____ _____ rice. You can use that.
Jack: What, to make chips??

Conversation 3
Tom: We can have a barbecue. ª_____ _____ _____ meat in the fridge?
Mum: Yes, there is but ᵇ_____ _____ . I need to go shopping again. Don't worry, though. I've got a recipe for vegetarian burgers.
Tom: Er …, well, maybe we can get a takeaway.

/5

5 **Complete the dialogue with *a, an, the* or Ø in each gap.**
Nathan: What's this?
Paula: It's <u>*a*</u> pancake. ¹___ American pancake.
Nathan: Great. I love pancakes. Are they easy to make?
Paula: Yes. I always use ²___ recipe for pancakes in this book. It's ³___ great book.
Nathan: I like ⁴___ cooking but I haven't got any books. I always look on ⁵___ Internet. Why buy books when you can get everything for free?

/5

6 **Choose the correct answers A–C.**

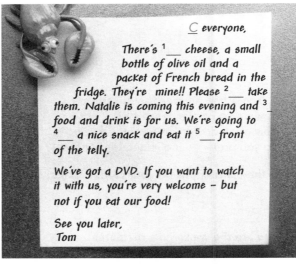

<u>*C*</u> everyone,

There's ¹___ cheese, a small bottle of olive oil and a packet of French bread in the fridge. They're mine!! Please ²___ take them. Natalie is coming this evening and ³___ food and drink is for us. We're going to ⁴___ a nice snack and eat it ⁵___ front of the telly.

We've got a DVD. If you want to watch it with us, you're very welcome – but not if you eat our food!

See you later,
Tom

	A	B	C
	A For	B Best	Ⓒ To
1	A a	B some	C any
2	A don't	B do	C not
3	A the	B a	C some
4	A do	B get	C make
5	A in	B on	C at

/5

Total /30

7 Complete each pair of sentences with the same word A–C.

She's going to the shop to buy a ___ of crisps and a drink.
I need a ___ of flour to make a cake.
A bar   B bag   C packet

1 Paella is a famous rice ___ from Spain.
Ben's favourite ___ is spaghetti bolognese.
A dish   B meal   C takeaway

2 There aren't any eggs. Can you get a ___ from the supermarket?
My family drinks a ___ of orange juice every day!
A loaf   B tub   C carton

3 Street ___ is very popular in Asia.
He doesn't eat meat – he only eats vegetarian ___ .
A food   B speciality   C snack

4 You can use butter or olive oil to ___ eggs.
Add some salt to the meat before you ___ it.
A mix   B slice   C fry

5 There aren't ___ mushrooms on this pizza.
How ___ bags of sugar do we need?
A any   B many   C much

/5

8 Put the words in the correct order to make sentences or questions.

Tim: food / the / I / best / think / is / fresh
         I think fresh food is the best.
Pedro: Yes, I agree.

1 Waiter: you / order / to / ready / are
         _____?
Lina: Yes, I'd like a pizza Margherita, please.

2 Amy: What do you want for dinner?
Paul: get / tonight / a / let's / takeway
         _____

3 Lucy: What do you do after school?
Dan: I / snack / make / usually / a
         _____

4 Jim: drink / would / to / like / you / what
         _____?
Cathy: Can I have some lemonade, please?

5 Sam: how / is / much / it
         _____?
Helen: It's two pounds fifty.

/5

9 Complete the text with the correct answers A–C.

blog

Easy chocolate cake

This cake is very easy to make! It's a quick and _C_ dessert. You cook it in a cup in your microwave oven. First, get your ¹___ . You only need four! Put ²___ egg, sugar, flour and cocoa into the cup. You don't need ³___ of sugar or cocoa. ⁴___ the egg, sugar, flour and cocoa together. Cook the cake in the microwave oven for one minute. It's ready! Do you have ⁵___ vanilla ice cream? Put it on top of the cake and enjoy your dessert!

	A grilled	B local	C delicious
1	A ingredients	B specialities	C dishes
2	A the	B some	C an
3	A a lot	B many	C much
4	A Chop	B Mix	C Boil
5	A many	B some	C any

/5

10 Choose the correct answers A–C.

I need ___ oil to fry the fish.
A a lot of
B much
C an

1 Is there ___ cheese in the sandwich?
A any
B many
C some

2 This is an amazing pizza. I just love ___ mushroom topping! Yum!
A –
B a
C the

3 There aren't ___ people in the restaurant.
A many
B some
C much

4 I have ___ flour to make a cake.
A much
B some
C lot of

5 Have you tried Szechuan chicken?
It's ___ spicy dish from China.
A –
B the
C a

/5

Total   /20

3 Work

VOCABULARY

3.1

Jobs • *work* and *job* • prepositions

SHOW WHAT YOU KNOW

1 Match the jobs with the descriptions.

> gardener ~~journalist~~ lawyer mechanic
> nurse plumber receptionist
> shop assistant waiter

This person …

writes for a newspaper.   *journalist*
1 fixes cars.   _____
2 welcomes people to an office or
  a hotel and answers the telephone.   _____
3 works with patients and people
  who are ill.   _____
4 helps people with legal problems
  and sometimes works in a court.   _____
5 fixes problems with water pipes.   _____
6 works with plants, e.g. trees,
  flowers and lawns.   _____
7 helps you buy things.   _____
8 brings you food in a restaurant.   _____

WORD STORE 3A | Jobs

2 Use the correct form of the words in brackets and write the names of the jobs.

Javed: What does your dad do?
Linda: He's an *engineer* (ENGINE).

1 **Dad:** So, Tom, what career are you interested in?
  Tom: Well, actually, I want to be a _____ (BUILD).
2 **Amy:** My aunt and uncle live in the countryside.
  Sally: Do they have animals? Like cows or sheep?
  Amy: Yes, they're _____ (FARM).
3 **Pam:** Is it easy to become a _____ (TEACH)?
  Jo: Well, there's a lot to learn. Not everyone can do it.
4 **Sue:** You've got a lovely voice. Why don't you join the drama club?
  Dan: No way. I'd hate to be an _____ (ACT).
5 **Phil:** You're really good at drawing.
  Cath: Thanks. I'd love to be an _____ (ART) in Paris or Florence.
6 **Tim:** My ambition is to become a _____ (SCIENCE).
  Mum: Well, if you work hard, you could be a really good biologist.
7 **Amy:** Why do you want to be an _____ ? (COUNT)
  Sam: I like working with details.

---

3 Complete the names of jobs. The last letters or endings are given.

I travel in space.
*astro*naut
1 I've got a class of primary school pupils.
  _____er
2 I design new buildings.
  _____ect
3 I stand in a big, noisy building all day and help to make cars.
  _____ _____er
4 I take people to the railway station, the cinema, the theatre and to many other places in my car.
  _____ _____er
5 I work with animals. I try to make them well when they are ill.
  _____t
6 I think my job is very important. People come to me when they have problems with their teeth.
  _____ist
7 I fight for my country when there are wars.
  _____ier

WORD STORE 3B | *work* and *job*

4 Complete the dialogue with *job* or *work* in each gap.

Woman: Can I help you?
Man: Yes, I'm looking for a *job*.
Woman: Do you want a part-time [1]_____ or do you want to [2]_____ full time?
Man: I want a full-time [3]_____ . I don't want to [4]_____ part time.
Woman: Can you [5]_____ at night?
Man: I don't mind when I [6]_____ but I'd like a well-paid [7]_____ . I can [8]_____ long hours and I always [9]_____ hard. I don't want to [10]_____ only eight hours a day – I can stay at work for twelve hours or more!
Woman: Well, we need factory workers. We pay £10 an hour.
Man: Have you got anything else? That's quite a boring [11]_____ and quite a badly-paid [12]_____ too. I'm hoping for £15 an hour or more.

---

5 Complete the text with the words from the box. There are three extra words.

(at   for   from   in (x2)   on   own   to   with)

HOW DO YOUNG PEOPLE SEE THEIR FUTURE?

Here are some of your responses.

I don't know what I want to do when I finish my education. My parents work _for_ large companies but I don't think I'd like that. I'd like to work ¹_____ home and be free to go shopping or sleep when I want. I definitely don't want to be a teacher. I couldn't work ²_____ a school ³_____ children. I don't think I'd be very good at working ⁴_____ a team, either. I like to decide what to do and when to do it. Yes, I believe it's a good idea for me to work alone, without any people around me. I could work ⁵_____ projects – at my own desk with my own computer. Yes, I would really like to stay at home.

Katy, 17

REMEMBER THIS

Some job names can have a different meaning in other languages even if they look similar.

Manager – someone whose job is to organise and control the work of a business/organisation or a part of it, e.g. *sales manager, personnel manager*.

Chief – someone who is the highest in authority, position or rank in a business/organisation, e.g. *a police chief, an army chief*.

Boss – the person who is in charge of you at work.

Chef – someone who organises cooking food in a restaurant/hotel.

6 Read REMEMBER THIS. Choose the correct option.

1 My *chief / boss* gets very angry when I'm late for work.
2 He's the finance *boss / manager* of a small company.
3 I'd like to be a *chef / chief* in a Greek restaurant.
4 Police *chiefs / chefs* from different countries often meet to discuss new ideas.

REMEMBER BETTER

If you do not remember the exact word to describe somebody's profession or job, describe what a given person does.

She works in a garden. (She is a gardener.)
He works with engines. (He's an engineer.)

Complete the mini-conversations with one word in each gap. The first letters are given.

Guido: Emily is … I don't remember the word. She **w**_orks_ in an office and she ¹**c**_____ money.
Paola: You mean an accountant.
Guido: That's it. Thanks!

Kazuo: Brian works in a hotel, in ²**r**_____ , you know, where people go when they first arrive.
Aiko: So, he's a receptionist.
Kazuo: Yes.

Diego: My sister works in a restaurant.
Manuel: Does she cook?
Diego: No, she serves customers. She's like a ³**w**_____ but there's a different word when it's a female.
Manuel: A waitress. You know the word *princess* – that can help you remember *waitress*.
Diego: Good idea!

Defne: I want to work in the theatre. I want to ⁴**a**_____.
Yusuf: You want to be an actress.
Defne: An actress, yes.

SHOW WHAT YOU'VE LEARNT

7 Choose the correct option.

1 I work *from / on / in* home, so I don't need to dress smartly.
2 My mum works *with / on / in* a supermarket but not on a checkout.
3 Kate is an *actor / acting / actress*. Her dream is to go to Hollywood.
4 I love working *with / for / from* animals. That's why I work at our local zoo.
5 I don't want a badly- *pay / money / paid* job. I want to be rich!
6 Do you always work *long / hard / team*?
7 My dad is a *lawyer / plumber / mechanic*. People often phone up in the middle of the night because there is water on their kitchen floor.
8 I work eight hours *in / the / a* day. I start at 7 a.m. and finish at 3 p.m.
9 Do you want a full-time or *part- / short- / half-* time job?
10 I don't want to work outside, so I don't want to be *an accountant / a gardener / a secretary*.

/10

SHOW WHAT YOU KNOW

1 Complete the sentences with the correct forms of the verb _be_. In negative sentences, use short forms where possible.

Hello. My name's John. _Are_ you English?

1 Paul's brother is here. What ____ his name?

2 John ____ (not) here today. He's at the dentist's.

3 That boy looks just like you. ____ he your brother?

4 Thanks for all your help. You ____ a really good friend.

5 Hi. Nice to meet you. Where ____ you from?

6 You can't come in. We ____ (not) ready.

7 I ____ (not) often late for school but sometimes I have problems waking up.

2 ★ Complete the text with the correct forms of the verbs in brackets. Use short forms where possible.

Henry V

I'_m sitting_ (sit) in my classroom. We ¹_____ (do) a History test. Paul ²_____ (write) quickly. Maggie ³_____ (not/write). She ⁴_____ (think) – but ⁵_____ she _____ (think) about the exam or something else? Our teacher ⁶_____ (watch) us. He's got a book but he ⁷_____ (not/read) it. Simon and Will ⁸_____ (talk). They ⁹_____ (not/try) to do the test at all. They don't care. They always do badly in tests. And I'm … What ¹⁰_____ I _____ (do)? I ¹¹_____ (waste) time. Come on, think … Henry V …

3 ★ ★ Complete the questions and answers with the phrases from the box.

> ~~are you doing~~   are you waiting   is she going
> they are having   they are washing
> 's going   ~~'m looking~~   'm waiting

Cathy: What _are you doing_?

Mum: I _'m looking_ for my phone. I can't find it anywhere.

Conversation 1

Phil: Hi, Ben. Who ¹_____ for?

Ben: I ²_____ for Elaine. She's late.

Conversation 2

Russ: Vicky's at the bus stop. Where ¹_____ ?

Tim: She ²_____ to the cinema. She's meeting Ted there.

Conversation 3

Claire: What's that noise?

Shelly: Colin and Ben are in the kitchen. ¹_____ the dishes.

Claire: I don't think so. I think ²_____ an argument.

4 ★ ★ ★ Use the words in brackets to make full dialogues.

Conversation 1

Amy: Hi, Mel. _Are you doing_ (you/do) anything at the moment?

Mel: Not really. ¹_____ (I/wait) for a phone call from Pete.

Amy: ²_____ (he/work) today?

Mel: Yes, ³_____ (he/help) his mum at her café. ⁴_____ (he/serve) the customers.

Conversation 2

Beth: Hi, Cathy. ¹_____ (What/you/cook)?

Cathy: A curry. Do you want some?

Beth: No, thanks. ²_____ (Joe/get/pizza).

Cathy: ³_____ (Where/he/buy) it?

Beth: I don't know. Why?

Cathy: Because there's a new pizza restaurant near the station. ⁴_____ (They/sell/pizzas) for half price this week.

SHOW WHAT YOU'VE LEARNT

5 Put the verbs in brackets in the correct form to make sentences and questions. Add the correct personal pronouns.

Will: _Why are you running_ (why/run)?

Dan: I'm late for work. I don't want to lose my job.

1 Hale: _____ (what/read)?

John: _Game of Thrones_. I think it's great.

2 Liam: Bye Mum. _____ (go) to school.

Mum: Bye. See you later.

3 Val: What's wrong? Where's Tom?

Belle: _____ (play) tennis with Steve and I'm all alone.

4 Andy: Hey, Stuart, _____ (use) your phone now?

Stuart: No. Do you want to borrow it?

5 Dad: _____ (write) an email?

Jack: No, I'm looking for a summer job.

6 Meg: Hi, Diana, hi, Sam. Good to see you two. Do you have a minute?

Diana: _____ (have) lunch right now. Let's meet in my office at 2.30, OK?

/6

GRAMMAR: Train and Try Again page 130

Verb–preposition–noun collocations
• *learn* and *teach*

1 Read the three texts. Complete gaps A–C with the
verbs from the box. There are two extra words.

> building   learning   making   teaching   working

Extract from Student's Book recording 🔊 **2.6**

Amy: I ¹*make / work* **with local teachers** and we
²*teach / learn* **young children** in the village.
The lessons are in a very old school, but we
are **A_____ a new school!** We work
on the building in the afternoons and on
Saturdays. It's hard work but I enjoy it. And
this place is so beautiful! […]

***

Terry: Hi. I'm **B_____ on a gardening
project.** We run a vegetable garden next to
the local hospital so we can ³*grow / eat* **fresh
vegetables** for the patients. I like ⁴*making /
working* **with my hands** and it's great to work
outside. Some of the patients also ⁵*help / sleep*
in the garden […]

***

Richard: Hello everyone. I ⁶*work / teach* **with
homeless children**, mainly teenagers. I talk to
them in the street and try to help them. We
also run a bakery together. The young people
⁷*do / make* **the bread**; they learn to work in
a team and they learn practical skills. They
⁸*do / make* **some money** and they always
have something to eat. The kids are great
and they're **C_____ me real street
Spanish!**

2 Choose the correct words 1–8 to complete
the recording extract in Exercise 1.

3 Match the beginnings 1–5 with the correct endings
a–f.

I **teach** ⬜ f

1 The most important thing is to **work** ⬜
2 We can't **grow** ⬜
3 Mum keeps promising to **make** ⬜
4 My parents are **building** ⬜
5 I haven't got time to **help** ⬜

a **flowers** because we haven't got a garden.
b **a chocolate cake**.
c **you with your homework** at the moment.
d **a house** by a lake where they can live when they retire.
e **with nice people**.
f **English** in a small school in a village.

4 Complete the collocations with the words from the box.

> a house   children   in   money   on
> vegetables   with (x2)

COLLOCATIONS WITH PREPOSITIONS

work ·········· *with* young people / your hands
¹_____ a project
²_____ the garden / kitchen

help ·········· you ³_____ your homework

COLLOCATIONS WITHOUT PREPOSITIONS

teach ·········· ⁴_____ / someone English /
a foreign language
learn ·········· English / a foreign language
make ·········· bread / a cake / pizza / ⁵_____
grow ·········· flowers / plants / ⁶_____
build ·········· ⁷_____

WORD STORE 3D | *learn* and *teach*

5 Complete the sentences with the correct words.

TEACH / LEARN
A You've got a lot of free time now that your exams
are over. You can *teach* your brother to swim.
B You've got a lot of free time now that your exams
are over. You can *learn* to swim.

1 **TEACH / LEARN**
A We _____ a lot in our Maths lessons.
B Our teachers always _____ us a lot during
our lessons. I'm always tired when we finish.

2 **TEACHES / LEARNS**
A I like the way our English teacher _____ us.
She makes the lessons fun and stress free.
B I work very hard at school but my friend always
_____ more than me. I don't know why.

3 **TEACH / LEARN**
A How can I _____ a new language?
Are there any good websites you know?
B I can't _____ my brother Spanish.
He's a terrible student!

4 **TEACHING / LEARNING**
A Now that I've got a job, I'm _____ a lot
about myself. I get nervous very quickly when
things go wrong!
B My dad is _____ me how to drive.
He gets nervous very quickly when I do
something wrong!

1 Read the texts and answer the questions. Write **T** (Tess), **M** (Matt) or **S** (Sylvie). Write **N** if a question doesn't match any of the people.

Who …
1 works outside?
2 works in the evening?
3 does the job because he/she can't find anything else?
4 sometimes wears special clothes?
5 works in an office?
6 doesn't always earn the same amount of money?
7 sometimes works with other people?
8 does more than one job?
9 works for different businesses?
10 can eat when he/she is working?

YoungPeople.ed   Home | Search | Contact

Young people and … money
How can you earn a bit of extra pocket money? Here are some ideas.

1
Tess, aged 20

I'm a student and, to earn a little bit of money, I do leafleting for local businesses. It's really <u>dull</u> work and quite tiring. I stand in the street all day on Saturday and give people leaflets for pizza restaurants, shops and children's play areas. Sometimes, the company I am working for gives me an <u>outfit</u> to put on – like a snail outfit for a French restaurant! I don't get paid much – £40 for a whole day. Sometimes, two of us work together. That's good because we can chat and laugh together.

2
Matt, aged 16

I live in a small town and there aren't many part-time jobs for people of my age. In fact, there aren't any. That's why I work for myself. I do tutoring. I'm very good at Maths and Sciences and a lot of children need help with these subjects. I go to their homes after school and help them with homework or <u>revision</u>. I only tutor one child a day, so I still get home by 5 p.m. I earn different amounts from different people. Some of the families don't have much money, so I don't <u>charge</u> much – but I never do it for free! When I have a lot of school work or when exams are coming up, I take a week off.

3
Sylvie, aged 17

I don't have a <u>regular</u> job, but when I need money, I do babysitting. The great thing is that I can say 'Yes' or 'No'. It <u>depends</u> on what my plans are, so I never miss any parties or concerts. I always work in the evening and it isn't hard work at all. The children I look after are asleep or getting ready for bed when I arrive. I tell them a story, switch their lights off and, after that, I can just sit and watch television. There is even food for me to eat and, for four hours, I earn £24.

GLOSSARY

businesses (n, pl) – companies or organisations that sell something or offer a service

amounts (n, pl) – quantities of something such as time, money, or a substance

miss (v) – not do something or go somewhere because you can't for some reason

2 Look at the underlined words in the text. Decide what part of speech they are: A *(adjective)*, N *(noun)* or V *(verb)*.

1	dull	A	N	V
2	outfit	A	N	V
3	revision	A	N	V
4	charge	A	N	V
5	regular	A	N	V
6	depends	A	N	V

3 Choose the correct meaning for the words in Exercise 2.

1 It's really <u>dull</u> work.
   A It's very interesting work.
   B It's very boring work.

2 Sometimes, companies give me an <u>outfit</u> to put on.
   A Sometimes, companies give me some special clothes to wear.
   B Sometimes, companies give me something to hold up and show people.

3 I help them with homework or <u>revision</u>.
   A I help them with homework or project work.
   B I help them with homework or studying for exams.

4 I don't <u>charge</u> so much.
   A I don't take so much money.
   B I don't work so hard.

5 I don't have a <u>regular</u> job.
   A My job is different to other people's.
   B I don't work at the same time, on the same day every week.

6 It <u>depends</u> on what my plans are.
   A After I make my plans, I decide when I can work.
   B After I get work, I make my plans for my free time.

4 Complete the dialogues with the words from Exercise 2. Change the form of the words if necessary.

Conversation 1
Peter: How much do you *charge* for your lessons?
Matt: That _____ on how rich the family is.

Conversation 2
Cath: Who are you working for today, Tess?
Tess: An Italian restaurant. I'm lucky. John's over there in the funny _____ but they've only got one.
Cath: What is it?
Tess: I'm not sure. I think it's some kind of pasta.

Conversation 3
Emma: Do you really like babysitting, Sylvie?
Sylvie: Yes, I love it. Why, don't you?
Emma: No, it's really ¹_____ . Nothing happens. I hate watching TV. And sometimes I work on Friday evenings, sometimes on Saturdays. I'd like to work ²_____ hours – and not in the evening.
Sylvie: Take your school books. You can do your ³_____ and get paid for it!

REMEMBER BETTER

It is important to learn the pronunciation of new words along with their meaning. You can use Internet dictionaries which give pronunciation in both oral and written form (audio recordings and phonetic transcription). What's more, they often give British as well as American pronunciation of particular words.

REMEMBER THIS

To strengthen the meaning of a message, we can use so-called intensifiers, e.g. *very* (*I'm tired – I'm very tired*), *at all, just, even, in fact, whole*, etc.

5 Read REMEMBER THIS. Find these phrases in the text and complete the missing words.

… £40 for a *whole* day
1 _____ , there aren't any.
2 … it isn't hard work _____ _____ .
3 There is _____ food for me to eat.
4 I can _____ sit and watch television.

6 Complete the text with one word in each gap to make the meaning stronger.

Meg: What's wrong?
Tanya: Oh, it's the World Cup. Jake talks about it the *whole* time. We don't go out ¹_____ _____ .
Meg: Well, it's only for a month. Why don't you watch a few matches? You might enjoy it.
Tanya: I watch quite a few matches but Jake doesn't ²_____ know I'm there. He ³_____ sits there looking at the television.
Meg: Simon's completely different. He doesn't really like any sports. ⁴_____ _____ , he always complains about me when we're out because I usually spend the ⁵_____ time looking at my mobile phone.
Tanya: Oh well, that's different. Mobiles are important!

VOCABULARY PRACTICE | Work

7 Look at the vocabulary in lesson 3.4 in the Student's Book. Complete the sentences with one word in each gap. The first letters are given.

They make chairs and other furniture in that **f***actory*.
1 Sandra is a nurse. Her job is **d**_____ and she works very hard.
2 I need more money – that's why I'm looking for a job with a good **s**_____ .
3 The assistants at this shop always speak politely to the **c**_____ .
4 Uncle Max is a headteacher – he's **r**_____ for organising school leaving exams in his school.
5 My parents prefer to pay more money and buy products that are of good **q**_____ .

WORD STORE 3E | Collocations

8 Put the words in the correct order.

I / salary / earn / a / don't / very / good
I don't earn a very good salary.

1 you / a lot / money / a shop assistant / of / as / earn / Do
_____ ?

2 enough / his needs / doesn't / My brother / earn / for
_____ .

3 £100 / earn / about / I / a week
_____ .

4 earn / living / How / does / her / Mrs Fisher
_____ ?

5 wants / Paul / a new computer / some / to pay / to / earn / money / for
_____ .

SHOW WHAT YOU KNOW

1 Complete the sentences with the correct forms of be or do. Use short forms if possible.

I *don't* (not) like my job. I work at night and I can never sleep during the day.

1 _____ you working at the moment? If not, can you help me in the kitchen?

2 Where _____ your mum teach? Are you happy she doesn't teach in our school?

3 Mr Brown _____ (not) work here. He works in our office in London.

4 A: Do you work every weekend?
   B: Yes, I _____ , but only on Saturdays.

5 What _____ your brother doing at the moment?

6 What _____ you want to do when you finish university?

7 A: Are you phoning the plumber?
   B: Yes, I _____ . I can't stop this water.

2 ★ Complete the sentences with the correct form of the verbs in capitals. Use short forms if possible.

PLAY
Dan usually *plays* tennis on a Saturday but today he*'s playing* golf.

1 MEET
We usually ª_____ outside the cinema but it's raining, so we ᵇ_____ in a café.

2 HAVE
My mum ª_____ a bath at the moment. She usually ᵇ_____ a shower but she wants to relax today.

3 DO
It's seven o'clock in the morning and my brother ª_____ his homework. I always ᵇ_____ my homework in the evening.

4 HAVE
We usually ª_____ Maths on Friday afternoon but our teacher is ill, so today we ᵇ_____ an extra English lesson.

5 SEND
My friends usually ª_____ me texts but my phone isn't working, so they ᵇ_____ me emails at the moment.

3 ★ ★ Complete the questions with the correct form of the verbs in brackets.

Conversation 1
Jason: Hi, Mark. What *are* you *doing* (do)?
Mark: I'm cooking dinner. Can you help me?
Jason: OK. ¹_____ your mum _____ (work) today?
Mark: Yes, she is. She's working late. ²_____ your mum _____ (work)?
Jason: Yes, she does. She works in a bank. That's why I know how to cook. Right. Let's start.

Conversation 2
Mandy: I can't believe your mum wants you to clean the whole house. ¹_____ Tom _____ (help) you?
Theresa: No, he isn't. He says he's got lots of homework.
Mandy: ²_____ you _____ (believe) him?
Theresa: No, but my mum does.
Mandy: What ³_____ you _____ (want) to do later, when the house is clean?
Theresa: I'm not sure. I'll phone and tell you.

Conversation 3
Sam: What ¹_____ you _____ (do)?
Kelly: I'm a teacher. I teach Chemistry.
Sam: Really? I've got a problem with my Chemistry homework. Could you help me?
Kelly: OK. Let me look. Oh, right. Well. It's like this … ²_____ you _____ (understand) now?
Sam: Er … I think so. Can you tell me again?

4 ★ ★ ★ Complete the advert with the correct forms of the verbs in brackets.

Do you work (you/work) very hard?
¹_____ (you/earn) a low salary?

Are you unhappy at work?

Danielle ²_____ (work) hard but she isn't unhappy.
She ³_____ (love) her job. She is a waitress at
FRESHFLAVOURFOODS.

FreshFlavourFoods is a new business but now
it ⁴_____ (grow) very quickly.
We ⁵_____ (open) new restaurants all over the
country and we ⁶_____ (look) for friendly,
hard-working people like Danielle to come and work for us.

⁷_____ (you/look) for a new job?
For more details and an online application form, go to
www.FreshFlavourFoods.uk

SHOW WHAT YOU'VE LEARNT

5 Complete the text with the correct form of the verbs from the box. There are two extra verbs.

do   get   ~~have~~   need   not complain
leave   open   sit   stand

Hi Kathy,
I'm at work. Don't worry! I*'m having* a break.
I ¹_____ down with my tablet for ten minutes.
I ²_____ up all day, so I ³_____ this rest. The restaurant is very busy today but the customers are nice. They ⁴_____ even when I bring them the wrong food. And they often ⁵_____ me quite a lot of money. I earn £30 and I often get another £20 from customers.
Oh no. The door ⁶_____ . It's my manager.
Time to go back to work. Only another four hours to go!
See you.
Rachel

/6

GRAMMAR: Train and Try Again page 130

1 Translate the phrases into your own language.

SPEAKING BANK

Describing a photo

Who? Where? What are they doing?

The photo shows
(a person/people)
in (a place).

_____
_____
_____

In the photo there is/
there are (a person/
people) in (a place).

_____
_____
_____

He/She is … /They are …
(*eat*) + *ing*

_____
_____

Details of the picture

On the left/On the right …

_____

In the background …

_____

We can also see …

_____

He/She's wearing …

_____

What you think

Perhaps … / Maybe …

_____

I think he is … / they are …

_____

2 Choose the correct option.

¹*On / In* the photo, there are two men. They are talking
and looking at a piece of paper. ²*Might be / Maybe* there
is a problem and they don't know what to do. ³*In / On* the
background, we ⁴*do / can* see a road. There aren't any cars.
It is a new road. The men are helping to build it. ⁵*In / On*
the left of the two men is a camera or other equipment that
they use in their work. ⁶*Might be / Perhaps* it is broken!
I think the men enjoy their work. ⁷*He's / It's* an interesting job.

3 Match questions 1–6 with answers a–g.

Who can you see in this photo? [g]
1 What is she doing?
2 How old is she?
3 What is she wearing?
4 How is she feeling?
5 Is the work difficult?
6 Do you think she likes her job?

a She isn't very young. I think she's about 35 years old.
b Maybe she's a bit worried about something she's
   reading but I think that generally, she isn't sad.
c Yes, definitely. She loves it. I am sure she doesn't like
   working in a boring, stress free job. She needs the
   excitement.
d She is looking at a computer. Maybe she's reading
   a report. Or perhaps she's reading a blog!
e I think it is very hard. She has a lot of responsibility.
f She's wearing a smart, dark, summer dress.
g We can see a woman. I think she's a business woman
   and she is working in her office.

4 Complete the description with the words from the box.

> asking   background   happy   likes   part-time
> ~~photo~~   singing   think (x2)   wearing   writing

In this _photo_, we can see a waitress in a restaurant.
She is young and she is ¹_____ a uniform and
a scarf in her hair. Perhaps she is a student and she works
²_____ . The photo also shows two customers,
a man and a woman. I ³_____ they are about
25 years old. They are ⁴_____ . Maybe they work
near the restaurant and go there after work. The waitress
is ⁵_____ the customers what they want to eat
and drink. She is ⁶_____ in a notebook. In the
⁷_____ , we can see three musicians. Two men
are playing instruments and a woman is ⁸_____ .
It's a friendly restaurant. I think the waitress ⁹_____
her job. The customers are nice to her but maybe it's
difficult to hear the customers because of the music!
I ¹⁰_____ she makes a lot of mistakes!

WRITING

An email of request

1 Complete the email with one word in each gap. The first letters are given.

To: Ben Taylor

From: Jane Simpson

Subject: Overtime

Ben,

We have got a p*roblem* – a nice problem but we ¹n_____ your help.

Our new holidays are very popular and we are getting hundreds of phone calls. Lots of people want information and our telephone sales staff can't answer them all. Could you do me a ²f_____ ? Could you ³p_____ find ten or more people to work an extra four hours every day this week, starting today? We can offer them £20 an hour for this.

Please ⁴c_____ you let me know how many people want the extra work before 2 p.m. I'm ⁵s_____ not to give you more time ⁶b_____ I need to tell Mr Collins at our meeting.

⁷T_____ very much.

Jane

2 Put the words in the correct order to make polite requests.

favour? / you / a / Could / me / do
Could you do me a favour?

1 you / please? / also / for me, / think / Do / check this email / you could

_____
_____

2 come / early / to work / you could / Do / tomorrow, / think / you / please?

_____
_____

3 Could / before 4 p.m.? / comments and suggestions / send it / with your / you please / to me

_____
_____

4 until / you / at work / this evening? / stay / 7 p.m. / Could

_____
_____

3 Complete the email with the requests from Exercise 2.

Hi Sandra,

I've got a problem. *Could you do me a favour?*
I need some help with the new computer program.
Mr Bryant wants to have it by tomorrow morning.
¹_____ ? I think we can finish it before 9 p.m. today. ²_____ ?
I want to send it to Mr Bryant but it has to be perfect.
³_____ ? Thanks a lot. I hate writing official letters and it's nice to have your opinion.
One last thing. ⁴_____ ?
Mr Bryant is coming at 9 a.m. and I want to make sure that everything is working OK. Can you be here by 7.30 a.m.? I'll get some breakfast for us.

Thanks a lot.
Helen

SHOW WHAT YOU'VE LEARNT

4 Imagine that you run a restaurant and one day you cannot come to work. It just happens that on that day health inspectors are to inspect your restaurant. On top of this, two new waiters are going to start work. Write an email to the head waiter/waitress. In your email:

- explain the situation.
- ask him/her to check that it's clean in the restaurant, to train the new waiters and to buy fresh food products.
- apologise for asking him/her to do all this work.
- thank him/her for his/her efforts.

SHOW THAT YOU'VE CHECKED

Finished? Always check your writing.
Can you tick ✓ everything on this list?

In my email:

- I have started the email with an appropriate greeting, e.g. *Greg, Hi Monica*, etc. ☐
- I have explained the situation. ☐
- I have listed all my requests in a clear and kind way. ☐
- I have mentioned my expectations. ☐
- I have apologised for the whole situation and expressed my thanks for helping me. ☐
- I have used contractions (e.g. *I'm / aren't / that's*). ☐
- I have checked my spelling. ☐
- My text is neat and clear. ☐

1 **In pairs, ask and answer the questions.**

PART 1

Talk about food.
1 What food do you like eating when friends visit you?
2 What food do you cook most often? Why?
3 How often do you eat fast food?
4 Do you prefer going to a restaurant or eating at home? Why?
5 What's the local speciality where you live?

PART 2

Talk about jobs.
1 What's your ideal job? Why?
2 Would you like to work with old people? Why?/Why not?
3 Do you prefer working in a team or on your own? Why?
4 What's good about working from home?
5 Would you like to work abroad? Why?/Why not?

2 **Look at the photos of people at work.**

PART 1

Take turns to describe the photos.

PART 2

In pairs, ask and answer the questions about the photos.

Student A's photo
1 What job does this photo show?
2 What is the woman on the left doing?
3 What is the woman on the right wearing?
4 What is the woman on the right doing?
5 Do you think the woman on the left likes her job? Why?/Why not?

Student B's photo
1 What's happening in this photo?
2 Where are these people?
3 What is the woman doing?
4 Do you think it's a nice conversation? Why?/Why not?
5 Why do you think the man on the left is filming?

3 **Read the instructions on your card. In pairs, take turns to role-play the conversation.**

Student A
You are a careers consultant. You are helping Student B to choose his/her future job. Ask Student B the questions.   • Ask Student B if he/she wants to do a full-time job or a part-time job.   • Ask if he/she is happy to work long hours.   • Ask if a good salary is important to him/her.   • Ask if he/she wants to do a demanding job or an easy job.   • Ask if he/she wants to work with customers.   • Say you can think of some job ideas for him/her. End the conversation.

Student B
Student A is your careers consultant. He/She is helping you choose a future job. Answer Student A's questions.   • Say that you want to have a full-time job.   • Say that you're happy to work long hours if you like the job.   • Say that a good salary is very important to you.   • Say that you want to do a demanding job.   • Say yes, you want to work with customers.

VOCABULARY AND GRAMMAR

1 Complete the jobs with one letter in each space.

Jennie: What do you want to do when you finish your studies?

Ashley: It's difficult. I like acting but I don't want to be an <u>a c t r e s s</u>. It's hard work and not many people become famous and rich.

Jennie: That's true. I'd like to become an
¹__ __ **c** __ __ **t** __ __ __.

Ashley: Our town needs one. The buildings here are horrible! I guess I could get a job with the local newspaper as a ²__ __ **u** __ __ __ **l** __ __ __. Then I could write about you.

Jennie: My brother wants to be a car ³__ __ **c** __ __ **n** __ __. My parents are very upset.

Ashley: Why? It's a good job. He can fix my old car.

Jennie: They want him to go to university. At least he doesn't want to be a ⁴__ __ __ **d** __ __ __. Rose's brother is on a UN peacekeeping mission in Africa. Her parents worry about him all the time.

Ashley: Anyway, first we've got exams and three or four years of university. For now, I'm happy with my job in the Seaview Restaurant. I'm a ⁵__ __ __ **t** __ __ **s** __. It's great!

/5

2 Complete the jobs with the correct form of the words in capitals.

You could be an <u>engineer</u> (ENGINE) and help to design and build roads, bridges or machines.

1 I'd like to be a famous _____ (LAW) and help people who have legal problems.

2 You like staying in hotels. You could be a _____ (RECEPTION) and spend your whole life in a hotel!

3 I don't want to be a shop _____ (ASSIST) and serve customers. Customers are sometimes so rude.

4 My aunt is an _____ (COUNT) and helps people with their finances and taxes.

5 Steve is a _____ (SCIENCE). He is working on a new theory of time.

/5

3 Complete the sentences with one word or phrase from the box in each gap. There are two extra words or phrases.

badly-paid   why   in   from   ~~eight hours a day~~
part-time   well-paid   with

I work <u>eight hours a day</u>, so I get home at about six o'clock every evening. Unfortunately, it's a ¹_____ job and I don't earn a lot, so I've also got a ²_____ job for two hours a day in the evening. The evening job is great. I work ³_____ a supermarket. I work on a checkout and there are always people there – customers and the people I work ⁴_____ . My other job is really boring. Not many people come in to the office or phone. I don't know ⁵_____ I'm there, really.

/5

4 Complete the dialogues with the words in brackets. Use the Present Continuous.

Sam: Hi, Kate. What <u>are you writing</u> (you/write)?

Kate: Hi, Sam. It's a story for a new travel magazine.

Conversation 1

Mr Bell: _____ (you/make) a cake?

Mrs Bell: Yes, but not for you! It's Mrs Kent's birthday today.

Conversation 2

Jackie: ª_____ (I/not/work) today.

Aaron: Why not?

Jackie: The owner of the restaurant ᵇ_____ (get) married. The restaurant is closed for the weekend.

Conversation 3

Manager: Why ª_____ (Seth/sit) down?

Waiter: He's tired. He ᵇ_____ (have) a rest.

/5

5 Complete the text with the correct form of the verbs in brackets. Use the Present Simple or Present Continuous. Add the correct personal pronouns.

Hi Sally,

How are you?

<u>Do you remember</u> (remember) Jake Samuels? He's in India at the moment. ¹_____ (work) as an English teacher for a few weeks. ²_____ (love) it. ³_____ (not/want) to come home! Do you know he's got a blog? ⁴_____ (write) it every day. It's really interesting. And now, because of reading his blog, ⁵_____ (dream) about life in a foreign country. I think that would be so cool! Maybe we can work somewhere for a year after we finish our studies? I know – it's a long way in the future, but I'm really excited!

All the best,
Jess

/5

6 Choose the correct answers A–C.

Hi Jess,

Thanks for <u>C</u> email. Of course I remember Jake. I ¹__ at his blog right now. You're right. It's amazing. I love the photos too. Are they really his pictures? Perhaps he ²__ them on the Internet! I'm joking! I know they are his photos. They're all selfies of him in amazing places!

Your idea about finding a job is great. My cousin is working in Greece at the moment. She's working ³__ a waitress. It's a good ⁴__ . She doesn't ⁵__ a lot but she gets a room and all her food.

See you soon,
Sally

	A	B	C
	A a	B Ø	Ⓒ the
1	A look	B am looking	C looks
2	A is finding	B find	C finds
3	A as	B for	C with
4	A work	B job	C paid
5	A earn	B paid	C pay

/5

Total /30

USE OF ENGLISH

7 Put the words in the correct order to make sentences and questions.

Joe: What does your mum do?
Pam: part / a shop / she / works / in / time
She works part-time in a shop.

1 Paul: favour / a / could / you / me / do
_____ ?
Kathy: Yes, of course. What do you need?

2 Jen: What can you see in this photo?
Mark: a / hospital / right / the / on / there's
_____

3 Ms Jones: OK, Lisa. like / a / new / to / project / on / would / work / you
_____ ?
Lisa: Yes, of course, Ms Jones.

4 Andy: am / you / to / sorry / bother / I
_____
Ezme: That's OK, Andy. I'm not working.

5 Henry: Look at this old photo. the / is / in / Grandpa Joe / background /
_____
Anna: He looks very happy!

/5

8 Choose the correct answers A–C.

He's a mechanic – he works ___.
Ⓐ with his hands
B his hands
C with hands

1 Oh no! Ben and Ted ___ again.
A have an argument
B they have an argument
C are having an argument

2 I always ___ work at nine o'clock.
A am starting
B start
C am at

3 At the moment, Carol ___ to a customer.
A is speaking
B speaks
C doesn't speak

4 We ___ today. Our team has got an extra free day this month.
A don't work
B are working
C aren't working

5 I prefer to work ___. It's good because we can help each other.
A in a team
B for a company
C full-time

/5

9 Complete the text with the correct answers A–C.

BLOG

Hi. My name's Alex.

I'm fifteen and I _A_ starting my first job today. I'm working ¹___ my uncle's café. It's only for a few months in the summer, but it's a ²___ job, every day for eight hours. There are two ³___ at the café – Ken and Sam – and they work very hard. Ken is ⁴___ me to make coffee. I hope I can make nice coffees! I want the ⁵___ to be happy!

Ⓐ am   B is   C are
1 A on   B with   C in
2 A part-time   B full-time   C well-paid
3 A waiters   B plumbers   C vets
4 A earning   B learning   C teaching
5 A workers   B customers   C assistants

/5

10 Complete the second sentence so that it has a similar meaning to the first. Use between two and five words, including the word in capitals.

Who is your English teacher? **TEACHING**
Who *is teaching you* English?

1 Mr Smith's office is in his house. **HOME**
Mr Smith _____ .

2 My cousin Tina earns a lot of money. **JOB**
My cousin Tina has a _____ .

3 Their mum is teaching them French. **LEARNING**
They _____ their mum.

4 Bob is a builder – that's his job. **LIVING**
Bob is a builder – that's how he _____ .

5 Gary is at his job from 8 a.m. to 8 p.m. **LONG**
Gary _____ .

/5

Total /20

4 People

VOCABULARY 4.1

Appearance • adjective order • personality

SHOW WHAT YOU KNOW

1 Complete the description with the words from the box.

ears eyes eyebrows eyelashes forehead hair ~~head~~ lips neck mouth nose

This is a description of a person's *head* from top to bottom. [1]_______ grows on the head. It can be short, long, curly or straight. You can even have dreadlocks. At the front of the head is the [2]_______ . If you have a fringe (short hair), it can cover a lot or all of this. Under this are the [3]_______ ; some people's are thick and some people's are thin. We see with our [4]_______ and, just above these are the [5]_______ – short hairs that protect them. At the side of the head, we have two [6]_______ . We can hear things with these. In the centre of the face, we have a [7]_______ with two holes in it which we use to breathe and to smell things.
Under this is the [8]_______ where we put food when we eat it. Around the mouth, we have two [9]_______ .
Under the face, we have a [10]_______ which joins the head to the body.

WORD STORE 4A | Appearance

2 Complete the table with the words in the correct places.

~~bald~~ blond brown blue curly fit green grey good-looking medium-length middle-aged pretty short slim sporty red teenager wavy well-built

Age	__________ , __________
Appearance	*bald* , __________ __________ , __________
Build	__________ , __________ __________
Hair type	__________ , __________
Hair length	__________ , __________
Hair and eye colour	__________ , __________
Hair colour only	__________ , __________
Eye colour only	__________ , __________

3 Complete the sentences with two opposite adjectives. The first letters are given.

I'm only 54. I'm not **o***ld*. I'm still **y***oung*!

1 I'm not saying that Chris is [a]**u**__________ . He's got a nice smile, but he's not exactly [b]**g**_____-_____ with his big nose and ears!
2 Helen hasn't really got [a]**f**__________ hair. Her eyebrows are [b]**d**__________ and that's her real hair colour too.
3 My parents have both got [a]**c**__________ hair but my hair is [b]**s**__________ . My sister's hair is wavy.
4 At our school, boys can't have very [a]**l**__________ hair. The strange thing is that girls can't have very [b]**s**__________ hair.
5 Why are you worried about what you eat? You aren't [a]**f**__________ . You are really [b]**t**__________ . I think you should eat more.
6 When my friends and I go out, we take a lot of photos but the [a]**t**__________ people always stand in the front, so you can never see the [b]**s**__________ people behind them.

WORD STORE 4B | Adjective order

4 Label the adjectives with the correct numbers.

1 = opinion 2 = length/size 3 = type 4 = colour

Helen: It's boring here. Let's play movie characters.
Elaine: OK. He's an (*1*) ugly, (*2*) small creature with [a](___) big, [b](___) blue eyes and a [c](___) big, [d](___) bald head.
Helen: Gollum.
Elaine: Very good. Your turn.
Helen: They are [e](___) tall, [f](___) blue people with [g](___) strange, [h](___) big ears.
Elaine: The Na'vi from *Avatar*. What about this one? He's a [i](___) nice, old man with [j](___) long, [k](___) straight, [l](___) grey hair and a long beard.
Helen: Gandalf?
Elaine: It could be. Or Dumbledore.
Helen: He's a [m](___) friendly, young boy with [n](___) medium-length, [o](___) red hair.
Elaine: Ron Weasley. But he's 30 now and he's going bald! Try this one. He's a [p](___) handsome, [q](___) well-built young man. He's got [r](___) long, [s](___) straight, [t](___) brown hair but then he cuts it short.
Helen: Jacob from *Twilight*. My turn.
Elaine: Here's our bus. Come on. You can tell me when we sit down.

WORD STORE 4C | Personality

5 Complete the text with the opposites of the adjectives in brackets. The first letters are given.

Application for summer camp volunteers

Describe yourself:

I'm a very s<u>ociable</u> (UNSOCIABLE) person. I love meeting people and talking to them. I'm not at all ¹s_____ (CONFIDENT). At school, I'm quite ²s_____ (FUNNY) and hard-working but, when I'm not working, I have a good sense of humour. I'm ³c_____ (STUPID) and do well with my school work. I am hoping to go to university next year to study law. I'm a very ⁴p_____ (NEGATIVE) person and I try to see the good in people. I think I'm an ⁵i_____ (BORING) person and that most people like me. I care about people and animals and I think I am ⁶k_____ (UNKIND).

Personal details:

Name: Janine

Surname: Terence

Age: 18

6 Rewrite the sentences using more polite forms.

British people are shy.
British people aren't very confident.

1 The boys in my class are funny.

_____

2 My brother is negative about other people.

_____

3 This film is boring.

_____

4 The new student is unsociable.

_____

5 Those girls are unkind.

_____

SHOW WHAT YOU'VE LEARNT

7 Choose the correct answers A–C.

1 Janet's sister is quite ___ . I think she's fourteen.
   A young   **B** short   **C** middle-aged

2 Emily's got ___ hair. I think it looks great.
   A short, curly, dark   **B** curly, dark, short   **C** dark, curly, short

3 Mark does a lot of exercise. He is really ___ .
   A well-built   **B** tall   **C** sociable

4 What ___ the new English teacher look like?
   A is   **B** does   **C** has

5 Grandpa hasn't got any hair – he's ___ .
   A wavy   **B** curly   **C** bald

6 Poor Colin never does well in his exams. He tries hard but he isn't very ___ .
   A positive   **B** interesting   **C** clever

7 It's difficult for Jackie to make friends at university because she is so ___ .
   A shy   **B** kind   **C** sociable

8 Paul never laughs. He is always so ___ . He's so different to his brother.
   A confident   **B** serious   **C** funny

9 What's your new teacher ___ ?
   A look   **B** look like   **C** like

10 My mum's hair isn't curly and it isn't straight. It's ___ .
   A bald   **B** wavy   **C** blond

/10

---

1 Write the opposite adjectives.

serious ≠ *funny*

1 fat ≠ _____
2 far ≠ _____
3 difficult ≠ _____
4 intelligent ≠ _____
5 good-looking ≠ _____
6 interesting ≠ _____

2 ★ Complete the dialogue with the correct comparative form of the adjectives in brackets.

Emily: Two boys want to go to the end of school dance with me.

Kirsten: Who?

Emily: Wayne and Theo.

Kirsten: Well, go with Wayne. He's *better-looking* (good-looking) than Theo. He's ¹_____ (thin) too.

Emily: Well, Theo isn't fat! Anyway, Wayne is ²_____ (boring) than Theo. Theo is ³_____ (funny) than Wayne and he's ⁴_____ (clever).

Kirsten: ... so, go with Theo.

Emily: Well ... Wayne has a lot of friends. He's ⁵_____ (sociable) than Theo. Theo is ⁶_____ (shy). Maybe it's better to go to the dance with Wayne, but it's a difficult decision.

Kirsten: Yes, but it's less difficult than deciding what to wear. That's impossible!

3 ★ ★ Complete the sentences with the correct forms of the adjectives in capitals.

My mum is *older* than my dad but the *oldest* person in our family is my dad's grandmother. She's 98. **OLD**

1 Harry isn't shy at all – he's the _____ boy in our class. In fact, he's _____ than our teachers! **CONFIDENT**

2 I'm not _____ than my mum. She's the _____ person in the house. **SHORT**

3 Who is the _____ person in my family? My baby sister. My brother Tom is _____ than me – he's ten and I'm twelve years old. **YOUNG**

4 I'd like to be _____ than I am but I'll never be the _____ person in my class. Seven people play sports for school teams. **FIT**

5 Ela's got _____ hair than me. She's got the_____ hair in our class. Some of the boys call her 'Rapunzel' but she doesn't mind. **LONG**

4 ★ ★ Complete the email with the correct form of the adjectives in brackets.

Hi Eleanor,

How are you? Life here at university is great. The *best* (good) thing about it is that we've got a lot of free time! I like the lessons too. The lecturers are ¹_____ (interesting) than our teachers at school and they are ²_____ (friendly) too. The ³_____ (nice) lecturer is our psychology teacher. She's great.

The ⁴_____ (bad) thing about university is that we have lectures at 8 a.m. every day. The other problem is my room. It's ⁵_____ (small) than my bedroom at home. It's ⁶_____ (tidy) too because my mother isn't here to tell me to put things away! It's a bit unfair because some of the rooms here are ⁷_____ (big) than the one I've got. Oh well. How is everything with you? Hope your marks are ⁸_____ (good) than last year!

See you soon,
Beverley

5 ★ ★ ★ Use the prompts to make full sentences.

The boy in that photo isn't Desmond. *Desmond has got darker hair than him* (Desmond / got / dark / hair / him).

1 I want Craig to win the school prize for best student.
   ᵃ_____
   (He / clever / boy / in the school). ᵇ_____
   _____
   (He / friendly / the other people) who are trying to win too.

2 We've got a book to read for English. The book I'm reading ᵃ_____
   (funny / and / interesting / book we are studying).
   Why do they always choose ᵇ_____
   _____ (boring / books in the world) to read?

3 Tim: Look at that dog. ᵃ_____
   _____ (That / ugly / dog in the world!)
   Phil: That's my dog!
   Tim: What? Oh, sorry. Sometimes ᵇ_____
   _____ (I / stupid / person I know)!
   Phil: Don't worry. I agree, he is a bit strange-looking but he's really friendly.

6 Find the word that is wrong in each sentence and correct it. One sentence is correct.

You look different. Your hair is shortest than before. *shorter*

1 This is, without doubt, the worse day of my life. _____

2 Who is the kinder person in your class? _____

3 Don't worry about what Chloe says. You're much more cleverer than she is. _____

4 This year at school is less difficult than last year. Maybe I'm less shy than before! _____

5 After my holiday, I want to be slimer than I am now. _____

6 This lake looks narower on the map than that one. _____

/6

GRAMMAR: Train and Try Again page 131

4.3

It and the -ing form as the subject of a sentence • life events

1 Complete sentences 1–4 with the words in brackets in the correct order.

Extract from Student's Book recording 🔊 **2.19**

Sara: _The most important life event for a young person is leaving home._ (is / life event / The / leaving home. / for a young person / most important) The best age is about eighteen or nineteen. Some people only leave home when they get married. But I think
1 _____
_____ (it / your own / a younger age. / is important / decisions / from / to make) I'm seventeen now and I don't want to go to university. When I leave school, I want to get a job and earn money. Then I can leave home. I want to buy my own flat one day […]

Mike: I think ² _____
_____ (most / to drive. / is learning / important / the / life event) Now my parents fetch me from my friends' houses – but they come at ten o'clock. I'm sixteen – I want to stay out later! I can't wait until next year when I can learn to drive!
A driver's licence can also help you get a better job. I think falling in love or buying your first flat are important … but for me, at the moment, all that is less important than learning to drive.

Grace: For me, ³ _____
_____ (is / going / important. / first date / really / on your) It's that first step in romance. And I think ⁴ _____
_____
(falling / life event. / is / in love / most important / the), just like your first date. This doesn't mean I want to get married now. I'm only fifteen! I want to do a lot of things before I get married – study, travel, get my first job. Anyway, I think it's better to get married when you're older ... so not eighteen but around thirty or later.

REMEMBER THIS

In English, a sentence must have a subject. There are a number of situations where the pronoun **It** is used as a subject, e.g. *It's cold, It's eight (o'clock), It's dark, It's Wednesday, It's important to…, It rains/'s raining.*

2 Read REMEMBER THIS. Rewrite the sentences correctly.

Is raining. *It is raining.*
1 Isn't fair! _____
2 Is so hot. _____
3 Is a nice day. _____
4 Is time for bed? _____
5 Is five o'clock. _____

3 Complete the second sentence in each pair so that it has the same meaning as the first one.

The most important life event is getting a job.
Getting _a job is the most important life_ event.
1 It is important to study hard at school.
Studying _____ important.
2 Saving money for the future is important.
It _____ future.
3 The most important thing in life is being happy.
Being _____ life.
4 Getting married is the most important life event.
The _____ married.
5 It is important to learn how to cook before you leave home.
Learning _____ important.
6 The best way to learn a foreign language is to live in a foreign country.
Living _____ foreign language.
7 It's fun to look at old photos.
Looking _____ fun.
8 Getting up early is difficult in the winter.
It's _____ winter.

WORD STORE 4D | Life events

4 Match verbs 1–6 with the correct endings a–f to make collocations. Then complete the sentences with the collocations. One collocation is used twice.

	learn	g	a	married
1	go on		b	a flat
2	fall in		c	job
3	buy		d	a date
4	get a		e	love
5	get		f	home
6	leave		g	to drive

I'd like to _learn to drive_ but the lessons cost a lot of money.
7 Ali is getting ready to _____ with Dave. They're going to a restaurant.
8 I'm going to _____ after my exams and earn enough money for a really good summer holiday.
9 I don't want to _____ . I like my bedroom and my dad's cooking.
10 I want to _____ when I start working. Then, when I get older, I can sell it and have some money for a house.
11 I'd like to _____ when I'm about 30 – if I meet the right person, of course.
12 I hope you won't _____ with Jamie. He's not right for you and you won't be happy.
13 We can _____ with two bedrooms and live there together. Think of the parties we can have!

1   **Read the text quickly. Who do you think is in the photo?**
   A   Megan and her boyfriend
   B   Henry and his girlfriend
   C   Steven and his girlfriend

Shopping and you

There is a popular idea that girls love shopping for clothes. They **shop around** for bargains all day. They **try on** clothes that they don't really want. Finally, they buy a lot of clothes but they don't keep them all. The next week, they **take back** the things they don't like and start all over again! Boys, on the other hand, buy the first thing they see which fits them. Then they don't enter a clothes shop again until their clothes **wear out** or they **grow out of** them, whichever happens first.

Is this true or not? We asked you for your own true-life experiences and here are a few of your replies.

Megan, aged 21, Bristol

In my opinion, it's totally true. I hate shopping for clothes with my boyfriend. He is always bored and totally unhelpful. He has two ways of reacting when I try on things. At first, he is too honest. He reacts with horror or makes jokes about the clothes I choose. Then, when he gets more bored, he says that everything is great or wonderful. Also, he has no idea about what is fashionable. I buy him things which are a little more elegant but he doesn't wear them. He's slim and looks good in close-fitting jeans but he prefers very loose clothes. Oh well, at least he's got a great personality!

Steven, aged 16, Leicester

The idea that boys don't like shopping for clothes is really old-fashioned. Boys now are not like boys from the 1980s. They spend more on cosmetics than girls and they care just as much about their appearance. They don't all wear shabby clothes. A lot of them want to look nice. What's your next article going to be about? Why don't young people buy video tapes anymore? Most of us live in the 21st century. Come and join us. It's great here!

Henry, aged 19, Bath

I love shopping with my girlfriend. We shop in places with a good choice of clothes for men and women. That way, we can both try things on at the same time. My girlfriend helps me a lot. She understands colours better than I do. She can see immediately what goes with what and which colours look wrong together. She also finds things that match my personality. In return, I help her. I **hang up** the clothes she doesn't want and **put back** dresses, skirts and T-shirts in the right place. It's true! She's much more untidy than I am.

GLOSSARY

bargain (n) – something you can buy cheaply or for less than its usual price

video tapes (n, pl) – special plastic boxes containing a length of tape that you can record sound and pictures on

join (us) (v) – to begin to take part in an activity that other people are involved in

immediately (adv) – at once

match (v) – look attractive together because they are a similar colour, pattern, etc.

2   **Read the text again and answer the questions.**
   1   How does Megan feel about shopping with her boyfriend?

   2   What does Megan like about her boyfriend?

   3   In Steven's opinion, which idea from the eighties is not true about modern boys?

   4   What do many boys of the 21st century want?

   5   Why do Henry and his girlfriend go together to clothes shops for men and women?

   6   How does Henry's girlfriend help him?

3 Look at the words in bold in the text and match them with the definitions.

	put on clothes to see how they look or fit	_try on_
1	return something to a shop because you don't want to keep it	_____
2	become too big for clothes because you are taller or fatter than before	_____
3	put clothes into a wardrobe or on hooks	_____
4	compare the price and quality of similar items in different shops before buying something	_____
5	become too old or damaged to use	_____
6	return something to its correct place	_____

4 Complete the dialogues with the correct form of the verbs from Exercise 3.

Conversation 1
Janice: You should _try on_ those jeans before you buy them. You can't _____ clothes to this shop.
Kelly: Really? What if there's something wrong with them?
Janice: You have to check them carefully here.

Conversation 2
Imelda: Don't buy the first thing you find. We should _____ and see if we can get them cheaper somewhere else.
Adrian: I haven't got the strength. I just want to go home.

Conversation 3
Sam: These jeans aren't very good quality.
Paul: It doesn't matter. You're growing so quickly, you'll ¹_____ them before they ²_____ .

Conversation 4
Simon: Can I borrow these CDs and DVDs?
Lisa: Yes, if you promise to _____ everything in the right place.

Conversation 5
Nick: Hi, Mum. I'm home.
Mum: _____ your coat. Don't leave it on the floor.

REMEMBER THIS

Most of the *phrasal verbs* in exercises 3 and 4 require an object. An object in phrasal verbs can appear after the whole phrasal verb, e.g. **try on** *a shirt* or between the verb and the preposition, e.g. **try** *a shirt* **on**. Sometimes phrasal verbs are inseparable.

When you check a phrasal verb in a dictionary, look at the position of *sth/sb*. If *sth/sb* is between the verb and preposition, it means this phrasal verb is separable, e.g. *take* **sth** *off*. If *sth/sb* is after the whole phrasal verb, it means this phrasal verb is not separable, e.g. *look after* **sb/sth**. Some phrasal verbs do not need an object, e.g. *get up*.

5 Read REMEMBER THIS. Look at these sentences. Are the verbs separable (S), inseparable (I) or is there no object (NO)? Use a dictionary if necessary.

	Try these trousers on. They look great.	S
1	Take these shoes back to the shop.	◯
2	Tommy grows out of his clothes very quickly.	◯
3	Hang your coat up when you come home.	◯
4	Can you put my clothes back in my wardrobe?	◯
5	I always shop around before I buy anything.	◯
6	Cheap clothes wear out quickly, so they aren't really a bargain.	◯

WORD STORE 4E | Clothes

6 Look at the photos and choose the correct option.

STYLISH or NOT? What do you think?

She's very trendy. She's wearing a ¹*hat / scarf / top* on her head, sunglasses and she's got a big ²*hat / scarf / sweater* round her neck. It's difficult to see what kind of ³*top / jacket / suit* she's wearing under her leather ⁴*jumper / coat / jacket* – is it a thin ⁵*skirt / jacket / jumper* ? I don't think it's a ⁶*T-shirt / suit / tracksuit*. She's wearing very close-fitting ⁷*trousers / tracksuits / dresses* – I think they are black jeans. On her feet … are they ⁸*jeans / shoes / socks* or ⁹*trousers / tracksuits / trainers*? It's difficult to say for sure. They aren't boots. They're too small. **She looks cool – and she knows it! 8/10**

He looks good. He's wearing a dark ¹⁰*skirt / suit / sweater*. It isn't too tight or too loose. The jacket and trousers fit him well. He's wearing a white ¹¹*shirt / coat / skirt* and a dark ¹²*scarf / top / tie*. His shoes are black. We can't see his ¹³*boots / trainers / socks* – I'm sure they are dark. **He is stylish and smart. 9/10**

VOCABULARY PRACTICE | Adjectives

7 Look at the vocabulary in lesson 4.4 in the Student's Book. Complete the dialogue with one word in each gap. The first letters are given.

Amy: I prefer to wear **c**_omfortable_ clothes, you know, like ¹**b**_____ sweaters and jeans. They're not ²**t**_____ – in fact, they look ³**o**_____-_____ , but I love them. I don't understand how people can wear ⁴**t**_____ clothes. I think they're very ⁵**u**_____ .

Ben: Yes, you're right. ⁶**C**_____ clothes are my favourite too. I love wearing jeans, and T-shirts – they're the best. But sometimes, you need to wear ⁷**s**_____ clothes. When someone gets married, for example, I wear a suit and tie – I can't wear ⁸**s**_____ clothes like a tracksuit then!

Amy: You? Wearing a suit and tie? I don't believe it!

Ben: OK, here's a photo from my cousin's wedding. See? I'm wearing a ⁹**s**_____ suit.

Amy: Yes, it's very fashionable. You look great!

VOCABULARY PRACTICE | Personality

8 Look at the vocabulary in lesson 4.4 in the Student's Book. Choose the correct option.

1 I can't sing, I can't dance and I can't play a musical instrument. I'm not very *generous / talented* .
2 Pablo is the most *creative / energetic* person I know – he has great ideas!
3 Many *relaxed / generous* people give money to this charity.
4 I like being with Alice because she's always *creative / cheerful* and happy.
5 My grandparents are always *relaxed / talented* and they never worry.
6 Young children are *cheerful / energetic* – they're always active.

4.5

Have to / don't have to

SHOW WHAT YOU KNOW

1 Complete the sentences with *can/can't* and the verbs in brackets. Check your answers at the bottom of the page.

○○○

Strange laws from around the world

The USA

In Gainesville, Georgia, you *can eat* (eat) fried chicken with your fingers.

1 In Cheyenne, Wyoming, you _____ (have) a shower on a Sunday.

2 In Oklahoma you _____ (wear) boots in bed.

3 In Gary, Indiana, you _____ (travel) on public transport after eating onions or garlic.

4 In Mesquite, Texas, children _____ (have) strange haircuts.

2 ★ Look at the information and complete the sentences with the correct form of *have to* or *don't have to*.

Survey on housework

Please complete the form and leave it in the box in Room 15 before 3 p.m. on Thursday. Thanks. Don't write your name.

Male / ~~Female~~

Tick the things you have to do around the house:

Make your bed	✓
Tidy your room	✓
Cook dinner	✗ *I can't cook!*
Take the dog for a walk	✗ *No dog!*
Wash the car	✓
Do the washing-up	✗ *We've got a dishwasher* ☺
Help in the garden	✓
Do the shopping	✗

He *has to make* his bed.

1 He _____ his room.

2 He _____ dinner.

3 He _____ the dog for a walk.

4 He _____ the car.

5 He _____ the washing-up.

6 He _____ in the garden.

7 He _____ the shopping.

Exercise 1, Answer key:
Example: You can. In fact, you have no choice. You can't eat it with a knife and fork. ¹You can, but you can't have one on Wednesday. ²You can't but you can wear shoes. ³No, you can't – for four hours. Then you can use public transport again. ⁴They can't, it's against the law.

54

3 ★ ★ Use the words in brackets to complete the questions and short answers.

Hannah: Hi, Gavyn. Can I ask you about housework?

Gavyn: OK.

Hannah: *Do you have to make* (you/make) your bed?

Gavyn: *Yes, I do* (✓). Every morning.

Hannah: ¹_____ (you/tidy your room)?

Gavyn: ²_____ (✗).

Hannah: No?

Gavyn: Well, my mum and dad never come into my room. But it is tidy. I like a tidy room.

Hannah: OK. ³_____ (you/cook dinner)?

Gavyn: ⁴_____ (✗) but I have to make breakfast.

Hannah: ⁵_____ (you/take) the dog for a walk?

Gavyn: ⁶_____ (✓). Twice a day. Before school and in the evening.

Hannah: Do you …

Gavyn: ⁷_____ (I/answer) these questions? My lesson starts in five minutes.

4 ★ ★ ★ Complete the dialogue with the correct form of *have to* and the verbs from the box. There are three extra verbs.

> do   get   have   not do   not get up   not go
> not make   take   stay (x2)   wear

Juan: I'm glad I'm not at an English school.

Pia: Why?

Juan: They *have to take* important exams when they are sixteen and eighteen. And they ¹_____ a uniform.

Pia: Yes, but they ²_____ very early. They start at nine o'clock. We start at eight.

Juan: But they ³_____ at school until 4 p.m.

Pia: My brother ⁴_____ at school until 4 p.m. and he ⁵_____ to school at 7.45 a.m.

Juan: Really?

Pia: Yes. He ⁶_____ any housework, though.

Juan: Why not?

Pia: Because he ⁷_____ so much homework. He doesn't have time for anything else.

SHOW WHAT YOU'VE LEARNT

5 Complete the text with the correct form of *have to*.

Hi Lisa,

Thanks for your email. I'm glad you can come to stay. On Saturday, my mum *has to* go to work, so I ¹_____ cook dinner and look after my little brother but we can go out later. We ²_____ get a bus – my dad can take us into the town centre. Usually, I ³_____ come home at 10 p.m. but, because you're here, I ⁴_____ be at home until midnight. What time ⁵_____ leave on Sunday? My mum ⁶_____ go to work, so she can cook us a nice Sunday lunch and then take you to the railway station.

Let me know. See you soon.

Rachel

/6

GRAMMAR: Train and Try Again page 131

SPEAKING

4.6
Going to the hairdresser's

1 Translate the phrases into your own language.

SPEAKING BANK

At the hairdresser's

How would you like it? _____

I'd like a haircut. _____
_____

I'm thinking of having _____
a new hairstyle. _____

What about/How about _____
(having a fringe/this _____
style/spiky hair)? _____

I'm not sure. _____

I'd like (shorter hair/ _____
a different style). _____

How about this style? _____
_____

That looks cool/ _____
fantastic/perfect. _____

Take a look. What do _____
you think? _____

Sit here, please. _____

2 Look at the photo and choose the correct words.

Where is the girl?
The girl is ¹in / on / at the hairdresser's.

Can you describe the girl's hair?
She ²has / is having ³shoulder-length / spiky hair and
a ⁴pony tail / fringe. I think her hair is ⁵dyed / shaved
at the front.

What is happening?
The hairdresser ⁶is cutting / cuts the girl's hair.

Why do you think she wants this hairstyle?
⁷Maybe / Might be she doesn't want to look boring.
⁸Possible / Perhaps she is going to a party and wants
to look different.

Do you enjoy going to the hairdresser's? Why?/Why not?
I like ⁹go / going to the hairdresser's. I want to look cool.
I usually look for a nice hairstyle in a magazine or on the
Internet. I show the picture to the hairdresser and she
gives me her opinion. Sometimes, she ¹⁰doesn't agree /
isn't agreeing with me!

**3 Complete the sentences with one word in each gap.
Then write down who says them.
Write H for hairdresser or C for customer.**

Hello. How can I help? [H]
1 I'm not _____ . ◯
2 How _____ this one? ◯
3 I'd _____ a haircut. ◯
4 What do you _____ ? ◯
5 I'm _____ of a new hairstyle. ◯
6 How _____ you like it? ◯
7 _____ here, please. ◯
8 Wow! It's _____ . Thanks! ◯
9 _____ about spiky hair? ◯
10 That _____ cool. ◯
11 Do you want the _____ style only shorter? ◯

**4 Match the questions in Exercise 3 with the correct
answers below.**

H: Hello. *How can I help*?
C: I'd like a haircut.

1 H: OK. Look at these pictures. _____ ?
    Do you like it?
    C: Wow! Shaved sides. That looks cool.

2 H: Sit here, please. _____ ?
    C: No, I've had it like this for a long time.
    I'd like something totally different.

3 H: Take a look. _____ ?
    C: Wow! It's perfect. Thanks!

4 C: _____ ? That's very different.
    C: Oh no! I don't think I'd like that.

5 H: _____ ?
    C: Well, I'm not sure.

**5 Complete the dialogue with the words from the box.
There are three extra words.**

dyed fringe hairstyle ~~help~~ how like
ponytail shaved shoulder-length spiky
what would

H: Hello. How can I *help*?
C: I'd like a new ¹_____ . Can you do it now?
H: Yes. Sit here, please. How would you ²_____ it?
C: Well, I'm not sure. I don't want it shorter because
   I like having a ³_____ . I just want it to look
   different.
H: Well, what about ⁴_____ hair? That's different.
   There are lots of great colours.
C: No, I don't think I'd like that.
H: OK. How about ⁵_____ sides? That's a very
   trendy style.
C: No, sorry.
H: OK. Look at these pictures. ⁶_____ about this one?
C: Wow! I love that ⁷_____ . That looks really cool.
Later …
H: OK. Take a look. ⁸_____ do you think?
C: It's perfect. Thanks!

1 Find six more mistakes in the profile. Underline them and write the correct words below.

Hi! I'm Luke

I have seventeen years old. I'm quite high – 1.82 metres – and I'm sporty and well-built. I've got short, dark hairs and green eyes.

I'm a very sociable person. I love meeting new people and going out with a group of friends. I play a lot of sports and I am very fit and strong. I'm not very serious. I enjoy laughing and joking. My friends say that I am funny but not very hard-working.

I've got a sister. She's youngest than me. She is fifteen years old. She's got dark hair but hers is long and wave. She's got big, brown eyes and she's quiet pretty. She's more serious from me and she does very well at school.

So, now you know something about me. And my sister.

```
        am
1  _____        3  _____        5  _____
2  _____        4  _____        6  _____
```

2 Put the words in the correct order to make sentences.

very / I'm / slim / not   *I'm not very slim.*

1 hair / medium-length / got / dark / I've
   _____

2 friends / I've / say / My / beautiful / that / eyes / got
   _____

3 serious / I'm / a / not / person / very
   _____

4 I / enjoy / going / really / discos / don't / to
   _____

5 is / than / brother / me / My / taller
   _____

6 like / really / going / long / walks / for / I
   _____

3 Complete the profile with one word in each gap. The first letters are given.

Hi!

I'm Abigail. I'm fifteen years o*ld*. I'm not ¹v_____ tall – I'm 1.56 metres. I've got medium-length, straight ²h_____ and blue ³e_____. I'm not a very sociable ⁴p_____. I ⁵e_____ being with my friends but I am shy when I meet new people. I'm clever ⁶b_____ I'm not very confident. I don't know why. I love reading and taking photos. I've got a website with my photos on it. I haven't got any brothers or ⁷s_____. I've got one cousin. His name is Gary. He's older ⁸t_____ me – he's twenty-five. We don't meet very often so I don't ⁹r_____ know him.

So, now you know something about me.

4 Julia is planning to put up her profile on a website for young people from all over the world to exchange emails in English. Julia is going to practise her English through writing emails herself, but she has asked you for help with her first email. Write her profile using the information below.

Name:	Julia
Age:	15
Height:	1.68m
Build:	not slim / not fat
Hair:	short, straight, brown
Eyes:	brown
Personality:	confident, positive, funny
Interests:	cycling, swimming
Family:	1 sister (Joanna) 18, tall, long brown hair, kind, sociable

Hi! My name's Julia …

Finished? Always check your writing. Can you tick ✓ everything on this list?

In my profile:

- I have included a description of Julia's appearance. ☐
- I have included information about her personality. ☐
- I have written about her interests. ☐
- I have described Julia's sister – Joanna. ☐
- I have used words such as: *very, really, quite.* ☐
- I have used comparative adjectives in the description to compare Julia and her sister. ☐
- I have used contractions, (e.g. *I'm / aren't / that's*). ☐
- I have checked my spelling. ☐
- My text is neat and clear. ☐

1 In pairs, ask and answer the questions.

PART 1

Talk about jobs.
1 Would you like to work with animals? Why?/Why not?
2 Would you prefer to work for a big company or a small company? Why?
3 What jobs do the people in your family do?
4 Would you prefer to have a well-paid boring job or a badly-paid interesting job? Why?
5 What voluntary work would you like to do? Why?

PART 2

Talk about people.
1 What does your favourite teacher look like?
2 How often do you go to the hairdresser's?
3 Can you describe your personality?
4 Who is the kindest person you know? Why?
5 Are you usually relaxed or energetic? Why?

2 Look at the photos of the students.

PART 1

Take turns to describe the people in the photos.

A

B

PART 2

In pairs, ask and answer the questions about the photos.

Student A's photo
1 Which girl has longer hair?
2 Who is the tallest person in the group?
3 Can you describe the students' clothes?
4 Who do you think is the most stylish? Why?
5 Do you think these students are friendly? Why?/Why not?

Student B's photo
1 Does the woman have longer hair than the men?
2 Who is the tallest person?
3 Whose hair do you like best? Why?
4 Do you think these people's clothes are trendy or old-fashioned? Why?
5 Do you think these people are confident? Why?/Why not?

3 Read the instructions on your card. In pairs, take turns to role-play the conversation.

Student A

You want to change your hairstyle. Ask your friend, Student B, for his/her opinion.
- Tell Student B you're thinking of a new hairstyle and ask him/her to help you choose a new style.
- Suggest getting a spiky haircut.
- Suggest having shorter hair.
- Show Student B a style you like in the Student's Book and ask his/her opinion.
- Ask if he/she can come to the hairdresser's with you.
- Thank Student B and end the conversation.

Student B

Your friend, Student A, wants your opinion about changing his/her hairstyle. Answer his/her questions.
- Agree to help Student A.
- Say that you aren't sure about the style he/she suggests.
- Say that you think the style he/she suggests is cool.
- Say that the picture looks perfect.
- Agree to go to the hairdresser's with him/her.

VOCABULARY AND GRAMMAR

1 Complete the text with one word in each gap. You can see a clue for the word in brackets and the first letter of each word.

The people I want to write about are my parents. They are very **p**_ositive_ (not negative) people. They are ¹**m**_____-**a**_____ (not old and not young). My dad is ²**t**_____ (not short) and well-built. He has got short, fair hair. My mum is ³**q**_____ (not very) short and ⁴**s**_____ (not fat). She has got long, ⁵**d**_____ (not fair) hair and brown eyes. They are both good-looking.

/5

2 Match the words in the box with the definitions. There are four extra words.

> boots   cheerful   kind   scarf   shy
> ~~sociable~~   socks   suit   tie   tracksuit

A _sociable_ person likes meeting people and talking to them.

1 A _____ person is always happy and smiles a lot.
2 A _____ person doesn't find it easy to talk to other people.
3 A _____ is something you wear when you play sport.
4 A_____ is something you wear around your neck to keep it warm.
5 You wear _____ on your feet to keep them warm under your shoes.

/5

3 Complete the text with the correct forms of the adjectives in brackets.

It's up to you!
What do you think about these celebrities?

| George Clooney | vs | Johnny Depp | vs | Leonardo DiCaprio | (TALENTED) |

George Clooney is more talented than Johnny Depp. Leonardo DiCaprio is the most talented.

1 Lionel Messi   vs   Serena Williams   vs   Cristiano Ronaldo   (ENERGETIC)
_____
_____

2 Chris Rock vs Adam Sandler vs Will Ferrell   (FUNNY)
_____
_____

3 Taylor Swift vs Katy Perry vs Angelina Jolie   (CREATIVE)
_____
_____

4 Queen Elizabeth   vs   Oprah Winfrey   vs   Madonna   (RELAXED)
_____
_____

5 Daniel Day-Lewis   vs   Hugh Laurie   (UNSOCIABLE)
_____

/5

4 Complete the text with the correct form of the words from the box. There are two extra words.

> boring   clever   ~~confident~~   energetic
> friendly   generous   good   negative

Dan and I are twins. We look exactly the same, but we're very different people. Dan is _more confident_ than me – I'm a bit shy. Dan plays a lot of sport, and I don't, so you can say he's ¹_____ than me! But I like reading. He's also ²_____ than I am – that's why everyone likes him and he has so many friends. I'm not unsociable – I just prefer to have a few really good friends.

Another difference is at school. I'm ³_____ student in our year. I always win prizes for my exam results because they're ⁴_____ ! So, my parents aren't happy that Dan gets B grades. They want to know why he can't get A grades like me. Maybe that's why he worries! Maybe my parents should be ⁵_____ !

/5

5 Complete the dialogue with the correct form of _have to_ + verb.

Alan: I'm going home. See you tomorrow.
Jeff: Are you going already? What time _do you have to be_ (you/be) at home?
Alan: I can stay out longer but I'm just tired. ¹_____ (I/get up) early in the morning.
Jeff: Why? You haven't got a job.
Alan: I know but ²_____ (my sister/catch) a train at 8 o'clock. ³_____ (I/drive) her to the railway station.
Jeff: ⁴_____ (You/not/take) her. She could go by bus.
Alan: She's got a heavy suitcase to carry. Anyway, the buses don't start until 8 on a Saturday.
Jeff: That's true. Why ⁵_____ (she/leave) so early?
Alan: She's going to Spain. The plane leaves at 11.

/5

6 Choose the correct answers A–B.

She has got __ hair.
A brown, beautiful, long   (B) beautiful, long, brown

1 My puppy has got a __ nose.
  A little, cute   B cute, little
2 Judy's got __ hair.
  A short, straight, dark   B dark, short, straight
3 Sally has got __ hair.
  A nice, medium-length, wavy
  B nice, wavy, medium-length
4 Harry has got __ eyes.
  A blue, small   B small, blue
5 My grandfather is seventy-two years old – he's got __ hair.
  A grey, spiky   B spiky, grey

/5

Total   /30

7 Complete the text with the correct answers A–C.

Eton College is probably the _C_ school in Britain.
It is very old, but other schools are even older.
So why do people know Eton better than other schools?
Eton is famous because of the people who go there.
When students leave the school, they are called
'Old Etonians'. Prince William and Prince Harry are
Old Etonians. So is Tom Hiddleston, who plays Loki
in the *Thor* and *Avengers* movies.

To get into the school, a student ¹__ pass an exam …
and be a boy. There are no girls at the school.
The students wear a special uniform with a long jacket,
called a morning coat, and a white ²__ around their
necks.

It is important for students at the school to work hard
in class. Every year, the ³__ students go to study
at Oxford or Cambridge University. Sports are also
important. Cricket is very popular in the summer
but the boys ⁴__ play that sport. They can choose
something else if they prefer. Character is also
important. Most Old Etonians are very ⁵__ people
who know what they want.

	A famous	B more famous	Ⓒ most famous
1	A have to	B doesn't have to	C has to
2	A tie	B shirt	C sweater
3	A most tolerant	B cleverest	C shyest
4	A don't have to	B doesn't have to	C have to
5	A confident	B well-built	C unsociable

/5

8 Choose the correct answers A–C.

Helen is ___ and has lots of friends.
A the least sociable
Ⓑ quite sociable
C more sociable than

1 '___'
'She's short and has black hair.'
A What is she like?
B What does she like?
C What does she look like?

2 ___
'Yes, we do. Hurry up!'
A Are we leaving now?
B Do we have to leave now?
C Do we leave now?

3 ___ this hairstyle?
A What do you think
B How about
C How would you like

4 I think Alex is ___ Paul.
A more kind than
B not kind as
C less kind than

5 ___ is difficult in the winter.
A Get up early
B Getting up early
C It's getting up early

/5

9 Complete each pair of sentences with the same word A–C.

Selena __ got a straight nose.
Daisy __ to go to work today.
A have   Ⓑ has   C had

1 What time does the next train __ ?
In Britain, many young people __ home at the age of eighteen.
A go   B leave   C come

2 Mark and Becky want to __ married.
Where can a teenager __ a job?
A go   B learn   C get

3 Is Gary older __ his brother?
My school is farther from my house __ the park is.
A than   B then   C more

4 My friend Bob is __ worst driver in the world!
This is __ happiest day of my life!
A a   B the   C most

5 Do you __ the latest album by the Arctic Monkeys?
You don't __ to pay for the tickets – they're free.
A have   B had   C has

/5

10 Complete the second sentence so that it has a similar meaning to the first. Use between two and five words, including the word in capitals.

Frankie and Andy are tall, but Jack is taller. **THE**
Jack is *the tallest* of the three boys.

1 It's Sunday today, so we're not going to school. **HAVE**
We _____ to school today because it's Sunday.

2 Her eyes are brown and they're big. **GOT**
She _____ eyes.

3 Anna is funnier than Emma. **LESS**
Emma is _____ Anna.

4 Stan asks his parents before he goes out with his friends. **TO**
Stan _____ permission from his parents before he goes out with his friends.

5 Uncle Tom and his neighbour Kelly are going out for the first time. **GOING**
Uncle Tom and his neighbour Kelly _____ their first date.

/5

Total   /20

5 Education

VOCABULARY

5.1 Types of school • at school • exams

SHOW WHAT YOU KNOW

1 Complete the sentences with one word in each gap. The first letters are given.

This classroom object is something the teacher can write on: b*lackboard*

1 These subjects are often called IT and PE: ªI_____ T_____ , ᵇP_____ E_____

2 These two subjects, and Biology, are ªS_____ : ᵇP_____ , ᶜC_____

3 Sometimes we call these people school students: p_____

4 This person is the most important person in the school: h_____

5 You have one of these for every subject. It has information and exercises in it: c_____

6 This person looks after a class: f_____ t_____

7 You sit at this and put your books on it: d_____

8 People who are good with numbers like this subject: M_____

9 This is something a teacher can write on but it can also be used with a computer to show information: i_____ w_____

REMEMBER THIS

College is a place where students go to study after secondary school. It is different from university.

If you leave school at the age of sixteen (after GCSE exams), you can go e.g. to a *college of further education* and train for a specific job, or you can go to a *sixth-form college* – which is a two-year preparation for A-level exams. When you have the right number of A levels, you can apply for a place at a university.

In old universities, such as Oxford and Cambridge, colleges are independent parts of the university. They can be located in different (often historic) buildings. They usually offer many different subjects.

WORD STORE 5A | Types of school

2 Find the words in the word chain and complete the sentences. You don't need to use all the words.

ABCqKINdERGarTENqfnuRSERYdGBOYS'ILEPLAYgrOUPSOPRMIXEDPQWERDJUSTATEbnMPRIVATEASCOLLEgeQWEPRIMARYLYTGIRLS'aqWUNIVERSITYBBDSingle-MNBSECONDARY

A Playgroups are for children between 3 and 4. Then children go to a *kindergarten* or a ¹_____ school. They are both for very young pupils before they go to ²_____ school.

B In our town, we have a ³_____ school for 11–18 year-olds. It's a ⁴_____ school, for boys and girls. My cousin, Mark, goes to a ⁵_____ school and his sister goes to a ⁶_____ school. I'm glad I don't go to a ⁷_____-sex school. I like having girls in my class.

C I go to a ⁸_____ school because it is very expensive to go to a ⁹_____ school.

D I don't want to go to ¹⁰_____ when I leave school. I am thinking about going to a ¹¹_____ . I want to be a car mechanic.

WORD STORE 5B | At school

3 Complete the text with the verbs from the box. You need to use some verbs twice.

be come do get leave miss start

blog

A new school year

My mum and dad often move and it's difficult to *start* school in a new place every year. Sometimes I don't ¹_____ very well but, this year, I want to have a good year.

This year, I want to:

make lots of friends, ²_____ on time for lessons, ³_____ good marks for my homework, ⁴_____ to lessons with a smile on my face and all my books in my bag!

This year, I don't want to:

⁵_____ any classes, ⁶_____ badly in tests, ⁷_____ bad marks, ⁸_____ late for lessons, forget my books.

Can I do it? When I ⁹_____ school next year, I want to go to university. I can't do that with bad marks.

4 Complete the dialogue between Simon and his mum with one verb in each gap.

M: Simon, this is a letter from your teacher.

S: Oh.

M: She says you sometimes _miss_ lessons. Is this true?

S: Well, once or twice, yes.

M: And you ¹_____ never on time. Why not? You leave here at 8.15. Where do you go?

S: I meet my friends. Sometimes we walk slowly because we are talking. But, I ²_____ well at school. I always ³_____ good marks for my homework.

M: I know, I know. Your teacher is happy with your work but you can't be late for school. People who ⁴_____ school and get a job can't be late in the morning.

S: I understand that. Don't worry. I can change. Anyway, I don't want a job yet. I want to stay at school for two more years, have good grades and then go to university.

M: Good. You can tell Mrs Taylor that when we meet her.

S: We???

M: Yes, she wants to talk to us both tomorrow at 4 p.m. Don't be late!

WORD STORE 5C | Exams

5 Complete the dialogue with the verbs from the box in the correct form.

(fail get into pass prepare retake revise take)

In the library …

Jade: Hi, Ned. What are you doing?

Ned: Oh hello, Jade. Well, I_'m revising_ for my History exam.

Jade: I see. When ¹_____ you _____ the exam?

Ned: It's on Wednesday, and I need to study hard because I don't want to ²_____ it.

Jade: Don't worry too much, Ned. You're a good student. I'm sure you can ³_____ your exam.

Ned: I hope so! I don't want to ⁴_____ it – once is enough! What about you? ⁵_____ you _____ for your exams yet?

Jade: Yes, I have. I started a few months ago.

Ned: Why did you start so early?

Jade: Well, I want to ⁶_____ the School of Fine Arts to become a painter and the entrance exams are really hard – all the best art students want to go there!

Ned: Good luck!

Jade: You too!

Complete the diagram with as many words as you can think of.

_____   _____   _____
_____   _____   _____
_____   Places in a school   _____
People at a school   Types of school

SCHOOL

Subjects   Objects

_____ _____   _____ _____
_____ _____   _____ _____
_____ _____   _____ _____

SHOW WHAT YOU'VE LEARNT

6 Choose the correct answers A–C.

1 Don't worry about your exams. Just __ your best.
   A do   **B** get   **C** be

2 In the UK, children go to __ school when they are 11.
   A primary   **B** high   **C** secondary

3 About twenty percent of the pupils __ their exams every year.
   A miss   **B** fail   **C** lose

4 My brother wants to __ school when he is 16.
   A leave   **B** miss   **C** start

5 Come on. Let's run to school. We don't want to __ late.
   A do   **B** get   **C** be

6 I never __ lessons because the school always writes to tell your parents.
   A skip   **B** leave from   **C** miss

7 Please be quiet. Paul is __ for his exams.
   A taking   **B** passing   **C** revising

8 Kelly is always __ time for school but she is always late when we go out!
   A early   **B** on   **C** at

9 I was very disappointed when I __ two of my exams.
   A failed   **B** retook   **C** passed

10 There aren't any boys here. It's a __ -sex school.
   A girl's   **B** single   **C** mixed

/10

GRAMMAR

5.2

must/mustn't
• should/shouldn't

SHOW WHAT YOU KNOW

1 Complete the text with the correct form of *have to* and the verbs in brackets.

Hi Jo,
I _have to make_ (make) a decision about next year.
I can stay here or go to the same *sixth form college
as you. So, I've got a few questions.
Firstly, ¹_____ (you/wear) a uniform?
Sixth formers at our school ²_____
(not/wear) a uniform but they ³_____
_____ (look) smart – they can't wear jeans, for example.
Next question, how much homework ⁴_____
_____ (you/do) every day? A friend who is a year
older than me here ⁵_____ (do)
about three hours of homework a day but he
⁶_____ (not/do) anything at the
weekend.
I think that's all for now.
Thanks,
Seth

* Sixth form college – the last years in the British school system.
Students aged 16–18 stay in the sixth form for two years while
they study for A levels, the highest level of school exams.

2 ★ Read the dialogue between Cathy and Damien and choose the correct option.

C: I'm not sure I want to be in the school play.
D: Well, you ¹*don't have to / mustn't* be in it. It's your
choice but it's great fun. Of course, it takes a lot of time.
People who want to be in the play ²*must / mustn't* go to
Drama Club every Tuesday and Thursday after school.
They ³*don't have to / must* learn their words and they
⁴*mustn't / don't have to* be late because everyone has
to wait for them. Of course, you ⁵*mustn't / don't have to*
act. You can help with the music or the clothes.
C: What do you think? ⁶*I should / Should I* do it?
D: Of course. I think it's a great idea. You ⁷*must / don't
have to* see Ms Lee at lunchtime and tell her.
She needs the list of names today.

SHOW WHAT YOU'VE LEARNT

5 Complete the sentences with the correct form of the modal verbs. Do not use the words in brackets.

You _shouldn't_ go to university just because your parents think it's a good idea. Do what is best for you. (don't)
1 We _____ finish our project tonight. We can give it to our teacher next Monday. (must)
2 I _____ tell my parents where I'm going and who I'm going with but I always tell them anyway. (should)
3 You _____ start doing your homework soon. It's getting late. (must)
4 You _____ write in this book. It's a library book. (should)
5 Dan, you _____ feed your cat only twice a day. It's really very fat. (should)
6 You _____ do all the housework. Ask your children to help you. (don't)

/6

3 ★ ★ Complete Cathy's email with the correct answers A–C.

Hi Sally,
Well, I'm in the school play! I ¹__ say much. I come on in the
middle of the play and say: 'Excuse me, is this the way to the
forest?' and that's it! The first meeting is tomorrow. We ²__ be
late. Ms Lee says that a good actor ³__ be well organised and
brave. That's why, in the first meeting, we all have to stand
in front of the group and say some lines from a play. Luckily,
we ⁴__ sing! I ⁵__ find something that I know well – maybe
something from *Romeo and Juliet*. I'm studying that in English.
Anyway, I ⁶__ do my homework now.
See you soon.
Cathy

1	A mustn't	B shouldn't	C don't have to
2	A don't have to	B mustn't	C have to
3	A have to	B shouldn't	C must
4	A don't have to	B mustn't	C have to
5	A shouldn't	B mustn't	C should
6	A mustn't	B don't have to	C must

4 ★ ★ ★ Complete the dialogues with the phrases from the box. There are three extra phrases.

don't have to speak   don't have to wait   must be
~~must say~~   should get   should go   should I do
should I go   should I say   shouldn't look   should sit
shouldn't wait   should wait   should look

Ms L.: Cathy, your turn.
C: This is from *Romeo and Juliet*. 'A rose by any other
name would smell as sweet.'
Ms L.: You _must say_ it louder. I can't hear you.
And you ¹_____ at us, not at the floor.
C: ²_____ it again?
Ms L.: Yes, please.
C: Er … er …'A sweet by any other name would smell
like a rose.'
Ms L.: Stop, stop. I think you ³_____ for a few
minutes. You're very nervous. Melanie, you go next.
***
C: I feel terrible, Damien. What ⁴_____ ?
⁵_____ home and forget about the
school play?
D: No, you shouldn't, Cathy. You ⁶_____
here with me and watch the others. Look, they're
making mistakes too. You ⁷_____ again
today. Ask Ms Lee if you can do it on Thursday.
C: No, I ⁸_____ . I ⁹_____
brave and try again now. It's like falling off a horse.
You ¹⁰_____ back on immediately.
The only problem is ... doing this is worse than
falling off a horse!

62

GRAMMAR: Train and Try Again page 132

Useful verbs and prepositions
• places at school • nouns and verbs

1 Complete the dialogue between Mark and Jane with the correct form of the verbs from the box. There are three extra verbs.

> borrow do give have lend make
> play put use wear

Extract from Student's Book recording 🔊 **2.35–2.36**

Jane: Now, you must always wait ᵃ*on / in* the corridor outside this room until the teacher comes. Students mustn't be in the room ᵇ*without / alone* a teacher. There is a lot of special equipment here. Students *do* experiments ᶜ*on / in* Chemistry and Physics lessons. You mustn't touch anything until the teacher tells you to.

Mark: What are all those books?

Jane: We keep all the Science books here, so everyone can use them in the lessons. You have to ¹_____ an overall ᵈ*in / for* here too over your school uniform, to protect it. […]
This is my favourite place in the school. I meet my friends here ᵉ*on / in* the breaks and we usually sit ᶠ*over / away* there. Teachers don't often come here because it's always very noisy – they prefer the staff room! You can buy all kinds of food and drinks here, so remember to bring your money! We take our food and sit ᵍ*in / on* the playground when the sun is shining. […]
We can go in here now but you mustn't talk ʰ*inside / in* and you mustn't use your mobile phone. There are lots of computers, so we can do our homework here. There's wifi too, so you can ²_____ the Internet. Oh, and you can ³_____ books ⁱ*for / until* three days, so you can read them at home.
You can also borrow DVDs and CDs from here. […]
We have a big school meeting here every morning before classes – called assembly. All the teachers and students have to come – that's [ʲ*round / around*] three hundred people! The headteacher ⁴_____ us important information and sometimes visitors come and give speeches. We don't ⁵_____ lessons in here, it's only for assembly and for doing exams. But we do drama here and sometimes we ⁶_____ sport in here if the weather is really bad.

2 Choose the correct words a–j in the dialogue in Exercise 1.

3 Complete the sentences with the correct prepositions from Exercise 1.

> I never get bored *in* English lessons.

1 I don't want to go out ____ my friends.
2 Is that Natalie ____ there?
3 Can we stay ____ today? It's raining and cold outside.
4 Can I borrow your phone ____ five minutes, please?
5 Don't run ____ the corridor. Walk quickly to your next lesson.
6 This isn't a very popular football team. Only ____ three hundred people watch them every match.

VOCABULARY PRACTICE | Places at school

4 Look at the vocabulary in lesson 5.3 in the Student's Book. Complete the dialogue between Noah and Jayne with one word in each gap. The first letters are given.

N: Excuse me, it's my first day here. I have to borrow some books. Where's the school l*ibrary*?

J: Walk along this ¹**c**_____ . Be quiet when you go past the ²**s**_____ **r**_____ . Don't wake the teachers up!

N: Eh?

J: Sorry. Just joking. So, go past the ³**c**_____ and the lovely smell of chips, then the ⁴**s**_____ **l**_____ . Careful, I think Class 8C are doing Chemistry in there at the moment! Go upstairs, walk by the ⁵**h**_____ – someone is giving a speech to all the Year 12 students now, and then go past the ⁶**g**_____ . The students aren't in there today. They're all outside playing football on the ⁷**s**_____ **f**_____ . So, at the top of the stairs, turn right. That's room 21 and the library is next to it. OK?

N: I think so. Thanks. Err …

J: Where are you going? That's the wrong way. That's the door to the ⁸**p**_____ . You can't go outside now. It isn't break time. OK, come with me.

REMEMBER BETTER

Learning collocations is a useful way to build up your vocabulary. Knowing which verbs collocate with which nouns, e.g. knowing when to use *make* and when to use *do*, makes your English better. It's also good to know that there may be different verbs which collocate with one noun, e.g. the Internet (*use, surf, access*).

WORD STORE 5D | Nouns and verbs

5 Cross out the words which do **not** collocate with the verbs. Use a dictionary if necessary.

	wear	~~equipment~~ / *a uniform* / *glasses*
1	**do**	*homework* / *dinner* / *experiments*
2	**borrow**	*a book from the library* / *a DVD from a friend* / *an email from someone*
3	**use**	*a computer* / *school books in lessons* / *a message*
4	**give**	*a promise* / *advice* / *a speech*
5	**have**	*a meeting* / *a party* / *a film*
6	**play**	*computers* / *sports* / *chess*

1 **Read the text quickly and decide which classroom, A or B, looks like a classroom in the Waldorf School.**

A ◯　　　　B ◯

2 **Read the text again. Are sentences 1–6 true (T) or false (F)?**

1 The writer gives four examples of how students and teachers can use technology. ◯
2 The staff and parents agree about not using technology at school. ◯
3 Students mustn't leave their desks during lessons. ◯
4 The writer doesn't say that students do better without technology. ◯
5 The lessons at the school are interesting for the students. ◯
6 The writer says that 160 students go to the Waldorf School of the Peninsula. ◯

ALTERNATIVE EDUCATION

Technology is changing our lives and many people believe that school pupils should all have laptops, look at interactive whiteboards and do all their homework online. Los Altos, California, is a city in an area **known as** 'Silicon Valley' because **it is home to** many technology companies **such as** Google, Apple, Yahoo and Hewlett-Packard. So the Waldorf School of the Peninsula is a **bit of a surprise**.

The staff and parents here believe that there shouldn't be any technology in our schools. There are no computers in the classrooms. No screens at all. The teachers write on blackboards and the classrooms are full of books, posters and magazines. There are wooden desks and pupils write on paper with pens and pencils. This doesn't mean that the teachers just stand at the front of the class and the students quietly do exercises. They get up and do fun activities and play games that help them to learn and remember.

Are the methods <u>successful</u>? It's difficult to **say for sure**. Most of the students <u>succeed</u> in their exams but is this <u>success</u> because of the school or because they have parents who think <u>education</u> is important? People who like the school say that the students use their <u>imagination</u> more. The teachers certainly work hard to create <u>imaginative</u> lessons and the students enjoy them. Parents also say that learning without computers helps the children to develop better problem solving skills and this actually helps them to use computers later in life.

However, others <u>disagree</u>. They say that students who study at the school are unprepared for our technological world when they leave. One thing is for sure. The schools are very popular. There are 160 Waldorf schools in the USA now and parents pay about $20,000 a year to <u>educate</u> their children at them.

What do you think? Do you <u>agree</u> with the parents or do you think students should use technology at school?

GLOSSARY

develop (v) – to grow or change into something bigger, stronger, or more advanced

unprepared (adj) – not ready to deal with something

REMEMBER BETTER

When you learn related parts of speech, you can talk about the same subject using different words.

*Our school basketball team is usually very **successful**. We don't always **succeed** in competitions but we have more **successes** than failures.*

A Complete the table with the underlined words in the text. Two of the words are not in the text. If necessary, use a dictionary to find them.

	Adjective	Noun	Verb
1	*successful*	a _____	b _____
2	a _____	b _____	imagine
3	educated / a _____ al	b _____	c _____
4	–	agreement / a _____	b _____ / c _____

B Complete the sentences with the correct form of the words in capitals.

1 SUCCESS

Our school basketball team are very *successful*. They win all their matches.

A Our students' _____ in their exams is because of our great teachers.

B Alex is very ambitious and he wants to _____ in everything he does.

2 EDUCATE

A _____ should be free for all students at university.

B They don't go to school. Their parents _____ them at home.

C There are many _____ videos on YouTube. You can learn about anything!

D My mum likes my new boyfriend. He's polite, smart and well- _____ .

3 IMAGINE

A You've got a great _____ . You should write children's books.

B This is a very _____ piece of writing. Well done, Katy!

4 AGREE

A I _____ with you about school sports. I can't see why all students should do some kind of exercise.

B I don't think young pupils should get homework. Do you _____ ?

C My parents and I often have a _____ about going out with my friends.

3 Look at the sentences from the text and choose the correct meaning (A or B) of the underlined expressions.

1 Los Altos, California, is a city in an area known as 'Silicon Valley'
   A Some people call the area 'Silicon Valley'.
   B The area is officially named 'Silicon Valley'.

2 … it is home to many technology companies such as Google, Apple, Yahoo and Hewlett-Packard.
   A … there are a number of technology companies in the area. Four of these are Google, Apple, Yahoo and Hewlett-Packard.
   B … there are four technology companies in the area: Google, Apple, Yahoo and Hewlett-Packard.

3 The Waldorf School of the Peninsula is a bit of a surprise.
   A The school is different to how people expect it to be.
   B The school is similar to the local companies.

4 It's difficult to say for sure.
   A The writer doesn't want to say.
   B The writer doesn't really know.

4 Complete the sentences with one of the phrases from Exercise 3 in each gap.

I'm *known as* Spiderman at school because I'm very good at climbing in the gym.

1 I want to go to the party but I can't _____ that I'm going. I have to ask my parents first.

2 The end of this film is _____ but I can't tell you what happens. Go and see it!

3 We do a lot of different sports at school, _____ football, cricket, volleyball and running.

VOCABULARY PRACTICE | Phrasal verbs

5 Look at the vocabulary in lesson 5.4 in the Student's Book. Complete the phrasal verbs in the sentences.

You can find *out* lots of interesting things online for your school project.

1 My friends know how to put ___ a tent because they go camping a lot.

2 Jack's family has to move ___ a lot because of his dad's job.

3 Turn off the television so that you can focus ___ your homework.

WORD STORE 5E | Collocations

6 Choose the correct option.

DO YOU HAVE ANY PLANS FOR THE SUMMER HOLIDAYS?

Why don't you [1]do / make **a course?**

It's a great way to [2]increase / improve your skills. And it isn't boring! You can [3]have / take part in interesting activities and [4]make / get friends. Sometimes, you can [5]win / take prizes too!

65

GRAMMAR

SHOW WHAT YOU KNOW

1 Complete the sentences with the correct positive or negative form of the verb *be* or *can*.

My brother *is* only three years old but he *can* swim quite well.

1 It ª_____ three o'clock in the morning. I ᵇ_____ in bed but I ᶜ_____ sleep.
2 Hey, Jackie? ª_____ you swim? ᵇ_____ you interested in a job? The swimming pool wants summer workers.
3 Louis ª_____ very good at Spanish. He ᵇ_____ say 'Hello', he ᶜ_____ count to ten and he doesn't know what 'Gracias' means! He ᵈ_____ the worst student in the class!
4 My mum and dad ª_____ angry with me because of my Maths test result. I work hard but I ᵇ_____ understand the Maths we are doing at the moment.

2 ★ Complete the text with the past form of the verbs in brackets.

○○○

Amazing children

William Sidis *was* (be) born in New York in 1898. He
¹_____ (can) speak more than ten languages and, when
he ²_____ (be) eleven he ³_____ (be) already a student
at Harvard University. He ⁴_____ (be) a professor
when he ⁵___ (be) twenty. He ⁶_____ (be) amazing but,
unfortunately, he ⁷_____ (not/be) a happy child.

3 ★ ★ Complete the dialogue between Elaine (E) and her grandmother (G) with the correct past forms of the verb *be* or *can*.

E: Hi, Grandma. What are those photos?
G: They're my old photos from when I *was* a teenager like you.
E: Wow. Is that your motorbike?
G: No, it ¹_____ my brother's.
E: ²_____ you drive?
G: Not then. Driving lessons ³_____ expensive and my parents ⁴_____ pay for them.
E: Oh, I like this one. Where ⁵_____ you?
G: We ⁶_____ in Wales on a school trip. The weather ⁷_____ very good – there ⁸_____ lots of rain – but we ⁹_____ very happy in the mountains. Every day ¹⁰_____ the same – breakfast at 8 a.m., a 20km walk and back to the hostel in the evening. We ¹¹_____ so tired, we ¹²_____ move in the evenings. There ¹³_____ any discos or parties – we ¹⁴_____ in bed before 9 p.m!
E: ¹⁵_____ you with Grandpa then?
G: No, I ¹⁶_____ . He ¹⁷_____ at the same school as me. Just a minute, ah, here's one of your grandfather and me. We ¹⁸_____ twenty-one or twenty-two then …

4 ★ ★ ★ Use the words in brackets to make full questions and answers.

Conversation 1: Marcus and Sam

M: Hi, Sam. *Where were you yesterday* (where/you/ yesterday)?
S: Hi. Sorry. ¹_____ (I/tired). ²_____ (I/not/phone) you because ³_____ (my phone/in) my bag at school.

Conversation 2: Jenny and Beverley

J: ¹_____ (David/really horrible) to me yesterday.
B: Really? Why?
J: ²_____ (We/with) Ellen and Mark at the Sports Centre for a game of tennis. You know I can't play any ball sports. ³_____ (I/not/hit) the ball! ⁴_____ (David/not/happy) with me! He hates losing.

Conversation 3: Mr Smith and Kate

S: ¹_____ (Why/you late) to school this morning?
K: ²_____ (My dad/not/find) his car keys.
S: ³_____ (Where/they)?
K: ⁴_____ (They/on the bathroom cupboard)!

SHOW WHAT YOU'VE LEARNT

5 Complete the sentences and questions with the correct Past Simple form of *be* and *can*. Use the words in brackets.

Why *were you sad* yesterday? **(you/sad)**

1 _____ at the age of seven? **(you/ swim)**
2 Why _____ after the party? **(Carole/ angry)**
3 Unfortunately, _____ me with my homework. **(Simon/help)**
4 _____ the guitar really well in primary school. What a talent! **(Nikki/play)**
5 'My _____ at the weekend.' 'Oh no, I'm sorry to hear that.' **(friends/ill)**
6 _____the pizza. Mega Supreme Pizza is really big. Too big! **(we/finish)**

/6

GRAMMAR: Train and Try Again page 132

1 Translate the phrases into your own language.

SPEAKING BANK

Asking for information

I'd like some information. _____

What are your opening times? _____

How much does it cost to get in? _____

How much are the tickets?/How much is a (family) ticket? _____

Can I book online?/ Are there any guided tours? _____

Is there a podcast? _____

Where is the (park/ museum/attraction) exactly? _____

Thanks very much. _____

Giving information

Can I help you? _____

What would you like to know? _____

Tickets are (£10) for adults and (£5) for children. _____

Children under (5) are free. _____

There are also discounts for groups. _____

A family ticket costs (£20). _____

The (museum/park) opens at (9 a.m.) and closes at (5 p.m.). _____

It's in/on (Green Street). _____

You're welcome. _____

Spinnaker Tower, Portsmouth

2 Look at the photo of the Spinnaker Tower in Portsmouth. Complete the answers with the words from the box.

> background   example   exciting   firstly
> looks   ~~modern~~   next   top   whole

1 **What can you see in the photo?**
I can see a big, _modern_ tower. It's ª_____ to the sea. There are some boats in the ᵇ_____ and some buildings. It ᶜ_____ like a big city.

2 **Why is something like this popular with tourists?**
There are a few reasons. ª_____ , of course, you get a great view from the ᵇ_____ . You can see the town, people, boats. In cities, you can see all the famous buildings and take great photos. In Paris, for ᶜ_____ , from the Eiffel Tower, you can see the Arc de Triomphe, Notre Dame, and other places. Also, it is ᵈ_____ to be high up.

3 **Do you like climbing towers when you are on holiday? Why?/Why not?**
Oh, yes. We always go up towers. The Eiffel Tower, the Leaning Tower of Pisa and smaller towers. The best is the Campanile di San Marco in Venice. You can see the _____ city and the canals. It's amazing.

3 Look at the information about the Spinnaker Tower and complete sentences a–g.

Useful information

Open: ▶ 10 a.m.–6 p.m. every day

Tickets: ▶ Adults £11.00 (online price £9.90)
Children (3–15) 8.50 (online price £7.65)
Under 3's – Free
Family ticket: £34.00
Seniors and Students: £10.00
Discounts for groups of 15 or more people.
Price includes a free audio guide.
See our website for more details.
We are also on Facebook and Twitter.

Address: ▶ Gunwharf Quays, Portsmouth.

a Yes, there is. A family ticket costs thirty-_four_ pounds.
b It's in ¹_____ Quays.
c They are ²_____ pounds for adults and ³_____ pounds fifty for children aged 3 to 15. It is free for children under the age of 3.
d Yes, there are. They are for groups of at least ⁴_____ people.
e Yes, you can and prices are lower. For example an adult ticket costs ⁵_____ pounds ⁶_____ online, a saving of 10% on the normal price.
f No, I'm afraid there aren't but we have free ⁷_____ guides for all visitors.
g The tower opens at ⁸_____ o'clock in the morning and closes at ⁹_____ o'clock in the evening.

4 Match questions 1–6 with answers a–g from Exercise 3.

What are the opening times? [g]
1 Are there any discounts for groups? [ ]
2 Are there any guided tours? [ ]
3 Can I book online? [ ]
4 Where is the tower exactly? [ ]
5 How much are the tickets? [ ]
6 Is there a cheaper ticket for families? [ ]

1 **Read the email and choose the correct words a–d.**

2 **Complete the email with the words and phrases from the box. There are two extra words or phrases.**

> about you   can't wait   else   hope   life   miss
> other news   plans   soon   things   up to   well
> you   your news

Subject: Hello from Spain

Attachment: jpeg picture – Fernando

Hi Stella,

How are *you* ? I ¹_____ you're OK. How's everyone at school?

I'm getting on ²_____ here in Spain. I couldn't understand anyone at first ᵃ*so / because* my Spanish was so bad ᵇ*but / and* it is getting better now. The food is great, the school is nice ᶜ*but / and* the people are friendly, ᵈ*because / so* I'm very happy. My ³_____ is that I'm in the volleyball team here. We play all over Spain. We were in Barcelona last weekend. It was great. What ⁴_____ ? Well, there's a boy called Fernando. He's very nice – I'm sending his photo with this email.

How ⁵_____ ? How's ⁶_____ ? What are you ⁷_____ ? How are Beth and Fiona and the other girls? Do you still go to the disco every Friday? What are your ⁸_____ for the summer? Can you come to Spain to visit me?

I ⁹_____ to hear all your news.

I ¹⁰_____ you all – but not English weather!

Write ¹¹_____ ,
Vicky

---

3 **Complete the sentences with one word in each gap. The first letters are given.**

A How are you?
   How are **t**hings?

B What are you doing at the moment?
   What are you ᵃ**u**_____ ᵇ**t**_____ at the moment?

C I'm getting on OK.
   I'm getting on ᶜ**w**_____ .

D Write soon.
   I ᵈ**h**_____ to ᵉ**h**_____ from you soon.
   I ᶠ**c**_____ ᵍ**w**_____ to hear all your news.

E I'm also …
   My ʰ**o**_____ ⁱ**n**_____ is that …

F It would be great to …
   I'd ʲ**l**_____ to …

4 **Complete the email with *and*, *but*, *so* and *because*.**

● ● ●   New Email

To: Tim James
Subject: Re: Hello my friend

Hi Tim,

Thanks for your email. How are things? I hope you aren't too busy with school work.

I'm getting on OK. I was ill for a few days *but* I'm fine now. It was nice to be at home at first ¹_____ it was boring after a while ²_____ there was nothing to do. We've got exams soon, ³_____ I'm working hard. What else? I'm doing a lot of sport ⁴_____ I'm also going out with a girl from my class. Her name's Elaine. She lives near me, ⁵_____ I see her a lot. My parents are a bit worried ⁶_____ I'm always tired ⁷_____ I'm happy ☺

How about you? What are you up to? I know you are on Facebook ⁸_____ I don't often go on there now ⁹_____ I haven't got time. I spend all my time doing school work, playing football ¹⁰_____ going to the cinema with Elaine.

Write soon.
Rob

SHOW WHAT YOU'VE LEARNT

5 **You are on holiday. Write an email to a friend at home.**

- Ask how your friend is.
- Give two pieces of recent news.
- Ask about your friend's news.
- Ask your friend to write back.

SHOW THAT YOU'VE CHECKED

Finished? Always check your writing. Can you tick ✓ everything on this list?

In my email:

• I have used the appropriate greeting and ending phrases.	⬭
• I have asked how my friend is.	⬭
• I have told my friend my news.	⬭
• I have asked about my friend's news.	⬭
• I have used linking words: *and*, *but*, *so* and *because*.	⬭
• I have used contractions (e.g. *I'm / aren't / that's*).	⬭
• I have checked my spelling.	⬭
• My text is neat and clear.	⬭

1 In pairs, ask and answer the questions.

PART 1

Talk about people.

1 Who is your favourite film character?
   What does he/she look like?
2 Can you describe his/her personality?
3 Who is the most creative person you know? Why?
4 Are you sociable or unsociable? Why?
5 What clothes do you never wear? Why?

PART 2

Talk about school.

1 What are your favourite and least favourite
   subjects at school? Why?
2 How do you revise for exams and tests?
3 Where do you go in your breaks at school
   and what do you do?
4 What do students do after primary school
   in your country?
5 What do you want to do after secondary school?

2 Look at the photos of the students' schools.

PART 1

Take turns to describe the people in the photos.

A

B

PART 2

In pairs, ask and answer the questions about the photos.

Student A's photo

1 What are the students doing?
2 What are they wearing?
3 Where in the school do you think they are?
4 What are they using?
5 Do they look like they're enjoying their lesson?
   Why?/Why not?

Student B's photo

1 Who can you see in the photo?
2 What do you think they're doing?
3 Where do you think they are?
4 What style of clothes are they wearing?
5 Do they look happy? Why?/Why not?

3 Read the instructions on your card. In pairs, take turns to role-play the conversation.

Student A

You're a tourist and you want to visit the
Old School Museum. Student B works at
the tourist information office. Ask him/her
questions.

• Start the conversation in a polite way.
• Say that you want information about
   the Old School Museum.
• Ask how much it costs to get in.
• Ask about opening times.
• Ask for directions to the museum.
• Ask if you can book online.
• Thank him/her for helping and end
   the conversation.

Student B

You work at the tourist information office.
Student A wants some information.
Answer his/her questions.

• Respond to how Student A starts
   the conversation.
• Ask what exactly Student A wants to know.
• Tell him/her ticket prices: £8 adults /
   £4 children / £20 family ticket.
• Tell him/her the museum opening times:
   8.30 a.m. – 5.30 p.m.
• Tell him/her that the museum is on North
   Street, next to the train station.
• Say yes and say that there is also an app.
• Respond and say goodbye.

VOCABULARY AND GRAMMAR

1 Complete the sentences with one word from the box in each gap. There are two extra words.

nursery   kindergarten   playgroup   mixed
~~primary~~   secondary   state   university

My five-year-old brother has just started _primary_ school.
1 Amber goes to a _____ school because she's only three years old.
2 Ellen loves studying at _____ . It's much more interesting than school.
3 All the children at the _____ that my brother goes to are four years old.
4 Every Tuesday at two o'clock, there is a _____ at Gina's house – her little boy and other children play and learn together.
5 I go to a _____ school because it's free. Private schools are very expensive.

/5

2 Complete the text with one word in each gap. The first letters are given.

○○○

School life. **Anthony, aged 15, UK**

I usually get to school early in the morning. I meet my friends and we play football in the p_layground_ but we are never ¹l_____ for our ²c_____ .
Lessons start at 9.00. The worst thing about our school is that it is a ³s_____-s_____ school.
It's just boys. I'd prefer to go to a ⁴m_____ school. Why? Because knowing how to talk to girls is an important part of our ⁵e_____ !

/5

3 Choose the correct option.

Hi Paul,

Thanks for the email. Sorry to hear about your problems at school and with Mum and Dad, but I'm not really surprised. You are never (on)/ in / at time for lessons and you don't often ¹make / get / do well in tests. You ²take / miss / lose one lesson a week or more because you 'are ill' and you ³get / do / make badly in subjects you should be good at because you don't try. When was the last time that you ⁴retook / revised / passed for a test? You just want to have fun. It's not really surprising that you often ⁵miss / fail / lose your exams.
Sorry, little brother, but I agree with Mum and Dad. I'm having a great time here at university, but you need to work harder if you want to study somewhere when you leave school.

See you at Christmas,
Clara

/5

4 Complete the dialogue between Mum (M), Peter (P) and James (J) with the verbs and phrases from the box. There are two extra verbs.

could   couldn't   don't have to   have to
~~must~~   mustn't   shouldn't   should

M: Peter, are you still here? It's ten o'clock.
P: I know but I _must_ find James' book.

An hour later …
J: Hi, Peter. You're late. You're always late. You ¹_____ get up earlier!
P: Sorry. I ²_____ find your book.
J: My book? You ³_____ give me back my book. You can keep it. I don't want it.
P: You ⁴_____ say that. It was a present from Melanie.
J: No, it wasn't. It was my brother's but he doesn't want it, either.
P: Are you sure? I'm talking about *The Hobbit* – that special book with photos from the film.
J: What? That book. Have you got it? Where is it? Go and look for it. I ⁵_____ have it today.
P: Why?
J: Melanie wants to borrow the book. She's having a *Hobbit* film night with her friends.
P: OK, let's go to my house and look together.

/5

5 Complete the text with *was, were, wasn't, weren't, could* and *couldn't*.

Stefani Germanotta _was_ born in New York City in 1986. Her parents ¹_____ quite rich and their home was in a good area of Manhattan. Stefani's school was an expensive, private, girls' school. Stefani was a good student. Her exam results were always very good but exams ²_____ the most important thing in her life. Stefani was very talented and she ³_____ play the piano and sing. Singing and acting were her main interests and she ⁴_____ think about anything else. Her dream was to be a star. It ⁵_____ easy but Stefani is now famous. Do you know her? She is now known as Lady Gaga.

/5

6 Choose the correct answers A–C.

You ___ say it louder. I can't hear you.
(A) must   B mustn't   C can
1 You ___ finish the exercise now. You can do it later.
   A mustn't   B shouldn't   C don't have to
2 The exam starts at 9 a.m., but you ___ be there at 8.45 a.m.
   A must   B can   C could
3 Where ___ yesterday afternoon?
   A was you   B you were   C were you
4 We were at the beach but we ___ swim. It was too cold.
   A mustn't   B couldn't   C shouldn't
5 I got a C in my Maths exam. ___ do it again to try to get an A or a B?
   A Should I   B I have to   C Was I

/5

Total   /30

USE OF ENGLISH

7 Choose the correct answers A–C.

Martin goes to a ___ school and it's very expensive.
A state
(B) private
C mixed

1 Tom ___ his exams now because he failed them in June.
A couldn't retake
B must retake
C retakes

2 Students ___ their school books during class tests.
A must use
B don't have to use
C mustn't use

3 ___ for lessons. Our teachers are very strict about that.
A You mustn't be late
B You could be late
C You don't have to be late

4 ___ in the canteen. Actually, it was closed.
A The student was
B The students weren't
C The students aren't

5 I don't want to ___ in my exams.
A fail
B go badly
C get bad marks

/5

8 Complete the second sentence so that it has a similar meaning to the first. Use between two and four words, including the word in capitals.

Andrew usually fails his exams. **BADLY**
Andrew usually _does badly_ in his exams.

1 There is an important discussion for the teachers about the exams. **HAVING**
The teachers _____
about the exams.

2 Jenny is two years old – she doesn't know how to write. **BECAUSE**
Jenny can't _____ she's only two years old.

3 At what age can you stop being a student in the USA? **LEAVE**
At what age _____ in the USA?

4 The headteacher is speaking to the new students in the auditorium. **SPEECH**
The headteacher _____
to the new students in the auditorium.

5 I want to study computers and I need some information. **COURSE**
I want to _____ in computers and I need some information.

/5

9 Put the words in the correct order to make sentences and questions. There is one extra word.

Ellie: Where are the students?
Tom: on / there / sports / are / the / field / they
They are on the sports field.

1 Pat: Do you have any brothers or sisters?
Kim: Yes, I have a sister. school / and / secondary / to / she's / ten / goes / primary / she
_____

2 Julie: I'm going to a camp in the summer.
Max: Great! lots / have / part / activities / can / take / of / in / you
_____?

3 Ben: I need help. take / tent / I / can't / up / this / put
_____
Lucy: OK, I can help you.

4 Alice: my / from / Spanish / want / to / skills / in / I / improve
_____
Mario: You should go to Spain.

5 Harry: I'd like to speak with Mr Jones, the Art teacher.
Mrs Smith: in / you / can / find / hall / room / him / the staff
_____

/5

10 Complete the text with the correct answers A–C.

```
● ● ●                New Email
```

Dear Danny,

How are you? How was your summer holiday? I hope it was great!

I'm excited because I'm starting at my new _B_ school tomorrow. I don't know any of the students there. I hope I can ¹___ some friends! It's difficult for me because my family ²___ around a lot – we usually stay in the same city for only a few years. But I know a good way to ³___ people – sports! I have to ⁴___ out what sports clubs they have at the school.

Well, it's late here and I should go to sleep. I have to be ⁵___ time for my first day of school!

Bye for now,
Jane

	A	B	C
	A kindergarten	(B) secondary	C nursery
1	A make	B have	C take
2	A goes	B moves	C runs
3	A find	B know	C meet
4	A look	B find	C put
5	A in	B on	C at

/5

Total /20

71

6 Health and sport

VOCABULARY

6.1

Types of sport • *go, do* and *play*
• sportspeople

SHOW WHAT YOU KNOW

1 Match the sports from the box with the sentences. There are three extra sports.

> badminton   cycling   football   climbing
> running   karate   sailing   skiing   table tennis
> tennis   volleyball   yoga

When I do this, it's more like fast walking! *running*

1 You need a bike to do this. _____
2 In this sport, people kick a ball into a net. _____
3 You can learn how to break something in half with your hand. _____
4 We do this in Greece. I love visiting different islands on our yacht. _____
5 Some people call this sport 'Ping Pong'. _____
6 In this activity, people sit in a special position and breathe slowly. _____
7 Players hit something over a net but it isn't a ball. _____
8 In this activity, you use your hands and feet to move up cliffs or rocks. _____

WORD STORE 6A | Sports

2 Complete the sports with one letter in each space.

At school, we play football, basketball and **v o l l e y** ball.

1 My friends and I sometimes go **c __ __ __ ing** on our BMX bikes.
2 In winter, people in our town go **i __ __ s __ __ __ ing** on the lake when it's very cold.
3 I do **Z __ __ __ a®** because I love dancing and I want to get fit.
4 Some girls in my class enjoy doing sports from Japan and China like karate and **k __ __ __ f __**.
5 In summer Amy spends all her time playing **ᵃt __ __ __ __ s** outside in the sun, and in the winter, she goes **ᵇs __ __ ing** in the mountains.
6 Mark and Jake often go **k __ __ __ __ ing** on a small river near our village.
7 Sam does a lot of **s __ __ m __ __ __ g** in the local pool, in a lake near his home and in the sea.
8 I'm very tall, so my teacher thinks I should play **b __ __ k __ __ __ __ __ l** but I don't like ball sports or team sports.

WORD STORE 6B | *go, do* and *play*

3 Complete the dialogue with *go, do* or *play*.

Rose: Do you do any sports?
Tim: Not many. I *play* table tennis at home with my brother because we've got a table. I ¹_____ cycling and, in the summer, I ²_____ swimming. I don't ³_____ football because I don't like it.
Rose: Do you ⁴_____ yoga or Zumba?
Tim: I don't even know what Zumba is!
Rose: It's a kind of dance. I ⁵_____ it twice a week. I ⁶_____ karate too.
Tim: Wow! What other sports do you like?
Rose: Well, we've got a yacht, so I ⁷_____ sailing quite a lot. I love the water. At school, I ⁸_____ volleyball for the school team.
Tim: Do you ⁹_____ running?
Rose: No. That's one thing that I don't enjoy but I ¹⁰_____ exercise every evening before I go to bed.
Tim: That's amazing. My favourite sport is basketball.
Rose: Do you ¹¹_____ it at school?
Tim: Oh, no. I don't ¹²_____ it. I like watching it on telly.

4 Answer the questions for yourself.

1 Do you do any sports?
_____ .
2 What other sports do you like?
_____ .
3 Which of the sports in the word cloud on page 73 would you like to try?
_____ .

5 Complete the name of the sportsperson in each sentence.

Cristiano Ronaldo is a great football*er* – he scores lots of goals!

1 Usain Bolt was the best run___ in the world and he won many Olympic medals.

2 During the Tour de France race in 2010, cycl___ Marcus Burghardt fell when a dog decided to cross the road!

3 Is LeBron James the greatest basketball play___ in the NBA?

4 Sir Francis Chichester was a famous sail___ who sailed around the world alone in a yacht in 1966–67.

5 Alberto Tomba is an Italian ski___ who won fifty World Cup events during his career.

REMEMBER THIS

The verbs *win* and *beat* are used in similar situations, but there is a difference between them.

Win something: *a match / a competition*
Beat somebody: *a player / a team*

---

6 Read REMEMBER THIS. Complete the sentences with the correct form of *win* or *beat*.

Tom's playing tennis right now. He's _winning_ the match at the moment but he looks tired.

1 This match is terrible. They're _____ us 5–0 and there's still half an hour to play.

2 On school sports days, I often _____ the 100 metres race but I usually come second or third in the 200 metres.

3 It isn't fair. Amy always _____ prizes for her school work but I never do. Why? My marks are better than her marks.

4 When I play tennis with Sara, she usually _____ me but I still enjoy the games.

7 In your opinion, which three sports below are ...

a the most dangerous? _____

b the most expensive? _____

REMEMBER BETTER

In English, names of sports appear also in the names of sports places, sports equipment or sportspeople, e.g. *cycling shorts, football boots, swimming pool, tennis court, running shoes*, etc. Learning how to make word collocations, you can enrich your vocabulary.

Try to complete phrases for these sports with the words from the box. Use a dictionary if necessary.

cap   costume   court   elbow   match   pool
shirt   shorts   race   trunks

football .... boots
.... kit
.... pitch

1 swimming .... _____
.... _____
.... _____
.... _____
.... _____

2 tennis .... _____
.... _____
.... _____
.... _____
.... _____

SHOW WHAT YOU'VE LEARNT

8 Choose the correct answers A–C.

1 I like football but I'm not good enough to play __ the school team.
   A with   B for   C at

2 Are you going to take __ in the school sports day?
   A part   B place   C off

3 My brother is bored with football and wants to start doing __ .
   A volleyball   B skiing   C kung fu

4 You're not __ running in this weather, are you?
   A going   B doing   C playing

5 It isn't easy to __ fit when you've got a broken leg.
   A make   B keep   C play

6 Why do you pay money to go to a gym when you can __ exercise at home for free?
   A play   B go   C do

7 I'm bored. Do you want to __ volleyball?
   A do   B play   C go

8 I'm afraid I don't __ a very healthy lifestyle now that I'm at university.
   A have   B keep   C leave

9 Don't disturb Kate. She's __ yoga.
   A doing   B playing   C going

10 Can you teach me how to play __ ?
   A sailing   B karate   C badminton

/10

SHOW WHAT YOU KNOW

1 Complete the dialogues with the correct past form of the verb *to be*.

1 Liam: Where <u>were</u> you this morning?
  Stella: I _____ at the gym. I go every Saturday.
2 James: ᵃ_____ the football match exciting?
  David: No, it ᵇ_____ . Their players ᶜ_____ much better than our players.
3 Sue: ᵃ_____ your parents worried about you going skiing?
  Alice: Yes, they ᵇ_____ . It ᶜ_____ strange. My dad ᵈ_____ more worried than my mum.

2 ★ Complete the text with the correct past forms of the verb in brackets.

On Saturday, I was bored. I <u>phoned</u> (phone) my friend. We ¹_____ (chat) for a while and then we ²_____ (agree) to meet at her house. We ³_____ (plan) to play tennis but it ⁴_____ (start) to rain, so we ⁵_____ (decide) to watch a DVD. Jackie's little sister was there. She ⁶_____ (want) to play with us but we said 'no'. Then she ⁷_____ (cry) and Jackie's mum ⁸_____ (ask) us to look after her. So, we all ⁹_____ (watch) a film that Jackie's sister ¹⁰_____ (like). It was terrible!

3 ★ Complete the sentences with one word in each gap. The first letters are given.

○○○

👍 💬 🌐 👤   **My Blog Space**

SARAH Brown

I first became interested in skateboarding a<u>t</u> the ¹a_____ of eight. Then, ²w_____ I was about ten or eleven, a new skatepark opened in our town. I went every day and got better and better. ³L_____ year, there was a competition and I won the under-18 skateboarding prize. I was really happy. A few months ⁴a_____ , I heard about a summer skateboarding camp. It starts today. I packed my clothes ⁵y_____ and sent messages to my friends. I went to bed late last ⁶n_____ but it's 6 a.m. now and I'm eating breakfast. The coach for the camp leaves at 11 o'clock but I can't sleep.

4 ★ ★ Complete the email with the words from the box. Put the verbs in the correct form. There are two extra words.

```
ago    do   drink   give   go   have   help
last   play   stay   take   watch   yesterday
```

Hi Chris,

How are you? We <u>had</u> a sports day at our school ¹_____ . It was quite good. I ²_____ table tennis and ³_____ some kung fu. Then I had a rest and ⁴_____ the running competition. After that, some friends and I stayed at school and ⁵_____ to clear up. The teachers ⁶_____ us some cans of drink, so we ⁷_____ them to the park and ⁸_____ them there. I ⁹_____ home quite early because I had a lot of work to do ¹⁰_____ night. We had a Maths test today and we've got exams all this week.

I must do some more work. Hope all is well.
Nick

5 ★ ★ ★ Put the words in the correct order with the verbs in the correct form to make sentences.

I / out / yesterday / be / but / phone you / you
I phoned you yesterday but you were out.

1 yoga /of / I / doing / age / at / start / the / twelve
_____

2 be / he / younger / Phil / want / doctor / when / a / to / be
_____

3 My / yesterday / a salad / sister / make / for lunch
_____

4 decide / Becky / last / a volleyball club / to join / week
_____

5 ago / I / this tennis racket / months / two / buy
_____

6 last month / my / find / old / in / skateboard / I / the garage
_____

SHOW WHAT YOU'VE LEARNT

6 Complete the dialogue with the words from the box. Change the form of the verbs. There are four extra words.

```
age   ago   cry   decide   go   hate   last
past   stop   watch   yesterday
```

Tim: Is this a good film?
Jan: Oh, it's lovely. I <u>cried</u> when I saw it.
Tim: Why? Is it sad?
Jan: Very. I saw it ¹_____ weekend. I ²_____ with Amelia. She ³_____ it. She wanted to leave before the end.
Tim: I can believe that. I remember when I was at her house a few weeks ⁴_____ . We ⁵_____ to watch a DVD. When I looked at her collection of films, they were all things most people like at the ⁶_____ of 12! In the end, we watched *The Lion King*!

/6

GRAMMAR: Train and Try Again page 133

Giving opinions • everyday
expressions • likes and dislikes

1 Complete the dialogue between Millie and Alfie with the words from the box.

care fair hate like ~~stand~~ think want

Extract from Student's Book recording ◄) **3.9**

M: Hi, Alfie. What's the ᵃ*happen / matter / worry*?
A: Hi, Millie. It's PE ... I really can't <u>stand</u> it.
M: But I thought you like sports.
A: I do – usually. But I ¹_____ team sports, like football or basketball, and especially rugby.
M: Why?
A: Well, I just don't ²_____ winning or scoring points is important. I don't ³_____ if my team is not the best. I hate all the competition.
M: Oh, I see ... But PE is ᵇ*so / real / such* fun. You can relax and enjoy yourself.
A: Fun? Relaxing? I have better fun in Science. Yesterday, Kevin missed a goal and the other guys yelled at him. They said, 'We lost because of you! You're rubbish!' I hate that ᶜ*form / sort / choice* of thing.
M: Yes, it's true that's not ⁴_____ .
A: I don't think we should have to do PE at school if we don't ⁵_____ to.
M: But it's important. We can't ᵈ*just / still / quite* sit at school for hours; we need some exercise.
A: ᵉ*Alright / True / Agree*, but there shouldn't be grades for PE. And we should have more choice of sports. I'd ⁶_____ to do some individual sports, like running. Or something with one other person, like squash maybe. We could have a climbing wall, or go to the swimming pool. We could have martial arts with a good instructor.
M: Yes! I'd love to do kung fu!

---

2 Complete the second sentence so that it has a similar meaning to the first. Use between two and five words. Use the word in capitals.

I hate doing PE at school. **STAND**
I *can't stand doing* PE at school.

1 I'm not interested in who wins the World Cup. **CARE**
I _____ the World Cup.

2 I want to go kayaking this summer. **LIKE**
I _____ kayaking this summer.

3 It's wrong that women tennis players earn less than men. **FAIR**
It's _____ women tennis players earn less than men.

4 In my opinion, children shouldn't play competitive sports at school. **THINK**
I _____ should play competitive sports at school.

3 Choose the correct words a–e in the dialogue in Exercise 1.

4 Complete the mini-dialogues with the correct words in italics from the dialogue in Exercise 1.

Antoine: Hi, Greg. What's the <u>matter</u>?
Greg: I think I broke a window with my football.
1 Mum: Beth, do you want to come shopping with me?
Beth: No, I'm looking at videos on the Internet.
Mum: Well, you can't _____ stay at home all day in front of the computer.
2 Janet: I'm glad our school started Zumba® classes. They are ᵃ_____ fun.
Alan: ᵇ_____ . It's much better than basketball.
3 Justin: What sports can you do at your school?
Liam: Football, rugby, basketball, that _____ of thing. Nothing very exciting or new.

WORD STORE 6D | Likes and dislikes

5 Put the words in order to make phrases. Then complete the dialogue. There is one extra phrase.

love / would / I _____
care / don't / about / I _____
prefer / I _____
into / are / you <u>Are you into</u>
enjoy / I _____
stand / can't / I _____

Ellen: <u>Are you into</u> skiing?
Sonia: No, I'm not. ¹_____ getting cold. ²_____ going to warm countries in the winter to being in the mountains. ³_____ lying on the beach with a good book. It's great! Actually, ⁴_____ to live in a warm country one day!

There are many stories of sports stars who **recovered from** serious injury or illness and became champions once again. However, there is one story that tells of not one, but two sporting heroes who made an impossible dream come true.

Bob Champion was a young jockey with a bright future. Then, one day, he fell off a horse which accidentally kicked him as it tried to get up. He went to the doctor because of his injuries and was shocked when he discovered that he had cancer. He needed medical help quickly. At that time, there was a new, but untested, treatment for the disease. It lasted many months and made him very weak. At times, he nearly died.

At the same time, there was a successful horse called Aldaniti. His trainer knew he was a great runner and jumper. Unfortunately, during one race, the horse suffered a serious injury. It was the sort of injury from which horses rarely make **a full recovery.** The vet advised the horse's trainer to put the horse down but the horse's owners refused. They looked after Aldaniti for a whole year and gradually the horse's injuries got better.

By this time, Bob Champion was out of hospital. He was weak and could only just stand up. However, he was determined to get better. Slowly, he **regained his strength.** Eight months later he returned to his job as a jockey. A month after that, he rode the winning horse in a race. Soon afterwards, Aldaniti also returned to training. His trainer was very careful with him. He didn't want the horse to get hurt again.

Early the next year, both Bob Champion and Aldaniti were almost **back to full fitness.** Now, there was a new plan. Bob decided to ride Aldaniti in the Grand National, one of Britain's most famous horse races. The thousands of spectators at the race and the millions more watching on TV knew all about the pair's **battles against ill health and injury.** Every one of them wanted the fairy tale to have a happy ending. And it was perfect. The next day, Aldaniti returned home. Thousands of people stood on the streets of the village to welcome him. Aldaniti, and Bob Champion, were real sporting heroes.

1 Read the text quickly and decide which title is the best.

A Illness and injury end two sporting careers ☐
B An amazing return for a horse and jockey ☐
C Heartbreak in the end for two sporting heroes ☐

2 Read the text again. Complete the gaps in the factfile with 1–2 words from the text.

1 The story of these two ¹_____ is like a fairy tale.
2 Jockey Bob Champion visited a doctor after he ²_____ a horse and found out he had ³_____ .
3 Aldaniti was a great race ⁴_____ but one day it had a ⁵_____.
4 Bob and Aldaniti made a successful comeback in a famous sporting event called the ⁶_____.

3 Match phrases 1–4 from the text with the correct meanings a–d. Use the context of the text to help you.

to recover from an illness or injury ☐ e
1 to make a full recovery from an illness or injury ☐
2 to regain your strength after an illness ☐
3 to be back to full fitness ☐
4 to battle against ill health or injury ☐

a to become strong again after an illness
b to get completely better after an illness
c to fight to get better when you are ill or injured
d to become 100% fit again after an illness
e to get better after an illness or injury

4 Complete the sentences with one word in each gap.

It takes a long time to recover *from* some diseases.

1 My dad was badly injured at work but doctors are sure he will _____ a full recovery.
2 I felt terrible after my illness but I'm _____ to full fitness now.
3 It took me almost a year to _____ my strength after my illness.
4 Mr Chambers died last month at the age of 87 after a long battle _____ ill health.

REMEMBER THIS

In English, there are many time expressions used to describe past events.

At the same time – used to talk about to two past events that took place simultaneously: *In 2013, I broke my leg and had to go to hospital. At the same time (= when I broke my leg), Helen fell off her horse and also went to hospital.*

By this time – used when one past event took place before the other: *We left hospital in July. By this time, (= at some point before July) we were in love.*

At times = sometimes, but not often: *I usually like my sister but, at times, she makes me angry.*

At that time = then: *When I was young, I played tennis. At that time, we lived near a tennis club.*

---

5 Read REMEMBER THIS. Complete the sentences with the correct time expression.

I left school in 2014. *At the same time* my brother left university and got a job.

1 On July 10ᵗʰ, I went back to the hospital. _____ my leg was much better.
2 I go jogging every morning. _____ , I hate it and want to stay in bed but usually I'm happy to get up and do some exercise.
3 I started to cross the road. _____ , a cyclist came round the corner. He hit me and I hurt my leg.
4 My dad started to support Liverpool in the 1980s. _____ , they were the best team in England.

VOCABULARY PRACTICE | Fitness

6 Look at the vocabulary in lesson 6.4 in the Student's Book. Complete the sentences with the words and phrases from the box.

> aerobics instructor   dance steps
> fitness centre   training videos   ~~workout~~

Natalia and Katya were very tired after they did a *workout* at the gym.

1 There are lots of great _____ that you can watch online.
2 Our _____ is really nice and her classes are fun!
3 I go swimming at the _____ near my house every morning.
4 These _____ are easy and anyone can learn them.

WORD STORE 6E | Collocations

7 Choose the correct option.

Amy: I want to ¹*keep / do* fit. What do you think I should do?
Lou: I think you should ²*go / join* a gym. There's a new one in the town and it ³*runs / gives* classes for teenagers.
Amy: That sounds great!
Lou: And there's a competition too, for new members. You could ⁴*win / take* the competition!
Amy: Wow! What is the prize?
Lou: A pair of Nike shoes!

GRAMMAR

6.5

Past Simple questions and negatives

SHOW WHAT YOU KNOW

1 Complete the Present Simple questions and negatives with the correct form of the verbs in brackets.

Ben: What time _do_ you _get_ (get) up?
Marie: I get up at seven o'clock.

1 Jake: ᵃ_____ your mum ᵇ_____ (take) you to school?
   Josie: No, she ᶜ_____ . She ᵈ_____ (leave) home before me.

2 Nigel: ᵃ_____ you often ᵇ_____ (feel) tired?
   Beth: Yes, I ᶜ_____ . All the time.

3 Cleo: How often ᵃ_____ your boyfriend ᵇ_____ (buy) you flowers?
   Jess: Never. He ᶜ_____ ᵈ_____ (buy) me anything!

4 Oliver: ᵃ_____ the teachers at your school ᵇ_____ (wear) ties?
   Jean: No, they ᶜ_____ but they look quite smart.

2 ★ Look at the information and complete the dialogue with the correct negative form of the verbs in brackets.

Alex,

I'm at work. Here are the things for you to do:

do the shopping, finish your homework, tidy your room, learn some French, read your English book, write to Aunt Louisa to thank her for your present.

See you at seven o'clock.   Mum

Mum: Hi, Alex, I'm home. Did you see my note?
Alex: Er …, yes.
Mum: Did you do everything?
Alex: Er … not quite.
Mum: So, what did you do?
Alex: Well, I _didn't do_ the shopping. I ¹_____ (know) what to buy. And I ²_____ (do) my homework but there isn't much to do.
Mum: Did you tidy your room?
Alex: Well, no. I ³_____ (tidy) my room and I ⁴_____ (learn) any French.
Mum: What about your English book?
Alex: Oh yes. I read some of that.
Mum: How much?
Alex: Well, I ⁵_____ (read) much. About half a page. It was really boring and I wanted to write to Aunt Louisa.
Mum: That's good. I've got a stamp here. You can go and post the letter.
Alex: Well, I wanted to write it but I ⁶_____ (write) it. Not all of it. It's not my fault. Jason came round and he stayed all day.

3 ★ ★ Complete the questions and negatives with the correct forms of the verbs in brackets.

Jo: So, how was the match? (you/win) _Did you win?_
Al: No, we ¹_____ (not/win) but we ²_____ (not/lose). It was 2–2.
Jo: ³_____ (Aggie/come) and see you play?
Al: Yes, but she ⁴_____ (not/stay) until the end. I scored a goal but she ⁵_____ (not/see) it.
Jo: ⁶_____ (you/phone) her and tell her?
Al: Of course!
Jo: What ⁷_____ (she/say)?
Al: Not much. She ⁸_____ (not/sound) very excited!
Jo: Oh well, never mind. You weren't very excited when she was in the school tennis tournament.
Al: I remember that. I ⁹_____ (not/go). I went to the cinema with Max. She ¹⁰_____ (not/speak) to me for three days!

4 ★ ★ ★ Use the words in brackets to make full questions and answers.

Brian: We went on a sports camp last month.
Harry: (What/activities/do?) _What activities did you do?_
Brian: We played volleyball, basketball, we went sailing.
Harry: ¹(have/a good time?) _____
Brian: ²(✓) _____ . ³(not/want/come home) _____ .
Harry: ⁴(Where/stay?) _____
Brian: We stayed in a hostel. ⁵(not/have/my own room) _____ . There were five of us together.
Harry: ⁶(know/any of the other people?) _____ .
Brian: ⁷(✗) _____ . Not at first. ⁸(But I/ not have) _____ any problems. I soon made lots of friends.
Harry: ⁹(What/do/in the evenings?) _____
Brian: There were parties and discos. ¹⁰(I/not/go out) _____ . I didn't have any money.

SHOW WHAT YOU'VE LEARNT

5 Complete the text with the words and phrases from the box. There are four extra words or phrases.

you did   got   did   didn't   get   did you do
did I   you went   did you go   do   I did

Hi Colleen,

I'm sorry I _didn't_ phone you last night, I was very tired. I didn't ¹_____ anything. ²_____ you have a nice time with Jerry? What ³_____ ? Where ⁴_____ ? Tell me all about it tomorrow!
⁵_____ tell you about the kayaking trip? Mrs Bryce told us about it on Friday when you were at home, sick. We didn't ⁶_____ any information about how much it costs or when we have to be at school. I don't think Mrs Bryce knows yet but I'm really excited about it.

See you tomorrow.
Ellen

/6

GRAMMAR: Train and Try Again page 133

78

1 Translate the phrases into your own language.

SPEAKING BANK

Asking for advice

Should I (see a doctor before I begin)?

_____
_____
_____

What should I wear/do/ eat?

_____
_____

Giving advice

You should (have a towel).

_____
_____

It's important to get enough to drink.

_____
_____

Make sure you always bring a bottle of water.

_____
_____
_____

Just try it!

_____
_____

You (really) shouldn't worry so much.

_____
_____
_____

2 Look at the photo. Match the questions to the correct answers. There are two extra answers.

1 Who are the people? ◯
2 What are they doing? ◯
3 How is the girl feeling? ◯

a They are walking in the forest. I don't think it's a one-day walk because their backpacks are big and full.

b She is in pain, so she is thinking about that. Maybe she is worried that she can't get home.

c Perhaps it isn't so serious and she can get up and walk in a few minutes.

d I think the girl is a university student. She looks about twenty years old. The other two are probably her friends.

e I enjoy walking with friends. My favourite walks are in the mountains.

3 Complete the dialogue between the people in the photo with one letter in each space. The first letters are given.

Ellen: Are you OK, Liz?
Liz: I think so. Owww!
Max: You **s** _h o u l d n_ 't try to stand up on your own. It's **¹i** _ _ _ _ _ _ _ **t** to be careful. In fact, don't stand up at all at the moment.
Ellen: **²S**_ _ _ _ **d** I phone your mum?
Liz: No, don't. She always worries a lot about me. I'm fine. I just need a rest.
Max: You should **³r** _ _ _ _ _ **y** go to the hospital and get an X-ray. I don't think it's broken but you should know exactly what's wrong. You should **⁴a** _ _ **o** put a bandage on it to protect it. I've got one here in my backpack somewhere.
Liz: OK. **⁵W**_ _ **t** should I do? Take off my boot?
Max: Yes, then we can put the bandage on it … It doesn't look very bad. Tell me if I'm hurting you.
Liz: No, it's fine.
Max: Let's have a rest and see how you feel in ten minutes.
Ellen: And **⁶m** _ _ **e s** _ _ **e** that you don't fall over again!
Liz: I'll try not to!

4 Complete the dialogue with the words and phrases from the box. There are two extra words or phrases.

> also   important not to   important to   I should
> make sure   ~~must~~   should I   should really
> you should   you shouldn't

Terry: Iza, I want to start jogging because I need to get fitter and lose some weight. You go jogging a lot. Have you got any advice you can give me?
Iza: Yes. First of all, you _must_ get some good running shoes.
Terry: OK, and how far **¹**_____ run?
Iza: Not very far when you start. It's **²**_____ do too much. It can be very dangerous. Some people have heart attacks.
Terry: Oh, wow! Anything else?
Iza: **³**_____ run on hard roads. It's bad for the legs. Try to find a path in the forest or a good running track. **⁴**_____ you take a lot of water to drink and you should **⁵**_____ take a mobile phone.
Terry: Why?
Iza: Because something could happen to you. When you're a long way from home, it's **⁶**_____ have some way to contact people who can help you. You **⁷**_____ go with someone else. It's safer and more fun.
Terry: Can I go with you?
Iza: Maybe when you're fitter. I go a long way and quite fast. You should go with someone who is starting to jog. Why not ask Carla? She wants to get fit too.

WRITING

6.7

A description of an event

1 Complete the short stories with the words and phrases from the box. There are two extra words or phrases for each story.

after   finally   first   the end   then

Steve started sailing when he was ten. At <u>first</u> , he only sailed in the summer holidays. ¹_____ a few years, he joined a club and sailed in the winter as well. He became a very good sailor. In ²_____ , he decided to sail around the world and, right now, he is somewhere in the Atlantic Ocean near Argentina.

after   at   in   suddenly   that

Melanie's parents were worried about her. She didn't do any exercise. ³_____ first, they took her for cycle rides or walks but she was never happy and, one day, she just said 'no'. After ⁴_____ , they decided to wait for her to change. It took a long time but, ⁵_____ the end, she met a boy who loved kayaking. Soon Melanie loved it too and now she goes every Saturday.

2 Choose the correct option.

I'm now a football fan!

I wasn't very happy when my boyfriend told me that he wanted to watch every match of the World Cup. ¹*At / For* first, I stayed away from the television. I went out with my friends and read a lot.

²*After that / After* a few days, I noticed that even my friends knew a lot about the World Cup. One day we went to a café. We sat outside in the evening sun. ³*Suddenly / Finally*, I realised that I was alone. My friends were inside, in front of a big television screen. I had a choice – sit outside alone or be with them. So, I joined them and watched. I really enjoyed it. ⁴*Then / After that*, I decided to watch all the matches. ⁵*Finally / At first*, my boyfriend was pleased but ⁶*after / then*, I noticed that he was very quiet when matches were on.

⁷*In / At* the end, I realised that he preferred watching the matches alone and I preferred watching them with my friends. So, that's what we did and it wasn't a problem. We both enjoyed the World Cup.

3 Choose the correct option.

1 I was happy *but / because / so* it was a sunny day.
2 Don't listen to music. Concentrate *on / in / with* your homework.
3 I was very *pleased / please / pleasant* that Jim wrote to me.
4 It's impossible to walk twenty kilometres *in / for / through* one hour.
5 We're organising a sports day to *lift / raise / spend* money for poor children.
6 There was a party and we all dressed *off / out / up* as famous people.
7 I hope you remembered to *do / make / have* your homework.

4 Complete the dialogue with one word in each gap. The first letters are given.

Bella: So, tell me about the walk you went on. What was it for?
Sarah: It was to **r**aise money ¹**f**_____ our local hospital.
Bella: Did people wear strange clothes?
Sarah: Some people did. I didn't ²**d**_____ up a_____ anything. I just wore shorts and a T-shirt.
Bella: How far was the walk?
Sarah: It was a thirty-kilometre walk.
Bella: Wow! Did you finish?
Sarah: No, it was ³**i**_____ to finish the walk. The day started sunny and warm but there was a big storm later on. The organisers told us to stop. I walked twenty-five kilometres.
Bella: Was it difficult?
Sarah: Yes. I was with a friend for the first twenty kilometres. She couldn't go any farther ⁴**b**_____ she had a hole in her shoe. She called her parents. I nearly went with them but I decided to continue. After that, I ⁵**c**_____ on singing the songs on my MP3 player. I was glad I ⁶**r**_____ to take that.
Bella: So, did you enjoy the day?
Sarah: Yes, I did. I was very ⁷**p**_____ that I walked so far. I want to do another long walk now, but maybe I'll check the weather forecast first!

SHOW WHAT YOU'VE LEARNT

5 Read the dialogue in Exercise 4 again. Write a post for the blog on behalf of Sarah, in which you describe the event she took part in.

In your post:
• give the reason for organising the event, the time and location.
• describe the clothes Sarah and other participants had on.
• describe what happened during the event.
• describe Sarah's feelings and emotions after the event.

SHOW THAT YOU'VE CHECKED

Finished? Always check your writing. Can you tick √ everything on this list?

In my blog post:

• I have included the reason for organising the event.	☐
• I have mentioned the time and location of the event.	☐
• I have described Sara's clothes as well as other participants'.	☐
• I have described what happened at the beginning, during and at the end of the event.	☐
• I have included time expressions showing the sequence of events.	☐
• I have described Sarah's feelings and emotions.	☐
• I have used contractions (e.g. *I'm / aren't / that's*).	☐
• I have checked my spelling.	☐
• My text is neat and clear.	☐

1 In pairs, ask and answer the questions.

PART 1

Talk about school.
1 How did you feel on your first day at secondary school?
2 What are the best and worst things about your school? Why?
3 What's your favourite place in your school?
4 What must you do when you use the science lab at school?
5 What subjects do most students study at university?

PART 2

Talk about sports.
1 How do you keep fit?
2 Do you prefer winter sports or summer sports? Why?
3 Do you think it's important to try new sports? Why?
4 Why do you think people enjoy extreme sports such as kite surfing?
5 Which sports are the most popular among boys and girls in your country?

2 Look at the pictures that show free time activities.

PART 1

Which of these sports do you do? Discuss in pairs.

PART 2

In pairs, ask and answer the questions.
1 Do you think skateboarding is dangerous? Why?/Why not?
2 Would you prefer to do yoga or kung fu? Why?
3 Do you like doing water sports such as kayaking? Why?/Why not?
4 What is good about doing a sport like karate?
5 What can you learn from playing a team sport like volleyball?
6 Do you prefer doing indoor sports or outdoor sports? Why?
7 Which of these sports do you like best? Why?

3 Read the instructions on your card. In pairs, take turns to role-play the conversation.

Student A

You want to go to basketball summer day camp. Talk to the camp leader, Student B, and ask for advice.

- Introduce yourself to Student B and say that you'd like to find out more about basketball summer camp.
- Ask if you can join the camp.
- Say that you're worried that you aren't very good at basketball.
- Ask what you should wear.
- Ask what you should bring.
- Thank Student B and end the conversation.

Student B

You work at the sports centre. Student A needs your help.

- Respond and ask how you can help.
- Say yes and explain that the camp is open to everyone.
- Tell him/her that he shouldn't worry and that everyone is welcome.
- Give advice on what Student A should wear (tracksuit, trainers).
- Say that it's important to bring a bottle of water and a packed lunch every day.

VOCABULARY AND GRAMMAR

1 Complete the text with one verb in each gap.

BLOG

How fit are you?

I think that I _have_ a very healthy lifestyle. I ¹_____ a lot of exercise. I ²_____ swimming twice a week and I often ³_____ part in swimming competitions. I don't often win but I enjoy them. I also ⁴_____ basketball for the school team. So, I do everything I can to ⁵_____ fit.

What about you? Are you worried about your fitness? Let me know. Maybe we can discuss what food people eat too.

/5

2 Choose the correct option.

The basketball (players) / playing / played stayed behind after the end of the match to sign autographs.
1 My brother loves cyclist / cycle / cycling. He takes his bike everywhere.
2 There was no snow, so the cafés were full of unhappy skiing / skied / skiers.
3 It's impossible to walk along this path because it is always full of jog / jogging / joggers.
4 I could never be a sailor / sailing / sail because I get seasick on the water.
5 We swimmers / swam / swimming half way to the island but it was impossible to get all the way there.

/5

3 Complete the text with the correct form of the verbs in brackets.

BLOG

How fit are you?

Replies:

Hi. I like your blog. I'm interested in keeping fit too.

Today I _did_ (do) very well. First of all, I ¹_____ (run) five kilometres. Then I ²_____ (play) volleyball with my friends. After that, I ³_____ (have) a short rest and later, I ⁴_____ (go) cycling in the park. I didn't go far. I was too tired. On the way home, I stopped at the local pizza restaurant and ⁵_____ (eat) an extra large pizza with ham, sausages and onions. …

I enjoyed my active day very much – the last activity was the best!

/5

4 Use the words to make full questions and answers.

Where / you / go / yesterday?
I / go / to the shopping centre.
Where did you go yesterday?
I went to the shopping centre.

Conversation 1
ᵃ What / you / do / last night?
ᵇ I / meet/ my friends
ᶜ we / see / a film / eat / burgers / and / have / a good time.

_____
_____
_____

Conversation 2
ᵃ you / play / any sports at school last week?
ᵇ x . We / have / exams / all week.

_____
_____

/5

5 Complete the dialogue with one word in each gap. The first letters are given.

Mike: What do you _prefer_? Individual sports or team sports?
Lindsay: Oh definitely individual sports. I ¹e_____ them much more than playing for a team. And I can't ²s_____ ball games like football and rugby. I'm ³i_____ dance and things like Zumba®. We do it at school. How about you?
Mike: I'm not ⁴r_____ into sports at all, to be honest. I do a lot of walking and cycling but that's just because I ⁵c_____ about my health, not because I like those activities. My favourite activity is sleeping!

/5

6 Choose the correct answers A–C.

Two months ago, there was a competition in Hawaii and George __ the under-18 surfing prize.
A win   (B) won   C wins
1 Who __ skiing with?
  A did you go   B you went   C you go
2 Mark __ healthy meals very often when he was younger.
  A doesn't have
  B didn't have
  C mustn't have
3 Lisa __ snowboarding a long time ago but I think she needs lessons again now.
  A learning   B learns   C learnt
4 Last year, I went to one karate lesson but I __ do any other martial arts.
  A don't   B didn't   C doesn't
5 __ sailing again last summer?
  A Do they go   B They go   C Did they go

/5

| Total | /30 |

7 Choose the correct answers A–C.

Can you show me the basic ___ for the waltz, please?
A dance class
B dance instructor
C dance steps ✓

1 This gym ___ – they can come and do exercises after work.
A runs lots of workouts
B has classes for young teenagers
C runs classes for adults

2 ___ tennis yesterday afternoon?
A Did you play
B Do you play
C Are you playing

3 It was cold, so the children ___ swimming.
A didn't went
B didn't go
C mustn't go

4 You should watch this great ___ video. It tells you how to eat healthily.
A training
B exercise
C fitness

5 Frank ___ karate three times a week.
A went
B played
C did

/5

8 Complete the second sentence so that it has a similar meaning to the first. Use between two and five words, including the word in capitals.

You shouldn't eat too much sugary food. **NOT**
It's important _not to eat_ too much sugary food.

1 Yolanda doesn't like football at all. **STAND**
Yolanda _____ football.

2 Don't start a diet before you see your doctor. **SURE**
_____ your doctor before you start a diet.

3 My sister enjoys kayaking, but I don't. **INTO**
My sister enjoys kayaking, but _____ it.

4 Winning isn't important to me – I just like playing sport. **CARE**
I _____ winning – I just like playing sport.

5 You can't ski – there isn't any snow on the mountain! **GO**
You can't _____ – there isn't any snow on the mountain!

/5

9 Put the words in the correct order to make sentences and questions. There is one extra word.

Rachel: What did you do in the afternoon?
Phil: did / friend / played / my / badminton / with / I
I played badminton with my friend.

1 Aida: What do you like doing in the summer?
Aileen: Well … going / Hawaii / like / surfing / in / I
_____

2 Carla: You're good at basketball. team / for / you / do / play / a / at
_____?

Ivan: Well, I play for my school.

3 Belinda: I want to do kung fu. class / with me / join / do / to / a / want / match / you
_____?

Sacha: Yes, I do!

4 Abby: Why was Andy so excited yesterday?
Donald: judo / a / lost / he / won / competition
_____ .
The prize is a holiday in Bali!

5 Henry: What did you do last weekend?
Anna: did / the / ice / I / skating / in / park / went
_____ .

/5

10 Complete the text with the correct answers A–C.

● ● ●   New Email

To: Tom Green
Subject: Volleyball

Hi Tom,

It's beautiful today. Let's do something! Do you want to _B_ cycling in the park? Or we could ride our bikes to the beach and then **1**___ volleyball on the sand. I want to be outside because it's a sunny day! Oh, and I want to **2**___ fit too. I think it's really important to **3**___ exercise.

So what do you think of my idea? Do you **4**___ cycling in the park to playing volleyball? They're both really good **5**___ !

Let me know soon,
Jake

	A	B	C
	A play	B go ✓	C do
1	A make	B have	C play
2	A live	B keep	C know
3	A have	B make	C do
4	A prefer	B enjoy	C love
5	A fitness	B workouts	C training

/5

Total /20

7 Travel

VOCABULARY

7.1 Holidays and transport • *book, make* and *visit* • accommodation

---

SHOW WHAT YOU KNOW

1 Complete the words with one letter in each space.

They travel on the road:

b<u>us</u>
1 b _ _ e
2 c _ _ _ h
3 m _ _ _ _ _ _ _ _ e

They travel on water:

4 f _ _ _ _ y
5 s _ _ p

They travel on tracks:

6 t _ _ _ _ n
7 t _ _ m
8 u _ _ _ _ _ _ _ _ _ _ d /
the T _ _ e

Ways of travelling

9 You d _ _ _ _ e a c _ _ r.
10 You s _ _ _ l a b _ _ _ _.
11 You f _ y a p _ _ _ _ e.
12 You c _ _ _ _ e when you
   are on a bike.
13 You r _ _ e a bike or
   a motorbike.

WORD STORE 7A | Holidays and transport

2 Read the descriptions and complete the types of holiday. The first letters are given.

> We had an amazing time. We climbed Kilimanjaro, went on a safari, flew in a balloon and other things. An a<u>dventure</u> holiday.

1 We helped on the farm and cleaned rooms at the hostel. A w_____ holiday.
2 We slept in a tent by a lake. A c_____ holiday.
3 We carried our clothes on our backs and walked from place to place. A b_____ holiday.
4 We stayed in a hotel in Spain and swam in the Mediterranean every day. A b_____ holiday.
5 We travelled on a coach through the Loire Valley looking at castles and palaces with a guide. A t_____ .
6 We went swimming, sailing, rock climbing and other things. An a_____ holiday.

---

3 Complete the texts with *go on*, *go on a/an* or *go by*.

HOLIDAY ADVERTS

– what they really mean

Do holiday adverts always tell the truth?
Not exactly, but the truth is there if you look carefully.
Here are a few of our favourites:

> '<u>Go on a</u> working holiday in Greece.
> A fantastic opportunity for a cheap holiday.'

What it means: You work for nothing and even have to pay to work!

> 'Perfect holiday town. You don't need transport.
> ¹ _____ foot to all the sights.'

What it means: This is a very small town with only one or two sights to visit.

> '² _____ six-day tour of Europe and see the sights. You ³ _____ coach and you don't pay for accommodation.'

What it means: You spend most of the six days and nights on the coach.

> 'You can now ⁴ _____ fast train from the airport to the city centre in just fifteen minutes or, a cheaper option is to ⁵ _____ bus.'

What it means: The train is <u>very</u> expensive.

WORD STORE 7B | *book, make* and *visit*

4 Complete the texts with the words from the box.

> accommodation   arrangements   excursions
> flights   holiday   hotels   ~~markets~~   museums
> reservations   seats   sights   tickets   transport

Do you want to visit the <u>markets</u> of Marrakech this weekend? Book cheap ¹ _____ on our comfortable and safe planes.
www.marockair.mv

At yourtrain.iz you can book ² _____ for trains in the UK and Europe. You can also book ³ _____ on trains and coaches.

Bookahotel.hs
is the best place to find cheap ⁴ _____ . From five-star ⁵ _____ to cheap hostels, come to bookahotel.hs.

When you book a ⁶ _____ with **Seymour WithusTravel**, you don't only get somewhere to stay, you get everything. We can make ⁷ _____ in popular local restaurants, we can book ⁸ _____ to see interesting ⁹ _____ and of course, we make all the ¹⁰ _____ for taxis to take you from the airport to your hotel and back again. Make Seymour Withus your travel agent.

When you come to London, get a one week city card. Visit all the city's ¹¹ _____ and art galleries for free. Book ¹² _____ (coaches and trains) and travel free on all the city's buses and underground trains.

5 Complete the text with one word in each gap. The first letters are given.

Hi Jo,

You asked me about places to stay. There's an expensive 4-star h<u>otel</u>. It's got a swimming pool and a nice restaurant but we can't stay there! There are some g_____ and b_____ and b_____ places but they are small with only three or four rooms. I'm worried about coming back late at night or making a noise. I don't want to stay somewhere which is just like being at home!

Another idea is to stay on a c_____. I've got a tent but what about rain? I think the best place to stay is the local y_____ _____. There are rooms for four or eight people. It's a good way to meet interesting people and it's very cheap.

What do you think?
Rebecca

REMEMBER BETTER

The verb *go* can be followed by many different prepositions.

Go to (a place)   **Go with** (a person)

Go for (a length of time)   **Go by** (transport)

Go in (a month/year)   **Go on** (a day/date)

Go at (a time)

In order to memorise those different combinations of *go* + **preposition**, think of a holiday and write sentences about it using all the phrases above.

Answer the questions about a holiday so they are true for you.

My holiday:

1 Where did you **go to**?
   I went to …

2 Who did you **go with**?
   I went with …

3 How long did you **go for**?

4 Did you **go by** car or some other form of transport?

5 Which month did you **go in**?

6 Which day of the week did you **go on**?

7 Did you **go at** night or at some other time?

---

6 Complete the text with the words from the box. There are four extra words.

> accommodation   arrange   beach   foot
> campsite   coach   flight   make   rode   sailed
> seats   sights   ~~travelled~~   visited   walking

BLOG

Holiday memories

Last year, my friends and I went to Portugal. We <u>travelled</u> by plane. When we arrived, we got a ¹_____ from the airport to the ²_____ where we stayed. It was very big and right next to the sea. The town was a nice size and we went to the beach and the shops on ³_____ .

It wasn't expensive, so we had some money to spend. We ⁴_____ around on motorbikes and visited the ⁵_____ . We had a great time but, really, it was a ⁶_____ holiday – lying in the sun and swimming in the sea. The only problem was that there was only one restaurant in the area and we couldn't ⁷_____ a reservation. Some days we waited an hour for a free table but the food was delicious.

On the last day, we ⁸_____ a local market and bought some clothes and souvenirs. We were worried the next day because we forgot to book ⁹_____ for the journey back to the airport but it was OK. There were three free places at the back.

All in all, it was a wonderful time. We're going again this year. Sally booked the ¹⁰_____ last week. London to Faro, July 10th!

/10

Portugal

7.2

Present Perfect
with *ever/never*

SHOW WHAT YOU KNOW

1 Complete the verbs with the past form.

Last year I …

was (be) in Greece
1 _____ (swim) in the sea.
2 _____ (eat) Greek food.
3 _____ (take) my laptop on holiday.
4 _____ (write) lots of emails.
5 _____ (visit) Athens.

2 ★ Complete the questions with the correct form of the verbs from Exercise 1.

ARE YOU A REAL TRAVELLER?

Answer the questions below:

Have you ever *been* to a different continent?
1 Have you ever _____ a town which wasn't in a guidebook?
2 Have you ever _____ a travel blog?
3 Have you ever _____ food which you thought people couldn't eat?
4 Have you ever _____ in a hot lake on a cold, snowy day?
5 Have you ever _____ a 'selfie' in front of a famous building?

Questions 1–4: 10 points for each 'Yes'; -40 points if you answered 'Yes' to number 5!

3 ★ ★ Use the words in brackets to make full dialogues.

1 **Debbie:** I've got a postcard from Adrian. He's in New York.
 Russell: *I've never been* to New York. (I / never / be)
 Debbie: ª_____ to the USA? (you / ever / be)
 Russell: Yes, I have. I've been to Florida and California.

2 **Patrick:** Do you want some Indian food?
 Lawrence: I don't know. ª_____ Indian food. (I / never / eat)
 Patrick: Really? ᵇ_____ Chinese food? (you / ever / have)
 Lawrence: Of course. I love it.

3 **Sandra:** Eric's late again.
 Tanya: ª_____ on time for anything? (he / ever / be)
 Sandra: ᵇ_____ late for a party. He loves parties. (he / never / arrive)

4 **Chris:** What's wrong?
 Amelia: ª_____ by plane before. (I / never / travel)
 Chris: Don't worry. ᵇ_____ a crash before. (The pilot / never / have)
 Amelia: ᶜ_____ a plane before??? (he / ever / fly)

REMEMBER THIS

When we talk only about visiting places we say *been* **to** … NOT ~~been in~~

*Have you ever been **to** France?*
*I've been **to** Paris but I haven't been **to** the south of France.*

4 ★ ★ ★ Complete the dialogues with the correct forms of the Present Perfect or Past Simple.

Conversation 1
Sonia: *Have you ever forgotten* (you / ever / forget) your passport?
Jake: *Yes, I have* (✓). Once.
Sonia: When ¹_____ (it / happen)?
Jake: ²_____ (it / happen) two years ago.
Sonia: ³_____ (you / miss) your plane?
Jake: ⁴_____ (✓).

Conversation 2
Jake: ¹_____ (your / friends / ever / be) camping?
Sonia: ²_____ (✓). ³_____ (they / go) camping last year.
Jake: Where ⁴_____ (they / go)?
Sonia: ⁵_____ (they / go) to Scotland.
Jake: ⁶_____ (they / have) a good time?
Sonia: ⁷_____ (✗). ⁸_____ (It / rain) every day.

SHOW WHAT YOU'VE LEARNT

5 Complete the sentences with the words from the box. Change the form of the verbs. There are four extra words.

~~be~~ do ever fly have never
ride see send swim take

Jim: My friends and I have never *been* on TV.
Derek: I've been on a radio show.
1 **Ollie:** Have you ever _____ on a camel?
 Jess: Yes, but only in a zoo.
2 **Mark:** William has _____ travelled by ferry.
 Phil: I'm not surprised. He gets travel sick on the bus to school!
3 **Pete:** _____ Lucy ever met your parents?
 Matt: Not yet but she's coming to dinner on Sunday.
4 **Angie:** Paul has never _____ me a postcard.
 Jill: He doesn't have to. He sends you messages on Facebook.
5 **Eva:** Have you _____ swum in the Red Sea?
 Don: No, I haven't but I'd love to go there one day.
6 **Jill:** I've been to Italy but I've never _____ in the Mediterranean.
 Frank: That's because you go to Italy to ski. ___/6

GRAMMAR: Train and Try Again page 134

LISTENING LANGUAGE PRACTICE

Verb + prepositional phrases
• travel

1 Complete the dialogues with one word in each gap. The first letters are given.

Extract from Student's Book recording 🔊 **3.27**

1 Check-in attendant and passenger

CA: Check in here for flights to Frankfurt, Madrid and Rome. Good morning, madam. Where are you travelling to today?

P: Well, actually I need to stop ᵃ*out / over* in Frankfurt and then fly ᵇ*on / up* to Rome tomorrow.

CA: That's fine. Can I have a look ᶜ*for / at* your ticket and your passport, please? […]

P: H*ere* you are.

CA: Have you got any luggage?

P: Yes, just this one. Can I have a ¹w_____ seat?

CA: No problem. ²H_____ a good flight.

2 Station announcement

³A_____ . There is a change of platform for the 11.15 to Manchester. This train is now arriving ᵈ*on / at* Platform 3 and not Platform 4 as originally announced. That's Platform 3 for the 11.15 to Manchester. This train stops ᵉ*at / in* Milton Keynes, Crewe and Manchester Piccadilly. All passengers for Manchester Piccadilly, please go to Platform 3.

3 Travel agent and woman

TA: Good morning. Can I help you?

W: Yes, I'd like to book a holiday to Spain.

TA: OK, where in Spain would you like to go?

W: I can't decide. Maybe Barcelona or Granada. My friend told me that the Basque country is beautiful.

TA: Why don't you look at these brochures? There are some great ⁴d_____ .

W: Does this price ⁵i_____ the cost of accommodation?

TA: Yes, in a three-star hotel.

W: OK, I'll think ᶠ*of / about* it. Thanks.

---

2 Complete the sentences with the words from Exercise 1.

> **A:** 'Passport, please.'   **B:** '*Here* you are.'
> **A:** 'Thank you. OK. That's fine.'

1 Two weeks in Spain for £150. It sounds great but it doesn't _____ transport or meals.

2 _____ . All passengers travelling to Rome, please go to Gate 7.

3 I never choose a _____ seat on a plane. It's difficult to get out if you need the toilet.

4 Wait with your booking until two days before you want to go on holiday. You can get some great late _____ .

5 I love America. Everyone is so polite. They always say '_____ a nice day' when you buy something in a shop.

3 Choose the correct words a–f in the texts in Exercise 1.

4 Match the base form of the verbs from the dialogues in Exercise 1 to their definitions or synonyms.

consider		*think about*
1 examine, check		_____
2 stop at stations so that passengers can get on and off		_____
3 continue a journey on a second plane		_____
4 get off one plane and wait for another		_____
5 come to a railway station		_____

5 Complete the text with one word in each gap.

ROME FORUM

Hi   18.34

I'm going to stop *over* in Rome for five hours on my way to Sicily. My plane arrives ¹_____ the airport at 6 p.m. and I fly ²_____ to Palermo at 11 p.m. Have I got time to get into Rome?

Hi   21.53

It isn't a lot of time but you could look ³_____ the Coliseum for half an hour. That's time to take a few photos. There's a fast minibus service to the main railway station that stops ⁴_____ the Coliseum first. It's quite cheap. Or you could think ⁵_____ getting a taxi. It's more expensive but quicker. Have fun!

WORD STORE 7D | Travel

6 Complete the sentences with the words from the box. There are three extra words.

> accommodation   arrangement   booking
> brochures   campsite   check in   flight   luggage
> passengers   ~~passport~~   platform   ticket

You can't travel to a different country without a *passport* or an ID card.

1 The _____ complained when their train arrived two hours late.

2 Hotels always look great in _____ but you should also read people's opinions on the Internet.

3 We've arrived. Let's _____ to the hotel, have a shower and then go for something to eat.

4 I've definitely got a _____ for this hotel. Look, here's the email you sent to me.

5 Would you like someone to carry your _____ to your room, sir?

6 I enjoyed the _____ to Cairo but I was bored waiting for two hours at the airport before we left.

7 Can you buy a _____ from the bus driver or do you have to get it earlier?

8 The train now arriving at _____ 8 is the 12.08 to London calling at East Croydon, Clapham Junction and London Victoria.

READING

7.4

Travel problems • adjectives • tourism

1 Read the text and match headings A–F with paragraphs 1–5. There is one extra heading.

A Can we join you?
B You haven't got a ticket
C An unexpected stopover
D We've arrived – but in the wrong country
E Right name, wrong place
F You haven't gone far enough!

Travel PROBLEMS

Travelling should be an exciting, relaxing, pleasant activity but sometimes, it is none of these things. Here are some true travel horror stories.

1

A few years ago, a couple from England booked a bargain flight to the Caribbean online. It was from the local airport in Birmingham to the island of Trinidad. At the airport, there was no information about the flight on any of the <u>departure boards,</u> so they went to ask at the <u>information desk</u>. That's when they discovered why the flight was so cheap. It was from Birmingham, Alabama in the USA, which is much closer to the Caribbean than Birmingham, UK.

2

The moment you are up in the air, you can relax – yes? Not always. On a flight from Newark to Denver, one passenger decided to relax and tried to use her <u>reclining seat</u>. **Unfortunately**, the man in the seat behind her wanted to work on his laptop and he used a special gadget called a 'knee defender' to stop the seat from moving down. The woman asked him to remove it. He refused. She threw a cup of water over him. The plane stopped in Chicago, left the two passengers there and continued its journey.

3

If travelling by plane is too stressful, why not take the train? A man from Darlington, in England, read that it was cheaper to buy a ticket to Durham than Darlington. **Strangely**, Durham was farther away. He thought it was OK, so, he bought a ticket and got off one stop early. When <u>station staff</u> checked his ticket, they said it was for the wrong station, and asked him to pay £155 extra!

4

For sure, the Eurostar train from London to Paris or Brussels is a nice way to travel? Not always. In December 2009, several trains stopped in the tunnel. One family said that there were no lights, no air conditioning, no food and no water on their train. After several hours, they got off and walked through the tunnel to find another train which was warmer. **Fortunately**, no-one told them they had the wrong ticket.

5

Finally, a story about ferry travel. During a bad storm one winter, the ferry from Portsmouth to Bilbao spent 36 hours at sea. **Eventually**, it came into a harbour – in Brest, northern France. Unfortunately, it was also Christmas Eve and there were no ferries back to the UK until after the holidays. Passengers were left in Brest, 1000 km from Bilbao. Their only choices were to find a local hotel, rent a car and drive all night or try to get to an airport and a very expensive, <u>last-minute</u> flight. Happy Christmas!

✉ DEPARTURES

TIME	DESTINATION	FLIGHT	GATE	REMARKS
12:39	LONDON	BA 903	31	CANCELLED
12:57	SYDNEY	QF5723	27	CANCELLED
13:08	TORONTO	AC5984	22	CANCELLED
13:21	TOKYO	JL 608	41	DELAYED
13:37	HONG KONG	CX5471	29	CANCELLED

Of course, events like these don't happen very often. For most of us, journeys are still relaxing – except for queues, delays, <u>security checks</u>, strikes and Icelandic volcanoes, of course.

GLOSSARY

remove (v) – to take something away from, out of, or off the place where it is
stressful (adj) – something that makes you worry a lot

harbour (n) – an area of water next to the land where the water is calm, so that ships are safe when they are inside it

delay (n) – a period of time when something happens more slowly than you expected, or the length of the waiting time

2 Read the text again. Choose the correct answers A–C.

1 The couple in the first paragraph had a problem because
   A the flight they booked didn't go to the place they thought.
   B the flight didn't leave from Birmingham.
   C they didn't check where the flight left from.
2 The man on the flight to Denver
   A asked the woman not to use her reclining seat.
   B had something that stopped the seat in front of him from reclining.
   C was angry because he couldn't use his reclining seat.
3 The man travelling to Darlington
   A was on the wrong train.
   B went past the station on his ticket.
   C didn't know that he couldn't travel to Darlington with the ticket he bought.
4 When the trains got stuck in the Eurostar tunnel,
   A some passengers moved from one train to another.
   B only people with the correct tickets could change trains.
   C passengers got out and walked to the end of the tunnel.
5 The passengers going to Bilbao definitely did <u>not</u> spend Christmas Day
   A in England.   B in Bilbao.   C on a ferry.

3 Match the underlined words in the text with the definitions below.

   People who work at a railway station.   <u>station staff</u>
1 Checks before you get on a plane to make sure you aren't carrying anything dangerous.   _____
2 A seat on a plane or a bus which can be moved back so that you can sleep.   _____
3 An adjective meaning something which is booked (a hotel, flight, etc.) very near to the time the person needs them.   _____
4 A place you can go to ask for help or information.   _____
5 Television screens or electronic screens in airports or railway stations which show when flights or trains leave and where passengers should go.   _____

4 Complete the text with one word in each gap.

○○○

17/7   *Holiday Day 1 (and 2)*

I was very happy when I booked a <u>last-minute</u> flight to Turkey. It was a great deal – £150 cheaper than the normal price. But the journey was terrible! What a nightmare! I got to the airport early and, of course, went to look at the departure ¹_____ to see where to check in. Next to my flight number, it said: *Please go to the information* ²_____ . So, I went and asked what was wrong. They said: *The flight is leaving tomorrow at 5 a.m.!* I decided to go home but the ticket office at the railway station was closed. The station ³_____ didn't know why. I bought a ticket on the train – it cost £10 extra. The next day, I got to the airport at 3 a.m. There were lots of security ⁴_____ . *Take your boots off, take your belt off.* You know the sort of thing. At last I got on the plane. I sat down with a cup of coffee from the airport. I put it on the tray and then the person in front of me suddenly put her ⁵_____ seat down. My coffee fell onto my jeans and I couldn't move.

REMEMBER THIS

We form regular adverbs by adding *-ly* to an adjective. Adverbs describe:

• how activities expressed by verbs are done, e.g. **Suddenly**,
• when the events in a sentence happened, e.g. **Finally**,
• our feelings about the events that are talked about, e.g.

   Unfortunately – it is/was unfortunate or unlucky,
   Strangely – it is/was strange,
   Eventually – in the end, after a long time,
   Amazingly / Surprisingly – it is/was surprising,
   Hopefully – with hope that something will happen, etc.

VOCABULARY PRACTICE | Adjectives

5 Look at the vocabulary in lesson 7.4 in the Student's Book. Complete the dialogues with one word in each gap. The first and last letters of the words are given.

Ava: Welcome back! How was your holiday in Greece?
Nick: It was great! The islands were amazing and the beaches were i<u>ncredibl</u>e!

Conversation 1

Gina: What did you like the most in Morocco?
Sia: I really loved the markets with the c_____l clothes and jewellery – I bought a red and gold scarf there.

Conversation 2

Mario: The Coliseum in Rome is really impressive.
Helen: Yes, it's s_____r! It's my favourite sight.

Conversation 3

Karl: Where did you stay in Switzerland?
Julie: We stayed at a c_____g hotel with a view of Lake Geneva. It was so beautiful!

WORD STORE 7E | Tourism

6 Complete the dialogues with the words from the box.

destination   ~~explored~~   highlight   monument
population   tourists

Fran: What did you do in Paris?
Leah: I <u>explored</u> the city. It was amazing!

1 Wayne: The _____ of Australia is 25 million.
   Jade: Really? I thought it was more!
2 Ruth: How many _____ visit France every year?
   Ian: Oh, more than 80 million!
3 Joe: Alan is going to Antarctica for his holiday.
   Rick: That's an unusual _____ !
4 Lisa: What was the _____ of your trip to America?
   Kelly: It was definitely New York. We loved it!
5 Dave: Which is the most famous _____ in China?
   Alice: It's the Great Wall – millions of people visit it every year.

GRAMMAR

7.5

Present Perfect
+ just/yet/already

1 Complete the sentences and questions with the correct Present Perfect form of the verbs. Use short forms if possible.

I *haven't booked* (not/book) the hotel.

1 My friends _____ (go) on holiday.
2 _____ (Amanda/call) you?
3 We _____ (not/find) our passports.
4 Lisa _____ (not/make) a reservation at the restaurant.
5 _____ (your parents/arrive) at the airport?
6 Sue _____ (go) to New York three times this year.

2 ★ Rewrite the sentences from Exercise 1 with the word in capitals in the correct place.

I haven't booked the hotel yet. **YET**

1 _____ **JUST**
2 _____ **YET**
3 _____ **YET**
4 _____ **YET**
5 _____ **YET**
6 _____ **ALREADY**

3 ★ ★ Complete the dialogues with the correct form of the verbs in brackets. Use short forms if possible.

Conversation 1

Meg: Do you want to get something to eat?
Mr Lee: No, thanks. I *I've already had* (already/have) lunch.
Mrs Lee: Really! It's only 12.30. I ª_____
_____ (not eat anything/yet).
I got up late and missed breakfast.

Conversation 2

Mrs Lee: ª_____ ?
(you send the postcards/yet)
Colin: No. I ᵇ_____
(just/buy) them. I ᶜ_____
_____ (not write them/yet).

Conversation 3

Mr Lee: Hi, Mum. We ª_____ (just/arrive)
at the hotel.
Mrs Lee: Well, we ᵇ_____ .
(not see the rooms/yet). Kelly
ᶜ_____ (already/
make) some friends in the children's play area.
Colin ᵈ_____
(just/get) the room key from the receptionist.
Oh, and Billy … Talk to you later.

4 ★ ★ ★ Complete the dialogue between Guy and Judith with the words from the box. Use the correct form of the verbs. Use short forms if possible.

already book   already invite   ~~just get~~   just go
just start   not have   yet (2)   you decide

G: Hi. You look nice.
J: Thanks. I *'ve just got* back from Turkey.
G: Wow. Lucky you.
J: What about you? Have you been anywhere nice?
G: I ¹_____ a holiday ²_____ .
I ³_____ a new job and my first holiday
is in December.
J: Oh dear! ⁴_____ where to go
⁵_____ ?
G: Oh, I know exactly. ⁶_____ the holiday.
To Cuba.
J: Cuba? My neighbour ⁷_____ there.
G: Oh right. I'd like to meet him and talk about his visit
when he gets back.
J: Well, I ⁸_____ him for coffee and cakes
when he gets back. He likes showing his photos to
people. You can come too. Sunday, August 17ᵗʰ,
about 4 p.m.
G: That's great. Thanks very much.

Trinidad, Cuba – The old town. UNESCO World Heritage Site.

5 Complete the sentences. Use the correct Present Perfect form of the words from the box and the words in brackets. Use short forms if possible. There are two extra sets of words in the box.

already/make   already/see   already/take   do
~~arrive / yet~~   just/find   just/hear   speak   take

We're at the railway station but *the train hasn't*
arrived yet. (the train)

1 _____ about your accident.
Are you OK? (I)
2 _____
six exams and he's got two more tomorrow. (Paul)
3 _____
this film. Can we watch something else? (I)
4 _____
any photos yet. Is your camera broken? (you)
5 _____ a flat to rent
and she's getting ready to leave home. (my sister)
6 _____ to you
about his holiday idea yet? (Ray)

/6

GRAMMAR: Train and Try Again page 134

90

SPEAKING

7.6

Asking for and giving directions

1 Translate the phrases into your own language.

SPEAKING BANK

Asking for directions

Excuse me, can you tell me the way to …? _____

How do I get to …? _____

Excuse me, where's the (post office)? _____

Giving directions

Go out of … and turn left/right. _____

Turn (left/right) into (High Street). _____

Walk along the (road) past the (post office) on your left/right. _____

Take/It's the first/ second/third turning on the left/right. _____

Go straight on. _____

Go across the (road). _____

The (museum) is opposite the (shop). _____

The (theatre) is on the left/right. _____

It's between the (station) and the (hotel). _____

It's next to/opposite the (station). _____

(Film City) is next door. _____

It's on the corner of (Shakespeare Road) and (King's Road). _____

2 Choose the correct word.

1 You know where Katy lives? Well, Jason lives next *house / door* to her.
2 Can you tell me the *way / get* to the post office?
3 Go out of the station and *take / turn* right.
4 Go straight *on / turn* for about 200 metres.
5 Walk *on / along* the road for a kilometre.
6 The bank is *opposite / between* the café.
7 The bookshop is ᵃ*on / in* the corner of Green Street and Hill Street, ᵇ*next / opposite* the cinema.
8 How do you *way / get* to school?
9 *Turn / Go* across the road here.
10 ᵃ*Take / Turn* the first turning ᵇ*on / in* the right.

3 Read sentences A–E and label the picture.

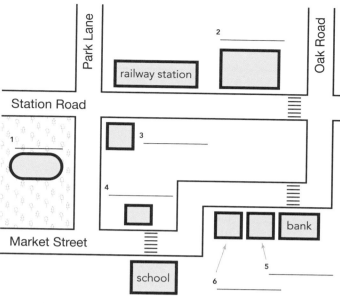

A The chemist's is on the corner of Station Road and Park Lane.
B The café is between the bank and the post office.
C The bookshop is opposite the school.
D The theatre is next to the railway station.
E The stadium is in the park.

4 Look at the map from Exercise 3. Complete the dialogue with one word in each gap. The first letters are given.

Max: Do you want to meet at my favourite café?
Abbie: OK. How do I g̲e̲t̲ to it? I'm coming by train.
Max: Come out of the railway station and ¹t_____ left. Go ²p_____ the theatre and then go ³a_____ the road. There's a crossing there. Go ⁴s_____ on, ⁵a_____ Oak Road. ⁶G_____ across the road again and the café is there. It's ⁷b_____ a bank and a post office.
Abbie: Great, thanks.

4 hours later …

Abbie: The train arrived and I started walking but I think I went wrong. I came out of the station and I turned ⁸r_____ . I went across Park Lane and then across Station Road into the park. I'm ⁹n_____ to the stadium now.
Max: Oh dear! Go back to Station Road and turn right. Then ¹⁰t_____ the first ¹¹t_____ on your right. That's Park Lane. Walk along Park Lane until you get to Market Street. Then turn ¹²l_____ . Not right! Go past the bookshop. That's ¹³o_____ a school. You can cross the road here. Keep going, straight on. The café is ¹⁴o_____ your right. It's next ¹⁵t_____ a bank.

91

1 Match beginnings 1–10 with endings A–M. There are two extra endings.

Dear   Ⓜ

1 I am writing to enquire if
2 I am writing in response to
3 Please reply to
4 Yours
5 You can email me
6 I would be happy to
7 I look forward
8 Would it be possible
9 Please could you
10 Thank you for your help in

A the offer on your website.
B at Craig_Donaldons@web.mail
C to hearing from you soon.
D for you to return my wallet to me by post?
E sincerely,
F this matter.
G you are able to help me.
H I left my diary at your hotel.
I pay for the phone calls.
J about your advertisement.
K send me more details of your offer?
L this email.
M Mr Salmond,

2 Complete the email with the words from the box. There are five extra words.

> at could enquire faithfully forward
> hope if in matter Mr number on
> organise possible reply response
> sincerely Sir soon would

Dear _Sir_ / Madam,

I have booked a room at your hotel for four nights from September 10th till September 14th this year. I am writing to
¹_____ about taxi transfers to and from the airport.
Would it be ²_____ for a driver to meet me at the airport and bring me straight to the hotel? My flight arrives at 11.50 p.m. and I am worried about transport at that time of night.
On the 14th, I have to leave at 4.20 a.m. I ³_____
you are able to ⁴_____ something, even at that time in the morning. ⁵_____ you please tell me the cost of a taxi ride? Also, do I pay the driver or the hotel? Naturally,
I ⁶_____ be happy to pay more than the normal price of a taxi for this service.
Could you please ⁷_____ to this email. You can email me ⁸_____ toby17@bleep.mail or contact me ⁹_____ my mobile. My mobile ¹⁰_____ is +44 7700 900889
Thank you for your help in this ¹¹_____ .
I look ¹²_____ to hearing from you ¹³_____ .

Yours ¹⁴_____ ,
Toby Blackstone

3 Read the leaflet below and write an email of enquiry.

In your email:
- explain why you are writing.
- ask for more details about the offer.
- ask about the website address and the possibility of receiving a brochure with all the information.
- say thank you for helping and ask for a prompt reply.

LATE SUMMER DEALS

One-week or two-week holidays in **Turkey** from £200 a person.
Flights and meals included.

Offer available from
September 3rd–20th

Email for more details at:
turkoffer@travel.co

Finished? Always check your writing. Can you tick ✓ everything on this list?

In my email of enquiry:

- I have used appropriate opening and finishing phrases e.g. *Dear Sir or Madam – Yours faithfully.* ☐
- I have explained why I am writing. ☐
- I have asked about the details of the offer. ☐
- I have informed about my expectations. ☐
- I have given my contact details. ☐
- I have said thank you for the help and asked for a prompt reply. ☐
- I have not used contractions (e.g. *I'm / aren't / that's*). ☐
- I have not used emoticons ☺, abbreviations or acronyms (*info / CU / gr8*). ☐
- I have checked my spelling. ☐
- My text is neat and clear. ☐

1 In pairs, ask and answer the questions.

PART 1

Talk about sports.
1 Do you prefer watching or doing sports?
2 What new sport would you like to try in the future? Why?
3 Do you prefer team sports or individual sports? Why?
4 Have you ever tried a sport you didn't enjoy? Why?
5 Which sport is the most popular in your country? Why?

PART 2

Talk about holidays.
1 How did you spend your last holiday?
2 What's the worst holiday you've ever been on?
3 What's your favourite way of travelling on holiday? Why?
4 Do you prefer to go on holiday abroad or in your own country? Why?
5 Would you like to go on holiday alone? Why?/Why not?

2 Look at the photos that show different types of holiday.

PART 1

Which of these types of holiday have you been on? Discuss in pairs.

PART 2

In pairs, ask and answer the questions.

1 Do you prefer winter or summer activity holidays?
2 What are the good and bad things about a beach holiday?
3 What places would you like to visit on a backpacking holiday?
4 What are the good and bad things about a camping holiday?
5 What type of working holiday would you like to go on?
6 Which types of holiday are the most popular with people in your country? Why?
7 Which of these types of holidays do you like best? Why?

3 Read the instructions on your card. In pairs, take turns to role-play the conversation.

Student A

You're looking for a train station.
Ask Student B for help.

• Stop Student B politely and ask if he/she speaks English.
• Ask which is the closest train station.
• Ask for directions.
• Listen and repeat back directions to check that they are correct.
• Ask if the station is far.
• Thank Student B for his/her help and end the conversation.

Student B

You're walking in your home town.
Student A needs directions.

• Say yes, you speak English.
• Tell Student A that Market Street Station is the closest station.
• Give directions: walk along Green Street past the library on the left, take the third turning on the left, the station is on the right.
• Listen and check that Student B has remembered the directions correctly.
• Tell him/her that the station is only a five minute walk.
• Respond and say goodbye.

VOCABULARY AND GRAMMAR

1 One word in each sentence is wrong. Cross out the wrong words and write the correct ones.

We're going out for dinner on Saturday. Have you ~~done~~ a reservation yet?   *made*

1 We didn't drive from Poland to Austria – we went with train.   _____
2 We visited all the main signs in the area and took photos of them.   _____
3 We booked three arrangements from our hotel. They were all interesting, especially the coach trip to a waterfall.   _____
4 We must get to the airport quickly. Our fly leaves in two hours!   _____
5 Have you ever stayed in a young hostel?   _____

/5

2 Look at the definitions and write the words. Write one letter in each space.

This is a place where you sleep and eat the first meal of the day.
<u>b e d   a n d   b r e a k f a s t</u>
1 This is the word for a journey by plane.
— — — — — —
2 This is a private home where people can pay to stay and have meals.
— — — — — — — — — —
3 This is a kind of ship that carries people and sometimes cars across a river or a narrow area of water.
— — — — —
4 This is a cheap place to stay and is sometimes only for young people.
— — — — — — — — —
5 When you go on this kind of holiday, you carry your things in a bag on your back.
A — — — — — — — — — — — — holiday

/5

3 Complete the sentences with one word in each gap. The first and last letters are given.

You don't need to get a **b**<u>rochur</u>**e** to see photos of the hotel. They've got a website.
1 The train to the airport leaves from **p**_____**m** 8. We should get there early because I don't want to miss it.
2 The other **p**_____**s** on the plane were quite noisy. I think a lot of them knew each other.
3 We haven't got much money, so we're staying in a tent on a **c**_____**e** near the sea.
4 In London, we travelled around by **u**_____**d**, or the Tube as people there call it.
5 You've got a lot of **l**_____**e** for a three-day trip! I'm only taking a small bag.

/5

4 Complete the dialogue between Jen and her mum with the words in brackets and the correct form of the verbs from the box. There are two extra verbs.

arrive   book   give   go   have   leave
look at   make

J: Hi, Mum. (We/just) <u>We've just arrived</u> at the airport.
M: ¹(you/the departure board/yet) _____
_____?
J: Yes, we have. Our plane ²(not/Spain/yet) _____
_____. It's about 5 hours late!
M: Oh no! What are you doing now?
J: Well, we're waiting with all the other passengers. Someone from the airline is here. Wait a minute …
³(She/just) _____ us £10 for food. We can check in our bags and go through security and spend the money after that. That's good.
⁴(I/not/breakfast/yet) _____!
I'm worried about our transport in Spain.
⁵(We/already) _____
seats on the 14.38 train from Madrid to Ronda. I don't think we can use them on any other train.
M: Don't worry about that now. Ask the woman from the airline and phone me later when you know more.
J: OK, bye Mum.

/5

5 Complete the dialogue with the phrases from the box. There are five extra phrases.

Did you enjoy   did you go   Have you enjoyed
~~Have you ever travelled~~   have you gone   I did
I have   We have been   We have slept   We slept
We went

Ross: <u>Have you ever travelled</u> by ferry?
Henry: Yes, ¹_____ . Once.
Ross: Really? Where ²_____ ?
Henry: ³_____ from Holland to England.
Ross: ⁴_____ it or was it boring?
Henry: It wasn't boring at all. ⁵_____
on the boat and, in the morning, we were in England.

/5

6 Choose the correct option.

Oh no! The train has (just)/ yet left!
1 I've been *to / at* Rome, but not Venice.
2 Has Tim *ever / never* travelled to a foreign country?
3 We haven't booked our accommodation *already / yet*.
4 They've *already / yet* visited the most important sights.
5 Sally *bought / has bought* a guidebook last week.

/5

Total   /30

7 Choose the correct answers A–C.

Max couldn't fly to Japan because he forgot to bring his __ .
A ticket
B brochure
C passport ⓒ

1 You can book all your __ – hotels, campsites and apartments on-line.
A arrangements
B accommodation
C reservations

2 Would you like to go on a tour to see the local __ ?
A sights
B signs
C destinations

3 Mike went on holiday three weeks ago and he hasn't arrived back __ !
A ever
B yet
C already

4 Has Steve __ anything on his travel blog yet?
A wrote
B write
C written

5 Emma's so excited about her school trip. She's __ packed her clothes and they aren't going until next week!
A already
B yet
C never

/5

8 Put the words in the correct order to make sentences and questions. There is one extra word.

Simon: plane / platform / train / which / is / from / our / leaving
Which platform is our train leaving from?
Kate: Hmm … three, I think. Let's go!

1 Helen: France / ever / in / to / have / you / been
_____
Daisy: Yes, I went there last year. It was great!

2 Liam: We have to buy our bus tickets.
Natasha: It's OK. them / yet / have / I / already / bought
_____

3 Serena: in / Germany / did / by / travel / car / you / to
_____?
Nick: Yes, we did and it was a very long trip!

4 Maria: What do you want to do in the summer?
David: to / trip / want / tour / go / on / I / package / a
_____

5 Ally: What do you want to do in London?
Will: museums / go / I / to / the / visit / want
_____

/5

9 Complete each pair of sentences with the same word A–C.

They love __ to foreign countries.
I'm __ to the island by boat.
A visiting
B travelling ⓑ
C exploring going

1 Hello. I'd like to __ a reservation.
We have to __ the arrangements for our summer holiday.
A do
B make
C book

2 I don't want to sleep __ a tent!
We can check __ at ten o'clock tomorrow morning.
A on
B to
C in

3 This looks like a great excursion. Let's __ it!
We can __ our hotel online. It's really easy.
A book
B go
C make

4 Bob is going __ an adventure holiday next week.
I didn't get a seat __ the train because there were too many people.
A at
B to
C on

5 My friend is __ in a guesthouse and she says it's very nice.
How long are you __ in Athens?
A staying
B visiting
C travelling

/5

10 Choose the correct answers A–C.

The __ of our trip to Egypt were the Pyramids and the museums. We loved them!
A monuments
B destinations
C highlights ⓒ

1 There were a lot of __ at the airport.
A passengers
B visitors
C flights

2 Did you visit the __ ?
A local specialities
B excursions
C local markets

3 Could you help me please? __ a ticket online.
A I've never bought
B I've already bought
C I bought

4 __ to Scotland two years ago.
A We've gone
B We went
C We've been

5 The travel agent gave me some __ about Iceland to look at.
A arrangements
B bookings
C brochures

/5

Total /20

8 Nature

VOCABULARY

8.1

Geography • animals • collocations

SHOW WHAT YOU KNOW

1 Find seven more words in the word search and write them under the correct headings.

S	E	M	O	N	O	F	F	P
C	R	O	C	O	D	I	L	E
O	T	N	A	T	O	S	O	N
M	A	K	B	U	S	H	W	G
T	R	E	E	B	T	I	E	U
U	A	Y	T	A	E	M	R	I
L	G	R	A	S	S	P	O	N

Plants	Animals
	crocodile

WORD STORE 8A | Geography

2 Complete the sentences with one word in each gap. The first and last letters are given.

We sailed to a small i_slan_d in the middle of the ocean.

1 The school children went for a walk through the f_____t to look at the trees and other plants.
2 This l_____e is very big; in fact, it's five kilometres across from one side to the other!
3 A r_____r runs through the middle of the town and it's a popular place for kayaking.
4 We walked up to the top of the m_____n and had an amazing view of the land below.
5 I love swimming in our local pool but swimming in the s_____a is much more exciting.
6 Lots of people come to see the w_____l. It's about 80 metres high and it's a beautiful sight.
7 I think Africa is the hottest c_____t in the world. Am I right?

WORD STORE 8B | Animals

3 Read the descriptions and write the names of the wildlife. Write one letter in each space.

The biggest land animal in the world. It lives in Africa and India.
_e l e p h a n t_

1 It's a big animal. It can be brown, black or even white. It can be dangerous but lots of young children have a toy version of it.
— — — —

2 This is a large cat which lives in Asia. It's got orange and black stripes.
— — — — —

3 This is an intelligent animal that lives in the sea. Sometimes, it looks like it's smiling!
— — — — — — —

4 This animal lives in the forest. It has long legs and is usually brown. Its babies are very cute!
— — — —

5 This is the biggest animal on Earth. It lives in the sea but it isn't a fish. There are different kinds – Blue (the biggest), Killer (it is black and white and also called an Orca) and others.
— — — — —

6 This is a dangerous kind of large fish. The Great White is the most famous. The film *Jaws* was about one of these.
— — — — —

7 This creature lives on the land but is a very good swimmer. It's got very big teeth which it uses to cut trees and build its home.
— — — — — —

8 This is the fastest animal in the world on land. It's a cat and it lives in Africa. There are black spots on its body.
— — — — — — —

4 Complete the text with the words from the box. There are four extra words.

> change destroy good heating hunting
> noise pollute ~~pollution~~ protect recycling
> toxic warming

A Greener World

Are you concerned about the environment? Do you want to do something about environmental problems locally, nationally and internationally? Why not join A Greener World?

We campaign against:

- air and water _pollution_ and all companies and countries that ¹_____ the air and water.
- companies that produce ²_____ waste.
- any activities which lead to global ³_____ and climate ⁴_____ .

We campaign for:

- waste ⁵_____ so that glass, paper and aluminium can be used again.
- projects that are ⁶_____ for the environment.

Join us today and help to ⁷_____ our world!

5 Complete the geographical names with one letter in each space. The first letters are given.

The five great **c** o n t i n e n t s in the world are:

1 **E** __ __ __ __ __ – from Portugal in the south-west to Russia in the north-east.
2 **A** __ __ __ __ __ – with the longest river in the world, the Nile, and the biggest hot desert, the Sahara. You can see it from the south of Spain.
3 North and South **A** __ __ __ __ __ __ – with natural sights like the Niagara Falls and the Amazon River.
4 **A** __ __ __ – the biggest continent from Istanbul, Turkey to Tokyo in Japan. Here you can find the world's highest mountains in the Himalayas.
5 **A** __ __ __ __ __ __ __ __ – the continent is also known as Australasia and Oceania. This land is famous for its kangaroos and the Great Barrier Reef, the world's largest coral reef.
6 The two biggest **o** __ __ __ __ __ __ :
7 The **P** __ __ __ __ __ __ – you can sail across this from San Francisco to Japan. There are many islands like Hawaii, Fiji and the Galapagos Islands.
8 The **A** __ __ __ __ __ __ __ – from Ireland to the USA or from Angola to Brazil. Columbus sailed across this great sea. He wanted to get to India, but he found a new world.

REMEMBER THIS

We use the definite article (*the*) with some geographical places but not with others.

6 Read REMEMBER THIS. Find examples of the following geographical places 1–4 in the sentences in Exercise 5. Write their names and *the* or Ø in each gap.

countries: _Portugal_, _Russia_, _Spain_, _Turkey_, _Japan_, _Ireland_, _Angola_, _Brazil_, _India_

countries which are groups of states: _the USA_

1 rivers: _____ , _____
2 cities: _____ , _____ , _____
3 seas and oceans: _____ , _____
4 continents: _____ , _____ , North and South _____ , _____ , _____

REMEMBER BETTER

Many geographical places may have similar names in English and in your language but the spelling is often different. In order to remember the English spellings and the correct article use, it is useful to practise writing the names of places. One way is to make a 'wish list' of places you would like to visit. Use different colours for different kinds of places, e.g. red for countries, blue for seas, black for cities, etc.

WISH LIST – Ten places I want to visit:

Venice, the Amazon River, the Dead Sea, …

SHOW WHAT YOU'VE LEARNT

7 Choose the correct option.

1 We didn't swim in the sea because we heard that there was a four-metre long *beaver / shark / deer* swimming close to the beach.
2 This was a forest but people have *cut down / cut out / cut off* all the trees.
3 Some people think that *air / climate / global* warming doesn't exist! Isn't it stupid?
4 We should do more to *destroy / protect / pollute* the environment before it's too late.
5 They went on a safari in Africa where they saw a family of *dolphins / lions / bears*.

8 Complete the sentences with one word in each gap.

Last year we went sailing in the Mediterranean _Sea_.

1 In the middle of the lake, there is a beautiful _____ with one tree on it.
2 Climate _____ is a good phrase because it isn't just temperatures that are different. There is more rain and there are stronger winds and other things.
3 There's a big problem with water _____ in our rivers.
4 All the fish in the river have died because of the _____ waste from factories nearby.
5 People who live near the sea are very worried about the effects of global _____ on sea levels.

/10

8.2 Future with *will*

SHOW WHAT YOU KNOW

1 Complete the positive sentences (+), negative sentences (–) and questions (?) using the subject, modal and verb in capitals.

1 WE / CAN / SAVE

+ _We can save_ the elephants.

– _____ all the animals.

? _____ panda bears?

2 WE / SHOULD / CYCLE

+ _____ every day.

– _____ after dark.

? _____ in the town centre?

2 ★ Complete the dialogue with the correct form of the verbs in brackets. Use *will*.

A Green World In 25 years …

Elephants _won't be_ (not/be) in danger.
There ¹_____ (not/be) any elephants.
Icebergs ²_____ (not/melt) in
the summer. There ³_____ (not/be)
any ice in our oceans. People ⁴_____
(not/cut down) the rainforests. Rainforests
⁵_____ (not/exist). Rivers ⁶_____
(be) more polluted and all the fish
⁷_____ (be) dead.
The Earth's climate ⁸_____ (get) hotter. Many plants
and animals ⁹_____ (die out). Scientists
¹⁰_____ (not/be) able to solve the problem of global
warming alone. We ¹¹_____ (destroy) the environment.

… or can we change our way of life?

We think people can. Let us show you how. **Join us today.**

SHOW WHAT YOU'VE LEARNT

5 Complete the second sentence in each pair. Use short forms of *will* where possible.

NOW: People use petrol in their cars.
IN 20 YEARS: _People won't use petrol_ in their cars.
All cars will use green energy.

1 **NOW:** I can't speak French.
IN 20 YEARS: _____ to speak French very well. I will live in France.

2 **NOW:** It sometimes snows in England.
IN 20 YEARS: _____ in England?
Or will global warming mean that temperatures are too high for snow?

3 **NOW:** People can go fishing in rivers.
IN 20 YEARS: _____ to go fishing in rivers. The water will be polluted.

3 ★ ★ Complete the questions about the future.

What will the world be like (What / the world / be like)
in twenty years? ☐ Better ☐ Worse ☐ The same

1 _____ (children / learn) at home or at school?
☐ Home ☐ School

2 _____ (Which country / win) the 2034 football World Cup?
☐ Thailand ☐ Indonesia ☐ Vietnam

3 _____ (Which language / children learn) in school?
☐ English ☐ Chinese ☐ Spanish

4 _____ (How many people / there be) in the world?
☐ >10 billion ☐ 6-9 billion ☐ < 6 billion

5 _____ (What / people / do) on the Internet?
☐ Go to virtual worlds ☐ Look at cat photos ☐ There won't be an Internet

4 ★ ★ ★ Use the correct forms of the words from the box to complete the interview with Alison. Use short forms of *will* where possible.

I know   It destroy   there be   they ask   they want   ~~we make~~   we not ask   we try   you like

I: Thank you for your interest in A Green World. Have you got any questions you'd like to ask before you join?

A: Yes. _Will we make_ the world cleaner and better?

I: Well, ¹_____ . We organise talks and meetings and other events. Don't worry, ²_____ you to do anything illegal. At the moment, we want to stop a new road. ³_____ the habitats of lots of animals. I'm sure ⁴_____ TV and newspaper reporters there. ⁵_____ to talk to some of us.

A: It all sounds very exciting. Oh wait … ⁶_____ me any questions? How ⁷_____ what to say?

I: Don't worry. Our organiser, Meg, has got all the details. She's great. I'm sure ⁸_____ her.

4 **NOW:** Planes travel to Australia in about 24 hours.
IN 20 YEARS: _____ to Australia in about 24 minutes. I'll go there after school!

5 **NOW:** You can download a film from the Internet in about half an hour.
IN 20 YEARS: _____ to download a film from the Internet in half a second.

6 **NOW:** There are thousands of cheetahs in Africa.
IN 20 YEARS: _____ any cheetahs in Africa? Or will they only live in zoos?

/6

GRAMMAR: Train and Try Again page 135

8.3

The weather • word building

1 Read the text. Complete gaps 1–4 with the words from the box. There are two extra words.

> bright   clear   ~~dry~~   heavy   light   strong   wet

Extract from Student's Book recording 🔊 **3.46**

P: And here's Nick Newman with the late-night weather.

NN: Good evening. Well, it seems spring's almost here. Across the British Isles, tomorrow will be warmer, but not everywhere …
So, let's look at the weather in more detail, and I'll start with the south. In all of southern England, tomorrow will be the sunniest day of the week; it will be *dry*, with ¹_____ skies and sunshine all day. In most places, there'll be a ²_____ wind, but it will still feel quite warm; temperatures will be around eighteen degrees in most of the area and will get to twenty in Cornwall.
Across Wales and the Midlands, the morning will be foggy, but the fog should soon clear. After that we can expect a sunny day with some cloud. There will be a few showers with the possibility of thunder in the late afternoon. The morning won't be very warm – only eight degrees, I'm afraid. But it should get warmer during the afternoon and the temperature will rise to fourteen degrees.
In the north of England, Saturday will be a windy day, and that ³_____ west wind will bring rainy weather from the Atlantic. It will be cloudy with showers most of the day but there will be some sunny moments. Temperatures will be around thirteen degrees, but it will feel colder in the wind.
Now for Scotland and Northern Ireland. Well, it's definitely not spring here yet. There will be a lot of cloud around and quite a lot of rain. The Highlands will have the wettest weather. The rain will be ⁴_____ there, and high up in the mountains it may still snow tonight and tomorrow night. Temperatures at best around eleven degrees.

WORD STORE 8D | The weather

2 Complete the collocations with the words from the box in Exercise 1.

sunshine: ·················· *bright*

skies: ········· ¹_____ (no clouds)
········· cloudy / overcast (clouds)

wind: ········· strong
········· ²_____

rain / snow: ········· ³_____
········· light

day / weather: ········· *wet* (rain)
········· ⁴_____ (no rain)

REMEMBER BETTER

Learning antonyms can help you keep talking about a topic even if you forget a word which you want to use. Compare these two students trying to say that *the wind was light*.

*The wind was very er … er … weak … er low … er soft … er
The wind was very … it wasn't strong at all.*

Complete the second sentence in each pair using the correct antonym.

There was pleasant, light wind, so we weren't too hot on the beach.
The wind wasn't <u>strong</u> and it was cool on the beach.

1 Wake up and look out of the window. The sky isn't cloudy at all.
Wake up and look out of the window. The sky is beautifully _____ .

2 I don't need a coat. It's raining but it's a light rain.
I don't need a coat. The rain isn't very _____ .

3 The weather in France wasn't great but, fortunately, it was dry.
The weather in France wasn't great but, fortunately, it wasn't _____ .

4 There was light snow but it was safe to drive.
It was safe to drive because the snow wasn't very _____ .

VOCABULARY PRACTICE | Word building 1

3 Look at the vocabulary in lesson 8.3 in the Student's Book. Complete the sentences with the correct form of the word in brackets.

A: Where's Verona?
B: It's in <u>northern</u> Italy. (north)

1 A: My cousins have a holiday house in Brest.
B: Oh? Where's that?
A: It's in _____ France. (west)

2 A: Where are you going for your holiday this year?
B: I'm not sure where exactly yet, but it'll be somewhere warm in _____ Europe. (south)

3 A: Does it rain a lot in the _____ part of the country? (east)
B: No, actually. It's very dry there.

VOCABULARY PRACTICE | Word building 2

4 Look at the vocabulary in lesson 8.3 in the Student's Book. Choose the correct option.

1 It's very *wind / windy* today. Be careful when you drive.
2 The *sun / sunny* is shining. It's a beautiful day!
3 We get a lot of *fog / foggy* here because of the lake.
4 It's very *cloud / cloudy*. Do you think it will rain?
5 It may *rain / rainy* later, so take a coat.
6 It was a *fog / foggy* morning when Dad crashed into the car in front of him.
7 It's a horrible, *rain / rainy* day today.
8 We had beautiful weather on holiday. It was *sun / sunny* every day.
9 What a lovely day. There isn't a *cloud / cloudy* in the sky.
10 There will be a strong *wind / windy* all day. Great for windsurfing.

1 Read the three sentences from the texts and match the places to the photos.

A The Bear Trail: It's a beautiful walk through forests and over rivers and lakes.

B Camino di Santiago: But in Spain, the walk often followed roads.

C GR20 Corsica: It goes … from two hundred metres to over 2,200 metres above sea-level.

A Hiking in Finland

I've just come back from Finland. My friends from university invited me to join them on an eight-day hike. The walk is called the Bear Trail and it is in the Oulanka National Park in north-eastern Finland. It's a beautiful walk through forests and across rivers and lakes. We stayed at campsites and carried clothes, food and tents on our backs. I'm not the fittest person in the world but I was able to finish. I loved the *incredibly clear* air, the beautiful views and the sounds of nature. In my opinion, it is perfect for anyone who wants to start long distance walking as it is almost *completely flat* and well-signposted. Just try not to fill your backpack up with things which you won't need.

B Camino di Santiago

It was the walk of a lifetime. Eight hundred kilometres from the south of France, over the Pyrenees mountains and across northern Spain to Santiago de Compostela. It all started so well. The path up to the Pyrenees was <u>magical</u> and it was good to meet other people doing the same walk. Everyone was <u>enthusiastic</u> about the walk ahead. But in Spain, the route often followed roads. It was noisy and <u>monotonous</u>, with unchanging views for hours and hours. More and more people joined the walk. They were *generally friendly* but it wasn't the experience I expected. I'd like to go back to the Pyrenees and hike there again but I'll stop there next time.

C THE GR20, Corsica

Corsica is a <u>magnificent</u> island with some *wonderfully picturesque* walks along the coast and inland. But for walkers, it is famous for the GR20, Europe's most difficult long distance walk. It goes from north to south and up and down from two hundred metres to over 2,200 metres above sea level. The *frighteningly steep* and rocky paths are beautiful but very <u>demanding</u>. Our guides will help you to complete the whole 180 km in fifteen days. The price includes transport, accommodation in tents and food. You should be in good health with experience of mountain walking and a good head for heights. No climbing experience is necessary.

GLOSSARY

flat *(adj)* – not going up or down
well-signposted *(adj)* – there are plenty of signposts and the information they give you is clear and easy to follow

steep *(adj)* – a road, hill, etc. that is steep slopes at a high angle
have a good head for heights – not afraid of being high above the ground

coast *(n)* – the area where the land meets the sea
inland *(adj)* – away from the coast

2 **Read the texts and choose the correct answers A–D.**

1 The text about Finland
   A gives practical information about the hike.
   B expresses the writer's opinion about the hike.
   C is a warning to people who want to go on the walk.
   D recommends places to see during the hike.

2 The writer of the first text
   A says he did the hike to get fit.
   B asked his friends to go on the hike with him.
   C slept in a tent.
   D mentions an animal he saw during the hike.

3 The writer of the second text
   A was disappointed by the experience.
   B would like to repeat the walk.
   C didn't like the behaviour of other people on the walk.
   D thought the walk was too long.

4 The third text
   A advertises an organised walk.
   B makes suggestions for different walks in Corsica.
   C invites someone to visit the area.
   D focuses on the natural beauty of Corsica.

5 The text about Corsica
   A tells us that the walk is suitable for anyone.
   B includes the total cost of the walk.
   C mentions the highest point in the north.
   D states the distance and the time needed to do the walk.

3 **Choose the correct meaning A or B for the underlined adjectives in the text.**

1 magical
   A amazing, wonderful
   B strange, frightening

2 enthusiastic
   A extremely tired
   B very interested in something or excited by it

3 monotonous
   A dangerous
   B boring

4 magnificent
   A beautiful, wonderful
   B very big

5 demanding
   A unattractive and boring
   B difficult to do

REMEMBER THIS

To add more information about adjectives, we can use adverbs before them. This will show your attitude towards what is described and can also make your writing more interesting for the reader. Look at the examples from the texts on page 100.

incredibly clear	*completely flat*
generally friendly	*wonderfully picturesque*
frighteningly steep	

4 **Choose the correct option.**

The Isles of Scilly are a ¹*magical / demanding / enthusiastic* place with the clear, blue sea and the golden beaches. It is the perfect place to relax. Teenagers who are looking for an exciting nightlife may find a holiday here quite ²*demanding / magnificent / monotonous* as there isn't a lot to do. Most people love the islands and some people decide to move here after a holiday. My parents did this before I was born. I'm glad. I go to a school with ten other children. Our teacher is very ³*enthusiastic / magnificent / monotonous* and always tries to make our lessons interesting. She also gives us a lot of ⁴*enthusiastic / demanding / magnificent* tests so we have to work hard.
My favourite island here is Tresco. It has a ⁵*magnificent / monotonous / demanding* tropical garden with beautiful flowers from all over the world. You should come here. You'll love it.

VOCABULARY PRACTICE | The natural world

5 **Look at the vocabulary in lesson 8.4 in the Student's Book. Complete the sentences with one word in each gap. The first letters are given.**

I saw a **c**<u>reature</u> in the forest – I thought it was a bear!

1 'What do you **f**_____ your dog?' 'Dog food!'
2 If you don't close the gate in the field, the sheep will **e**_____ .
3 After the long climb to 2,500 metres above sea level, his **l**_____ hurt and he couldn't breathe easily.
4 Their cottage is in beautiful **s**_____ – there's a forest and a river nearby.
5 It's good for your **b**_____ to do puzzles and other activities that make you think.
6 Koalas have thick grey or brown **f**_____ which keeps them warm in winter.

WORD STORE 8E | Word families

6 **Complete the sentences with the correct form of the words in capitals.**

The environment is *important* for all of us. Why don't people care more about it? **IMPORTANCE**

1 Most of the world's _____ snakes and spiders are in Australia. **POISON**
2 The _____ of a species depends on its environment. **EVOLVE**
3 It's _____ to swim in the sea when the waves are very big. **DANGER**
4 The police caught the _____ and he finally went to prison. **ATTACK**
5 Bees are actually much more _____ than you think. **INTELLIGENCE**

SHOW WHAT YOU KNOW

1 Use the words to make future plans and hopes. Add extra words where necessary and use short forms if possible.

I want to get (I / want / get) into the school basketball team.

1 _____ (I / should / be) more friendly.
2 _____ (I / not / want / fail) my exams.
3 _____ (I / like / go) travelling.
4 _____ (I / must / get) fit.
5 _____ (I / not / want / waste) my time.
6 _____ (I / planning / get) a job.

2 ★ Look at the plans and complete the sentences with the correct form of the verbs.

Plans

✓	✗
study ~~every day~~	play ~~computer games~~
write ~~a blog~~	eat ~~fast food~~
read ~~some books~~	be ~~late for school~~
help ~~my parents~~	argue ~~with my girlfriend~~

I'm going *to study* for my exams every day.

1 I'm not going _____ fast food.
2 I'm going _____ my parents.
3 I'm not going _____ with my girlfriend.
4 I'm going _____ a blog.
5 I'm not going _____ computer games.
6 I'm going _____ some books.
7 I'm not going _____ late for school.

3 ★ ★ Put the words in the correct order.

1 **Tom:** university / are / at / study / What / you / to / going
   What are you going to study at university?
   Adam: I'm / study / going / Maths / to
   _____ .

2 **Jon:** invite to / people / to / How many / party / going / are / your / you
   a _____ ?
   Lucy: not / to / I'm / party / going / have / a / this / year
   b _____

3 **Neil:** going / project / Is / our / to / Bob / us / help / with
   a _____ ?
   Tammy: he / No / isn't
   b _____ .

4 **Abigail:** weekend / Steve and Mark / Are / going / visit you / to / this
   a _____ ?
   Ruth: they / Yes / are
   b _____ .

4 ★ ★ ★ Complete the dialogue with the correct form of the words in brackets.

Mark: *What are you going to give* (What / you / give) Angela for her birthday?

Rick: I don't know. I haven't thought about it yet.
¹_____ (I / go) shopping on Saturday and try to find something. Do you want to come?

Mark: I can't. ²_____ (My dad / give) me a driving lesson.

Rick: Really? ³_____ (you / have) lessons with a teacher as well?

Mark: ⁴_____ (Yes / be) but Dad said I should have one lesson with him so that I know what I'm doing.

Rick: ⁵_____ (I / not / drive).

Mark: Why not?

Rick: I don't like cars. They're bad for the environment.

Mark: So ⁶_____ (how / you / get) to the town centre on Saturday?

Rick: Oh, ⁷_____ (my mum / drive) me there.

SHOW WHAT YOU'VE LEARNT

5 Choose the correct answers A–C.

1 What __ going to do next year?
   A you   B you are   C are you

2 I __ lend my phone to Harry again. He spoke to his friends for half an hour!
   A not going   B 'm not going   C 'm not going to

3 We're going __ married in June. I hope the day will be sunny.
   A to get   B get   C getting

4 Are you going to wear a dress to the party? Yes, __ .
   A I am.   B I'm going.   C I'm wearing.

5 Felicity __ phone us this evening.
   A is going   B going to   C is going to

6 Is your dad going to take us to the airport? No, he __ .
   A isn't going   B isn't   C not

/6

GRAMMAR: Train and Try Again page 135

SPEAKING

Agreeing and disagreeing

1 Translate the phrases into your own language.

SPEAKING BANK

Agreeing

I think so (too). _____

(Yes,) I agree. _____

Exactly./Absolutely. _____

That's/You're right. _____

Disagreeing

I'm not sure. _____

I don't think so. _____

I disagree. _____

To be honest, I don't think it makes much sense. _____

Agreeing in part / Agreeing and disagreeing

Perhaps/Maybe, but … _____

Maybe you're right … _____

_____

I see what you mean, but … _____

_____

You have a point, but … _____

2 Choose words and phrases that have a similar meaning to the underlined words and phrases.

1 **Al:** I think we should stop using plastic bags immediately.

Ben: <u>I see what you mean, but …</u>
You have a point, but … / Exactly.

2 **Max:** Governments should stop cigarette smoking in parks.

Elaine: <u>I think so too.</u> *I agree. / I disagree.*

3 **Josh:** Tourism is a bad thing for poorer countries.

Sue: <u>I'm not sure.</u> *Absolutely. / I don't think so.*

4 **Pauline:** Children should learn environmental studies at primary school.

Heather: <u>Perhaps,</u> but first they need to learn reading, writing and Maths. *Exactly, / Maybe,*

5 **Stella:** Free plastic bags in supermarkets are terrible for the environment.

Linda: <u>Exactly.</u> *Absolutely. / Perhaps.*

6 **Jocelyn:** They should close all the factories because the air in the town is very polluted.

Rebecca: <u>I don't think</u> that's a good idea.
I disagree. / I think so too.

3 Complete the text with one letter in each space.

HAVE YOUR SAY | ENERGY SAVING IDEAS

I think all electrical devices should automatically switch off if people don't use them for thirty minutes. Some people leave computers and lights on all night.

Darren, aged 15

I think so <u>too</u>.

¹A _ _ _ _ _ _ _ _ _ y!

²I a _ _ _ _ _

Sam, aged 14

³You're r _ _ _ _ _

Alison, aged 16

⁴M _ _ _ _ _ you're right. At school we have lights that go off after two minutes – in the corridors, not the classrooms!

Chris, aged 16

⁵I d _ _ _ _ _ _ _ e. How does a TV know if you are using it?

Simon, aged 17

⁶I'm not s _ _ _ this is a good idea. What about old people or children? They may need to have a light on all night.

Toby, aged 17

⁷To be h _ _ _ _ _ _ , I don't think this idea makes a lot of ⁸s _ _ _ _. Why not make electricity more expensive at night?

Jane, aged 18

⁹You have a p _ _ _ _ but electricity is expensive already!

Carla, aged 18

4 Choose the correct answers A–C.

Andy: This is my idea for our new environment campaign. What do you think?

Heidi: Well, to be ¹__ , I don't think it makes a lot of sense.

Andy: Why not?

Heidi: Well, the Earth is smiling. It seems to me that it's saying that everything is OK and the Earth is happy.

Andy: I see what you ²__ but I ³__ you're right. It says here: 'Put a smile on the Earth's face'. That shows people what it's all about.

Heidi: ⁴__ , but people will look at the picture first.

Andy: Hmm. You're ⁵__ . We need bigger writing, below the picture. Like this … What do you think?

Heidi: I'm not ⁶__ it's better. I've got a different idea. We have a sad looking, dark Earth and it's dreaming and the happy face is its dream. Like this …. Do you like it?

Andy: ⁷__ ! Yes, I ⁸__ with you. It's great.

1	**A** sure	**B** honest	**C** right
2	**A** say	**B** agree	**C** mean
3	**A** disagree	**B** don't	**C** 'm not sure
4	**A** Maybe	**B** Exactly	**C** To be honest
5	**A** right	**B** agree	**C** honest
6	**A** agree	**B** honest	**C** sure
7	**A** Absolutely	**B** Agree	**C** Perhaps
8	**A** disagree	**B** think	**C** agree

WRITING

8.7

Expressing an opinion, presenting arguments

1 Put paragraphs A–E in the correct order.

The Lindon Observer | **WHAT'S WRONG WITH OUR TOWN?**

Your chance to send your ideas about how to improve Lindon.

Ray, aged 16

A ☐ Also, there is a lot to do. We have good shops, cafés and restaurants. There is a cinema, a theatre and an art gallery. I go to a very good sports centre once a week. I know there aren't any concerts here and some teenagers say it's boring but I disagree.

B ☐ People always think their town should be better, but I don't think anyone is really unhappy here. In my view, it's simply impossible!

C ☐ I realise that people may disagree with me, but I think our town is a nice place to live and I'm going to try to explain why.

D ☐ Finally, the countryside outside the town is beautiful. You can swim in the lakes, walk in the forests and, in the winter, you can go skiing in the mountains just 50 km away.

E ☐ Firstly, it's safe. The people are friendly and there aren't any real problems here. I can go out at night and I don't have to worry. The schools are excellent and the park is very pleasant.

2 Complete the text with the words from the box. There are three extra words.

> addition   all   finally   first   firstly   opinion
> secondly   seems   think   view

The Lindon Observer |

Your chance to send your ideas about how to improve Lindon.

Lucy, aged 17

In my *opinion*, our town centre is unattractive because there are so many cars. Why is this a problem? ¹_____ of ²_____ , the air is polluted. I can taste the pollution when I go to the town centre. The air is cleaner in bigger cities which are car free. ³_____ , it is dangerous. The cars go very fast and there aren't many places to cross the road. In ⁴_____ , the old buildings are always dirty and it costs a lot of money to clean them. ⁵_____ , tourists enjoy walking around quiet, clean towns. It ⁶_____ to me that we don't get many tourists, because they don't like the town centre. It isn't a nice place to visit. I understand that people need transport but I think cycle paths, buses and trams are more environmentally friendly than cars.

3 Write which picture shows Lindon from Ray's text (R) and which from Lucy's text (L).

A ☐    B ☐

VOCABULARY PRACTICE | Environment protection

4 Look at the vocabulary in lesson 8.7 in the Student's Book. Match sentence beginnings 1–6 with their endings a–g.

When you brush your teeth, turn ☐ g

1 It's good to buy ☐
2 Try to throw ☐
3 It's important to plant ☐
4 Before you go to bed, turn ☐
5 You can save ☐
6 You should sort ☐

a water by taking shorter showers.
b away less and find other ways to use what you have.
c trees because they produce oxygen for the atmosphere.
d off the lights in the rest of the house.
e your rubbish for recycling – you know, glass, paper and aluminium.
f recycled things, like paper for your printer.
g off the tap water so that you don't waste it.

SHOW WHAT YOU'VE LEARNT

5 You also live in Lindon and find it boring and not a good place for teenagers to live. You have decided to present your views about the town on the *The Lindon Observer* website. Write an opinion essay.

- state what you think the main problem with the town is.
- give reasons for your opinion.
- put forward ideas for possible changes.
- explain why your ideas can help.

SHOW THAT YOU'VE CHECKED

Finished? Always check your writing. Can you tick ✓ everything on this list?

In my opinion essay:

- I have included a short introduction expressing my opinion. ☐
- I have used phrases to introduce my opinions such as *In my opinion/view*, *It seems to me*, etc. ☐
- I have clearly ordered my ideas using phrases such as *In addition*, *First of all*, *Finally*, etc. ☐
- I have given arguments to support my opinions. ☐
- I have explained why my suggestions are good ideas. ☐
- I have finished the essay appropriately. ☐
- I have checked my spelling. ☐
- My text is neat and clear. ☐

1 In pairs, ask and answer the questions.

PART 1

Talk about holidays.
1 What's the best holiday you've ever had?
2 Where do you think you'll go on your next holiday?
3 Would you prefer to stay in a youth hostel or at a campsite? Why?
4 Which foreign countries have you visited?
5 Which continent in the world would you most like to visit? Why?

PART 2

Talk about the environment.
1 Which wild animal would you most like to see in its natural habitat? Why?
2 Would you prefer to live in a forest, in the mountains, on a small island on a lake or at the seaside? Why?
3 What's your favourite type of weather? Why?
4 What do you think is the biggest danger to the environment in your country at the moment?
5 What things can we all do to help the environment?

2 Look at the photos of the animals.

PART 1

Take turns to describe the photos.

A

B

PART 2

In pairs, ask and answer the questions about the photos.

Student A's photo
1 What types of landscape does the photo show?
2 What can you see in the photo?
3 What are the people doing?
4 What is the animal doing?
5 What do you think will happen to this animal's home in the future?

Student B's photo
1 What can you see in this photo?
2 What animals does the photo show?
3 What are the animals doing?
4 What other things can you see in the water?
5 What do you think will happen to this animal in the future?

3 Read the instructions on your card. In pairs, take turns to role-play the conversation.

Student A

You and Student B are talking about eco-week. Tell Student B your ideas. Then listen to his/her ideas and say if you agree/disagree.

- Say that planting a tree in the playground will help the environment.
- Say that all students should walk to school during eco-week because this will help stop pollution.
- Agree that Student B has a point.
- Listen, disagree and explain why.
- Listen and agree.
- Say yes and end the conversation.

Student B

You and Student A are talking about eco-week. Listen to Student A's ideas and say if you agree/disagree. Then tell him/her your ideas.

- Listen and agree with Student A.
- Listen, agree in part with Student A and explain why.
- Now share your ideas with Student A. Say that everyone should turn off all the lights and electrical devices all week to save electricity.
- Agree that Student A has a point. Suggest that going vegetarian for the week will help the planet.
- Offer to tell your teacher the ideas you both have.

VOCABULARY AND GRAMMAR

1 Complete the sentences with one word in each gap. The first letters are given. Use 'landscape' vocabulary.

We spent some time taking photos of a beautiful **w**aterfall.

1 Did you know that African **e**_____ are much heavier than those in Asia?
2 We went kayaking along a dangerous **r**_____ . The water was very cold but, luckily, we didn't fall in.
3 Crete is a beautiful **i**_____ in the Mediterranean Sea. In Greek mythology, the first King of Crete was Minos, son of Zeus and Europa.
4 It's dangerous to swim at some beaches in Australia because there are **s**_____ in the sea.
5 More rain falls in Africa than in Antarctica. That's why Antarctica is the driest **c**_____ in the world.

/5

2 Complete the words with one letter in each space.

Hi Monica,

Wow! What an amazing holiday! We are by the sea. It's quite **w** i n d **y** but warm. The sky is blue all the time. I don't think I've seen a ¹**c** _ _ _ **d** at all. We have been to an aquarium. My sister loved the ²**d** _ _ _ _ _ _ _ **s** which jumped and caught fish in the air. We've also been on a boat trip to look at the ³**w** _ _ _ _ **s** that swim in the sea here. They were really big! I was quite worried when they came close to the boat! Dad wanted to take a helicopter ride to an island about 20km away but it was very ⁴**f** _ _ _ **y** that morning. The pilot couldn't see more than fifty metres in front of him and it was ⁵**d** _ _ _ _ _ _ _ **s** to fly. I'm quite glad – I hate flying! I'll tell you more when I see you.

Abigail

/5

3 Match sentence beginnings 1–5 with their endings A–I. There are three extra endings.

The biggest problem facing our rivers is toxic ☐ I
1 After they built the new road, air ☐
2 Every time we have cold weather, my friends ask me what happened to global ☐
3 I think more and more people are now worried by climate ☐
4 Don't throw away glass bottles – put them in a waste ☐
5 If you care about the environment, you should do something ☐

A warming.
B the water.
C to protect it.
D environment.
E change.
F recycling bin.
G pollution was much worse.
H the bush.
I waste from factories.

/5

4 Put the words in the correct order.

will / planes / 2050? / fast / in / how / travel
How fast will planes travel in 2050?
1 not / summer. / going / plane / travel / I'm / this / to / by
_____
2 going / a job / year? / is / to / next / Miranda / get
_____
3 it / sunny / weekend? / will / be / this
_____
4 going / project / to / our / tonight. / we're / finish
_____
5 won't / cars / 2049. / there / any / in / be
_____

/5

5 Complete the text with the verbs from the box in the correct future form.

going/join   not/be   not going/drive
not/going/join   they/live   you/going/do

BLOG

There's an island in the middle of the Indian Ocean. It's very beautiful but, in the near future, it *won't be* there. It will be under the sea. The people will lose their homes. Where ¹_____ ?
I read about the island in a magazine. It was a sad story and I want to do something to change the world. So, I' ²_____ an environmental group. My parents are also interested. They ³_____ the group but they are going to change the things they do. For example, my dad ⁴_____ to work, he's going to cycle.
I'm not sure we can save the island but … maybe. What ⁵_____ to help? Please, let us know your ideas.

/5

6 Correct the underlined words in the sentences.

Dolphins are famous for their <u>intelligent</u>.
intelligence
1 The shark bit the surfer. It was a terrible <u>attacked</u>.
_____
2 Do you know Charles Darwin's theory of <u>evolved</u>?
_____
3 All parts of that plant are <u>poisoned</u> to eat, including the flowers.
_____
4 Run if you see a bear in the forest – bears are <u>dangers</u>!
_____
5 Pronghorns are good runners probably because in the past they had to escape cheetahs, which are the fastest <u>attack</u> in the world.
_____

/5

Total /30

106

7 Choose the correct answers A–C.

There'll be some ___ in the morning. Don't get wet!
A sunshine
(B) showers
C fog

1 How can we get rid of ___ ? It's too dangerous for the fish in the river.
A global warming
B toxic waste
C air pollution

2 I think the planet ___, and that's terrible.
A is going to get hotter
B is heating itself
C will get hotter

3 Unfortunately, we ___ to meet you tomorrow.
A won't be able
B are going
C won't

4 There are many ways to ___ water around the home.
A throw away less
B save
C turn off

5 People have always been scared by ___. Storms can be really frightening!
A air pollution
B global warming
C thunder and lightning

/5

8 Put the words in the correct order to make sentences and questions. There is one extra word.

Mum: turn / the / of / to / off / don't / lights / forget
Don't forget to turn off the lights.

Mike: Don't worry, Mum. I'll remember.

1 Jane: tomorrow / skies / have / we / clouds / will / clear / I / hope

_____

Ivan: Me too! I don't want it to rain during our picnic!

2 Sam: We should start recycling at home.
Nicky: too / so / to / think / I

_____

3 Toni: climate / some / don't / believe / that / weather / people / change / a problem / is

_____

Lina: Well, I think those people are crazy!

4 Angie: how's / weekend / for / what's / the / the / weather / forecast

_____?

Jason: Rain! It always rains here!

5 Bryan: Do you think life will be better in the future?
Christina: I / right / be / honest / think / to / so / don't

_____

/5

9 Complete the sentences with the correct form of the words in capitals.

It wasn't a good day to take photographs because it was very *cloudy*. CLOUD

1 France and Spain are in _____ Europe. WEST

2 There are rocks in the water and it's _____ to swim there. DANGER

3 It was very _____ in the morning and I couldn't see very far. FOG

4 There was a _____ gas in the air and many people became sick. POISON

5 You can measure a person's _____ in many different ways. INTELLIGENT

/5

10 Complete the text with the correct answers A–C.

Hi Ben,

I've joined a great group. It's called Earth Now. It's a group for young people who want to *B* the environment.
We do lots of cool things. Next Saturday we're going to ¹___ some trees. We're going to go to a ²___ where there was a fire and many trees died. Trees are really important – they're like the ³___ of the planet because they give us oxygen when they breathe. They're also a home for many small ⁴___ . Would you like to come with me? We won't go if it's ⁵___ because that will damage the young trees, so I hope it's a nice day!

I hope you can come,
Annie

	A	B	C
	A sort	(B) protect	C recycle
1	A plant	B grow	C feed
2	A sea	B forest	C continent
3	A brains	B lungs	C surroundings
4	A creatures	B whales	C lions
5	A sunny	B cloudy	C windy

/5

Total   /20

VOCABULARY BANK

Translate the words and phrases into your own language.

People

Personal information

adult
age
at the age of (ten)

birthday
identity
identity card
middle-aged
old
person
young

Nationality

American

Australian

Brazilian

British
Canadian

Chinese
English
German
Polish
Portuguese

Russian
Scottish
Spanish
Swiss
Welsh

Appearance

Hair colour

black
blond
brown
dark
dyed
fair
grey
red

Hair type

curly
fringe
ponytail
shaved hair
shoulder-length hair

spiky hair
straight
wavy

Hair length

bald
long
medium-length
short

Eye colour

blue
brown
green
grey

Height

short
tall

Build and looks

fat
fit
flexible
good-looking
pretty
similar in looks
slim
sporty
thin
ugly
well-built

Clothes and accessories

black leather strap

boots
coat
dress
hat
jacket
jeans/pair of jeans
jumper
make-up
scarf
shirt
shoes
shoelaces
skirt
slippers
socks
sunglasses
suit
T-shirt
tattoo
tie
top
tracksuit
trainers
trousers
watch

Adjectives describing style

attractive
baggy
casual
colourful
smart
stylish
tight
trendy
(un)comfortable

Features of character

ambition
be afraid/scared of sth

boring
calm
charming
cheerful
clever/intelligent
confident
creative
dog lover
energetic
funny
generous
(hawve) a sense of humour

interesting
kind
laugh
music taste
old-fashioned
negative
personality
play jokes on sb
positive
reflect
relaxed
responsible
serious
shy
smile
sociable
stupid
successful
talented
tell jokes
(un)friendly

unkind
unsociable
worried

Feelings and emotions

be interested in sth _____

be into sth _____
be keen on sth _____
believe _____
can't stand _____
care about sth _____
enjoy sth/have fun _____

get on with _____
hate (Twitter/rollerblading) _____

have an argument _____

like (films/reading) _____

love (weekends/cooking) _____

prefer (rap/to relax at home) _____

worry _____

Home

Places where we live
city _____
countryside _____
house _____
village _____

Rooms in a house
bathroom _____
bedroom _____
garage _____
kitchen _____
living room _____
room _____
upstairs _____

Furniture and equipment
armchair _____
bath _____
beanbag _____
bed _____
candle _____
carpet _____
chair _____
cooker _____
cupboard _____
desk _____
dishwasher _____
door _____
fridge _____
freezer _____
key/room key _____
kitchen equipment _____

lamp _____
poster _____
roof _____
shower _____
sink _____
sofa _____
stairs _____
table _____
toilet _____
wall _____
wardrobe _____
water pipe _____
window _____

Describing a house – prepositions of place
behind _____
between _____
in _____
in front of _____
next to _____
on _____
opposite _____
over _____
under _____

Other
bricks _____
buy your first flat/house/home _____

leave home _____
neighbour _____

School

School subjects
acrobatics class _____
Art lessons _____
Biology _____
Chemistry _____
Geography _____
English _____
History _____
IT (Information Technology) _____

Maths _____
PE (Physical Education) _____

Physics _____
Science _____

Types of school
boys' school _____
college _____
film school _____
girls' school _____
kindergarten _____
mixed school _____
nursery school _____

playgroup _____
primary school _____
private school _____
secondary school _____
single-sex school _____

state school _____
stunt school _____
summer school _____
theatre school _____
higher education _____

university _____

Places at school
canteen _____
corridor _____
gym _____
hall _____
library _____
playground _____
Science lab _____

sports field _____
staff room _____

Classroom objects
coursebook _____
desk _____
IWB (interactive whiteboard) _____

(special) equipment _____

whiteboard _____

People at school
form teacher _____

head teacher _____
professor _____
pupil _____
teacher _____

School activities
acting _____
end-of-year sports competition _____

outdoor activities _____

sports team _____
studies _____
theatre group _____
trials _____
workshop _____

VOCABULARY BANK

Translate the words and phrases into your own language.

Verbs and phrases about school

be good at (foreign languages) _____

be late/early/on time for lessons _____

be late for school _____

borrow a book/CD/DVD from the library _____

cheat in exams _____

come to class _____
do a course _____
do experiments _____

do extra activities _____

do your homework _____
do tests _____
do well/badly in the exam/test _____

do sth useful _____

entrance exams _____
exchange _____
experimental _____
fail an exam _____
find out _____
finish school _____
focus on _____
get a good/bad mark (for sth) _____

get lost _____
get the most from sth _____

give a speech _____
good/bad grades/marks _____

go to university _____

have a meeting _____

improve (your skills) _____

in the breaks _____
last _____
learn (practical) skills _____

learn Spanish from a friend _____

learn to drive/make bread _____

leave school _____
lecture _____

life choices _____
life experience _____

miss school/classes _____

pass an exam _____
play sport _____
practical activities _____
retake an exam/a test _____

revise for an exam _____

rubbish at _____

run inside the school _____
start school _____

study a subject _____
study for a test _____
take lessons at a driving school _____

train to become (a vet) _____

use a tablet/mobile phone (in class/ during lessons) _____

use the Internet _____

wear a school uniform/an overall _____

Classroom language

alphabet _____
ask/answer questions _____

check _____
choose (the correct answer) _____

complete the table _____

discuss _____
listen to the dialogue _____

look at (the photos/the board) _____

look for information on the Internet _____

match (the words with opposite meanings) _____

noisy _____
put (the words) in the correct order _____

read the text _____
repeat _____
speak (in English) _____

subject _____

talk _____
teach children Spanish/teach Spanish to children _____

teach Spanish _____
teach sb about sth _____

think of sth _____
tick _____
underline _____
use a dictionary/pen/pencil _____

work in pairs/groups of three _____

write in your notebook _____

Work

Jobs
astronaut _____
accountant _____
actor/actress _____
architect _____
artist _____
au pair _____
author _____
builder _____
chef/cook _____
courier _____
dentist _____
doctor _____
engineer _____
factory worker _____
farmer _____
gardener _____
guide _____
hairdresser _____
journalist _____
lawyer _____
mechanic _____
nurse _____
photographer _____
plumber _____
receptionist _____

scientist _____
shop assistant _____

soldier _____
stunt performer _____
taxi driver _____
teacher _____
vet _____
waiter/waitress _____
zoologist _____

People at work

boss _____
co-worker _____
colleague _____
customer/client _____
guest _____
manager _____
patient _____
staff _____
worker _____

Workplaces

café _____
factory _____
hospital _____
hotel _____
office _____
supermarket _____

Types of jobs

full-time job _____
extra work _____
holiday job _____
office job _____
part-time job _____
physical work _____
weekend job _____

Job duties

build _____
do projects _____
duty _____
email sb / write/send an email to sb
_____
_____
explain _____
learn a skill / practical skills _____
_____
learn sth / about sth / to do sth
_____
look after a child/a pet _____
_____
make coffee _____
meet people _____
meeting _____
order _____
organise _____
phone _____
play with the kids _____
prepare sth/for sth _____
_____
quality _____
repair _____
sample _____
serve customers _____
service a car _____
sign _____
talk on the phone _____
_____
teach (sb) sth / (sb) about sth / sb to
do sth _____
_____

Working conditions and employment

abandon _____
driver's/driving licence _____
_____
finish work at (5 p.m.) _____
_____
gain experience _____
_____
get your first job _____
_____
have a job (in one's family's business)
_____
_____
interview people _____
_____
run (a bakery) _____
work (eight) hours a day _____
_____
work abroad _____
work alone/in a team _____
_____
work as (a programmer/a teacher)
_____
_____
work for (a company) _____
_____
work for money _____
_____
work from home _____
_____
work full-time/part-time _____
_____
_____
work in (a hospital/restaurant/
supermarket) _____
_____
_____
work in education/health _____
_____
work long hours _____
_____
work on a project/the details _____
_____
work outside _____
work well _____
work with people/children/adults _____
_____
work with numbers _____
_____
work with your hands _____
_____

Adjectives to describe work and jobs

badly-paid/well-paid (job) _____
_____
boring _____
demanding _____
difficult _____
easy _____
exciting _____
normal _____

Work and money

earn a good/high/low salary _____
_____
earn a lot of/some money as
(a waiter) _____
_____
earn enough to pay the rent/for my
studies _____
_____
earn (350 pounds) a week _____
_____
earn your living _____
make money _____
salary _____
support (your family) _____

Family and social life

Family

aunt _____
brother _____
child/children _____
cousin _____
father/dad _____
grandmother _____
grandfather _____
grandparents _____
husband _____
mother/mum _____
parents _____
sister _____
son _____
uncle _____
wife _____

Friends

best friend _____
friend _____

Relationships

do sb a favour _____
_____
fall in love _____
get married _____
_____
go on your first date _____

Everyday life

be busy (with sth) _____
_____
do the washing-up/wash the dishes
_____
_____
get dressed _____
get out of bed (in the morning)
_____
get pizza (from a pizzeria) _____
_____
go to bed (early) _____

VOCABULARY BANK

Translate the words and phrases into your own language.

have breakfast/lunch/dinner/supper
_____
_____

lie/sit on the sofa _____

learn about yourself/the world ____

run a vegetable garden _____

start _____
study _____
take the dog out (for a walk) _____

take/drive sb to school/to playgroup
_____

take care of _____
tidy your room _____
wake up/get up (first/early/late) __

wake up your (sister) _____

wash the car/the dishes _____

work in the garden/kitchen _____

Time expressions

always _____
at night _____
at noon/at midnight/at one o'clock
_____

at the weekend _____
every day/Saturday/weekend
_____

in the morning/afternoon/evening
_____
_____

never _____
often _____
on Friday afternoon/night _____

on Friday/Saturday _____
on Saturdays/Sundays

on Sunday mornings _____

on a typical weekday _____

sometimes _____
usually _____

Days of the week

Monday _____
Tuesday _____
Wednesday _____
Thursday _____
Friday _____
Saturday _____
Sunday _____

Free time

aquarium
build a rocket
challenge
collect wood for a fire _____

collect/fetch _____

demonstrate tricks _____

do jigsaw puzzles _____

do (stretching) exercises _____

do (yoga/karate/kung fu/Zumba®)
_____

dream of _____
drive around _____

driving lessons _____
go dancing
go for a coffee/a walk _____

go for a run/swim _____

go jogging _____
go on the Internet

go out (a lot/with friends) _____

go out for a meal _____

go rollerblading _____
go shopping/to the shops _____

go to a party/concert _____

**go to the park/cinema/shopping
centre/museums/the gym** _____
_____

go walking in the mountains ___

hang-gliding
hang out with friends _____

have a party
have fun/a good time _____

hike _____
hot-air balloon _____

identify stars _____
indoor skydiving _____
listen to music
lie down and rest _____

life event _____
make friends _____
move around

play a musical instrument _____

play the piano/guitar/drums ____

play chess/video games
_____

play sports _____
play together
post photos (on Facebook) _____

put (a model) together _____

read books/magazines/things __

on the Internet _____
on TV
on YouTube /Facebook

record videos _____
relax _____
social media _____

**spend time alone/with friends/with
family** _____

spend time at home/in my room

stay at home _____
take photographs/photos _____

talk about books/films/sports/people
_____

visit friends/my family _____

visit different places _____

vlog _____
**watch films/TV/videos/sports/TV
series** _____

zip wire _____

Parties
birthday party _____
bring-your-own party _____

fancy dress party _____

invite _____
post-exam party _____

Adjectives
awesome
awful _____
brilliant _____
good
great
terrible _____

Food

Fruit
banana _____
orange _____
strawberry _____

Vegetables
mushroom _____
onion _____
potato _____
tomato _____

Dairy
milk _____
(mozzarella) cheese _____
ice cream _____

Meat and fish
ham _____
tuna _____

Drinks
cola _____
juice _____
lemonade _____
(mineral) water _____

Other products
basil _____
bread _____
brownie _____
(dark/milk) chocolate _____

cornflakes _____
crisps _____
egg _____
flour _____
honey _____
ketchup _____
mayonnaise _____
oil _____
olive oil _____
pasta _____
pepper _____
rolls _____
salt _____
seafood _____
speciality _____

spicy food _____
street food _____

vanilla _____

Dishes
(cheese/egg and tuna) sandwich _____

hamburger/burger _____
noodles _____
omelette _____
pancake _____
pizza _____
salad _____

sauce _____
soup _____
spaghetti _____

Meals
dessert _____
dish _____
for breakfast/for dessert _____

snack _____
tea _____

Preparing food
boil (potatoes) _____
chop (fruit) _____
cook _____
fry (on both sides) _____

fry meat/an omelette _____

half-empty _____
heat _____
ingredients _____
make a snack _____
mix (eggs) _____
mixture _____
pan _____
prepare _____
put sth on top of sth _____

recipe _____
slice (cheese) _____
squash (tomatoes) _____

spoonful _____
take out (of the pan) _____

try _____

Containers
a bag of onions _____
a bag of potatoes _____

a bag of sugar _____
a bar of (chocolate) _____

a bottle of (ketchup) _____

a bottle of oil _____
a can of (lemonade) _____

a can of soup _____
a carton of eggs _____
a carton of (milk) _____
a carton of orange juice _____

a cup of (flour) _____
a jar of (honey) _____
a jar of mayonnaise _____
a jar of tomato sauce _____

a loaf of (bread) _____
a packet of butter _____
a packet of cocoa _____

a packet of cornflakes _____

a packet of crisps _____
a packet of flour _____
a packet of Parmesan _____

a packet of spaghetti _____

a tin of peas _____
a tin of (tuna) (BrE)/a can of (tuna) (AmE) _____
a tub of (ice cream) _____

Food adjectives
classic _____
delicious _____
fantastic _____
favourite _____
floating _____
fresh _____
grilled (salmon) _____
healthy _____
hot/spicy _____
local _____
per person _____
strong _____
traditional _____
typical _____
unhealthy _____
vegetarian (food) _____

yummy _____

Eating out
Anything else? _____
chef _____
cook _____
Enjoy your meal! _____
expensive _____
fast food _____
food festival _____
food stalls _____
get a takeaway _____

go out for a meal _____
Here you are. _____
large/small _____
menu _____
order _____
price _____
serve _____
waiter/waitress _____

Other
feed _____
have _____
hungry _____
taste _____
vegetarian _____

VOCABULARY BANK

Translate the words and phrases into your own language.

Shopping and services

Types of shops and services

bookshop
courier
postage
service
supermarket

Buying and selling

confirm
cost
customer
discount
enquire
expensive
free
open
opening times
shop assistant

Fashion

look
haircut
hairstyle
quality
trim
wear

Travelling and tourism

Forms of transport

air transport
coach
ferry
hot-air balloon
moped
motorbike/motorcycle
plane
ship
train
tram
underground/the Tube

Types of trips

activity holiday
adventure holiday

backpacking holiday

each holiday
camping holiday / camping trip

cycling trip
excursion
guided tour
package tour
trip abroad
working holiday

Planning a holiday

book a car
book a flight
book a holiday
book a hotel
book a room
book a seat on the train/bus

book a train/bus ticket

book an excursion

book my transport

book the accommodation

book online
brochure
experience

happen
have a booking
make the arrangements

make/change a reservation/
a booking

organiser
recommend
special/top offer

travel agency/travel agent's

Accommodation

bed and breakfast (B&B)

campsite
check in
guesthouse
(luxury/three-star) hotel

reception desk
space hotel
staff
stay in (a hotel)/at (a campsite)

youth hostel

On the journey

airport check-in desk

arrive
be on a plane

check in
destination
drive a car
engine
explore

family ticket
flight
fly in a plane
get into a car
get out of a car
get on the train/a bus

get off the train/a bus

get on a bike
get off a bike
go on holiday
go on a package tour

go on foot
go out of (the station)

highlights
make an announcement

monument
on the way back
on time
passenger
platform
population
realise a dream
ride a moped
road
street
take the metro
train station
travel/go by (train/plane/boat/ship/
bus/car/coach/ferry)

waiting room
wheels
window seat

Adjectives

fantastic
incredible
spectacular
unique

Holiday activities

at the camp
be active
campfire
climb
climbing
climbing partner
escape to the countryside

explore
go cycling/sailing

go hang-gliding/paragliding

go ice-skating/swimming/running

go kayaking

go mountain biking _____

go on holiday _____
go to/visit museums _____
guided tour _____
half way up _____
main square _____
make way _____
put up a tent _____
reach the peak / get to the top _____

relax (by the sea) _____

ride a camel/an elephant _____

rock climb/go climbing _____

scuba dive _____
see the sights _____
try different kinds of activities _____

visit a castle/local markets/museums/
tourist sights/a foreign country
_____

People on holiday
climber _____
guest _____
guide _____
hiker _____
owner _____
passenger _____
tourist _____

Places to visit
attraction _____
bazaar _____
beach _____
castle _____
desert _____
(elephant) sanctuary _____
island _____
local market _____
mountain _____
museum _____
rainforest _____
theatre _____
(top) tourist sights _____

town hall _____
World Heritage Site _____

Things to take on holiday
camera _____
case _____
guidebook _____
luggage _____
passport _____
sleeping bag _____
tent _____
ticket _____

Giving directions
along _____
between _____
close _____
get to ... _____
go across the road _____

next door _____
next to sth _____
on the corner _____
on your right/left _____

opposite _____
straight on _____
take the (second) turning on the
(left) _____

tell sb the way to ... _____

turn left/right into (High Street)
_____

walk past sth _____

Accidents
die _____
disaster _____

Culture

Art
artist _____
draw _____
paint _____

Music
band _____
dance class _____
sing _____
singer _____

Kinds of music
pop _____
rap _____
reggae _____
rock _____

Literature and film
actor/actress _____
audition _____

author/writer _____

comic _____
drama _____
fantasy _____
film/movie _____
film star _____
read a lot _____
science fiction _____
true life films _____
vampire stories _____

Sport

Sports
badminton _____
basketball _____
boxing _____
bungee jumping _____
cycling _____
diving _____
exercise _____
football _____
golf _____
hang-gliding _____
hockey _____
ice skating _____
karate _____
kayaking _____
kite-surfing _____
kung fu _____
Latin dance _____
long jump _____
rugby _____
running _____
sailing _____
skateboarding _____
skiing _____
ski jumping _____
squash _____
sumo _____
surfing _____
swimming _____
table tennis/Ping-Pong _____

team _____
tennis _____
triathlon _____
white water rafting _____

windsurfing _____
volleyball _____
yoga _____
Zumba® _____

Types of sport
individual sports _____

martial arts _____
summer sports _____
team sports/games _____

water sports _____
winter sports _____

Sports equipment
stretchy top _____
silver cup _____
towel _____

VOCABULARY BANK

Translate the words and phrases into your own language.

Doing sports

ancient ___
(aerobics/fitness/dance) instructor ___

challenge ___
chariot race ___
coach a football team ___

competition ___
complete ___
concentrate on ___
dance lessons ___
dance steps ___
finish line ___
first/second half ___

fitness centre ___
get fit ___
get a medal ___
goal line ___
join a class ___
join a gym ___
imitate ___
long-distance running ___

marathon ___
Olympic Games / Olympics ___

Olympic sport ___
Paralympics ___
play for a team/for your school ___

play (table) tennis/badminton/
basketball/hockey/football/volleyball ___

prize ___
run classes (for adults/children/all
age groups) ___

run fast ___
score (ten points/a goal) ___

speed ___
sports event ___
success story ___
succeed ___
swim ___
take part in (kung fu) competitions ___

take place ___
(tennis) match ___
throw ___
train ___
training video ___

win (a prize) ___
win a gold/silver/bronze medal ___

win a competition ___

workout ___
would love ___
yell ___

Places to do sport

gym ___
swimming pool ___

People in sport

athlete ___
basketball player ___
champion ___
competitor ___
cyclist ___
footballer/football player ___

gymnast ___
instructor ___
long-distance runner ___

professional sportsperson ___

runner ___
sailor ___
skier ___

swimmer ___

Health

Parts of the body

big/green/round/tired eyes ___

brain ___
ear ___
heart ___
lungs ___
flat/narrow/wide/straight/thin nose ___

tongue ___

Illnesses and treatment

be sick ___
break an arm/leg ___
breathe ___
dentist ___
disabled ___
doctor ___
health problem ___
hurt ___
neurological problems ___

nurse ___
painful ___
patient ___

Healthy lifestyle

do (stretching) exercise(s) ___

get enough sleep ___
go to the gym ___
keep fit ___
relax ___
rest ___
go walking ___

Science and technology

Electronic equipment

CD player ___
digital camera ___
e-book reader ___
gadget ___
games console ___
headphones ___
laptop ___
memory stick ___
mobile phone ___
MP3 player ___
smartphone ___
tablet ___

Computers

type ___

Technology

do experiments ___
exist ___
hoax ___
intelligence ___
inventor ___
International Space Station ___

meet scientists ___
scientist ___
solve problems ___
structure ___
use strategies ___
use tools ___

The natural world

Seasons

spring ___
summer ___
autumn (BrE)/fall (AmE) ___
winter ___

Months

January ___
February ___
March ___
April ___
May ___
June ___
July ___
August ___
September ___
October ___
November ___
December ___

Weather

bring rain ___
clear ___
clear sky ___
cloud ___
cloudy ___

cold _____
degree _____
dry _____
expect _____
fog _____
foggy _____
hot _____
rise _____
rain _____
rainy _____
shower _____
snow _____
sun _____
sunny _____
sunshine _____
temperature _____
thunder and lightning _____

warm _____
weather forecast _____
wet _____
wind _____
windy _____

Animals

bear _____
beaver _____
bill _____
cheetah _____
cow _____
creature _____
crocodile _____
deer _____
dolphin _____
evolution _____
evolve _____
fish _____
(forest) elephant _____
fur _____
Highland pony _____

lay eggs _____
lion _____
octopus _____
(polar) bear _____
poison _____
poisonous _____
platypus _____
pronghorn _____
run away/escape from _____

(sea) bird _____
scare away _____
shark _____
sting _____
tail _____
tiger _____
whale _____

Plants

cereal _____

Landscape

beach _____
continent _____
desert _____
island _____
jungle _____
lake _____
mountain _____
ocean _____
prairie _____
river _____
sea _____
surroundings _____
strait _____
(tropical) forest _____
waterfall/falls _____

Location

area _____
high up _____
north/south/east/west _____

northern/southern/eastern/western
_____
_____

Environmental protection

air/water pollution _____

climate change _____
danger _____
dangerous _____
destroy _____
die out _____
disappear _____
disaster _____
global warming _____
good/bad for the environment _____
_____

green _____
grow _____
habitat _____
hunt _____
melt _____
(nuclear) energy _____
plant trees _____
pollute the air/water _____

power station/power plant _____

predict _____
produce CO_2 _____

protect the (natural) environment
_____
_____

(radioactive/toxic) waste _____

recycled _____
recycling _____
safe _____

save energy/water _____

sea ice _____
sort rubbish _____
throw away _____
turn off the water tap _____
_____

turn on/off the light/electrical
devices _____
_____

use public transport _____

waste energy/water _____

waste recycling _____
wildlife _____
wind farm _____

Adjectives describing wonders of nature

amazing/incredible _____
unusual _____
wild _____

society _____

State and society

The state

agriculture _____
attack _____
attacker _____
education _____
education centre _____
_____

emblem _____
foreign _____
government _____
Peace Corps _____
soldier _____
vote in an election _____

Charity

charity _____
government programme _____

promote peace and friendship _____
_____

raise money _____

send volunteers to work _____
_____

support _____
voluntary work _____
volunteer _____

Culture of English-Speaking Countries

A-levels/Advanced Level (end of school exams) final exams at the end of secondary school in the UK

Australia the smallest of the seven continents and the sixth largest country in the world

BBC (the British Broadcasting Corporation) the main British public radio and television broadcaster

Bloom, Orlando a British actor; he is famous for playing Legolas in the *Lord of the Rings* film trilogy and Will Turner in the *Pirates of the Caribbean* film series

Broberg, Skye a female performer from New Zealand; she is thought to have the most flexible body in the world

Cake Off a baking competition which takes place during the Great British Food Festival

Canada the second largest country in the world

Cheshire Food Festival a two-day food festival which takes place in Arley Hall & Gardens in Northwich in the UK every year in September

Cornwall a county located in south-western England

Edinburgh the capital of Scotland

Eminem a popular American rapper, actor and film producer

England the biggest country in the United Kingdom of Great Britain and Northern Ireland

Facebook a social networking site created in the USA in 2004 by Mark Zuckerberg

Fanning, Dakota and Elle sisters and popular American actresses

fish and chips a popular British dish

Freeman, Martin a British actor; he is famous for playing Bilbo Baggins in the *Hobbit* film series; he won a BAFTA award for the best supporting actor and is also well known for playing Doctor Watson in the *Sherlock* film series

Garfield, Andrew an actor famous for his role in the *Amazing Spider-Man*

GCSE Exams (General Certificate of Secondary Education) exams at the end of Year 11 of school education in England, Wales and Northern Ireland; students need to take them to continue studying for two more years in the Sixth Form and to prepare for A-level exams

Halloween a special tradition of remembering dead people celebrated in many countries, especially in English-speaking ones on 31st October

Harry Potter a series of very popular fantasy novels about the adventures of a young wizard, Harry Potter, written by J. K. Rowling

Ireland an island in the North Atlantic; it is divided into the independent Republic of Ireland and Northern Ireland which is part of the UK

Jerome K. Jerome an English writer and playwright; he is best known for his humorous novel *Three Men in a Boat* (*To Say Nothing of the Dog*)

Jones, Norah Geetali Norah Jones Shankar is an American singer and eight-time Grammy winner (an award presented for achievements in the music industry)

Jordan, Michael an American basketball player, a six-time NBA champion, the winner of two gold Olympic medals; he has been honoured in the Naismith Memorial Basketball Hall of Fame

Just the Way You Are Bruno Mars' hit song from his debut album The Doo-Wops & Hooligans

Lawrence, Jennifer an American actress; she received an Oscar for her role in *Silver Linings Playbook*

Leeds a town in northern England

Little Folk a Welsh music band

Loch Lomond Food and Drink Festival a food festival which takes place near Glasgow by the Loch Lomond lake

London the capital of England and the United Kingdom

London Marathon a marathon which, because of its sponsor, is now called Virgin Money London Marathon; it has been organised every year since 1981

MacArthur, Ellen a British female sailor; she set a new world record for the fastest solo sailing journey around the world

Meyer, Stephenie an American writer; she is famous for the fantasy novels *The Twilight Saga*

Miami a city in Florida in the USA, located on the coast of the Atlantic Ocean

mile a unit of measurement in many English-speaking countries which is the equivalent of 1,609.344 metres

Natural History Museum in London one of the museums in London where it is possible to see a blue whale skeleton (25.5 metres long!)

New Year's Day 1st January, the first day of the new year

New Zealand a country located on two islands in the south-western Pacific Ocean

Niagara Falls a famous waterfall on the Niagara River, located on the border between the USA and Canada

Northern Ireland the northern region of the island where the Republic of Ireland is located; it belongs to the United Kingdom of Great Britain and Northern Ireland

Oxford a town in southern England located by the River Thames which is the home of the University of Oxford, the oldest university in the English-speaking world

Peace Corps a programme for American volunteers which was created to help developing countries; it is run by the American government

Phelps, Michael an American swimmer, 23-time Olympic champion, 26-time world champion; he won 8 gold medals during the Olympic Games in Beijing in China in 2008

pence British money is called pounds (£); there are 100 pence in £1

Perry, Katy   an American pop singer and a UNICEF Goodwill Ambassador

Portman, Natalie   a popular American film actress; she received an Oscar for her role in the *Black Swan* film

pound   the money used in Great Britain

Pratchett, Terry   a British fantasy and science fiction writer; he is best known for the Discworld series of novels

Princess Elizabeth Windsor   the title Princess Elizabeth had before she became Queen Elizabeth II

Queen Elizabeth II   the head of the British royal family; she has been the Queen of the United Kingdom since 1953

Radcliffe, Daniel   a British actor; he is best known for playing the title role of a young wizard in the *Harry Potter* film series

Scotland   a country located to the north of England; it is part of the United Kingdom of Great Britain and Northern Ireland

Scottish Highlands   a mountainous region located in northern Scotland

Senior Space School UK   a summer school for students who are interested in space and are preparing for their A-level exams; it is run by the University of Leicester

Spider-Man   a fictitious superhero appearing in a comic series published by Marvel and in many films

Starbucks (Starbucks Corporation)   the biggest chain of American coffee shops in the world

Sydney   the largest city in Australia

Shakespeare, William (1564–1616)   English playwright, poet and actor; he wrote plays such as *Hamlet*, *Macbeth*, *Romeo and Juliet* and *A Midsummer Night's Dream*

Stewart, Kristen   an American actress; she is best known for playing Bella Swan in the *Twilight Saga* film series

Stoeberl, Nick   the host of Tongue Show on YouTube; he is also called 'the lick' because he has the longest tongue in the world (10.1 cm)

The Colour of Magic   Terry Pratchett's first novel in the Discworld series

the UK (the United Kingdom)   the United Kingdom of Great Britain and Northern Ireland

the Thames   the main river in southern England; it flows through London

The Twilight Saga   a series of American fantasy novels by Stephenie Meyer; it describes the adventures of Bella Swan and a family of vampires

The Great British Food Festival   a series of food events in the UK; they take place in several places at weekends between May and September; the event is free for those who decide to take part in the Cake Off baking competition

The Hobbit   a fantasy film trilogy based on the novel by J. R. R. Tolkien

The Science Museum   a museum in London

Three Men In A Boat: To Say Nothing Of The Dog   a humorous novel written in 1889 by Jerome K. Jerome; it is about three men on a boat trip along the River Thames

the USA   the United States of America

Valentine's Day   14th February is the day which celebrates love and people who are in love

Wales   a country located to the west of England; it is part of the United Kingdom of Great Britain and Northern Ireland

Walton Hall   a 16th-century country house in Warrington, Cheshire, England; the house is on a special list of very important old buildings

YouTube   a video-sharing platform on the Internet

PEOPLE

1 Complete the text with the correct words. The first letters are given.

> ## We are family
> ### – but are we the same?
>
> When there is more than one child in a family, everyone starts looking for similarities and differences between them. For example, my two cousins (my aunt's daughters) are not similar in looks. Jo (17) is short, but her sister Anna (18) is really _tall_. Jo's hair is curly, but Anna's is ¹s_____ . Jo is well-built, but her sister is ²t_____ . Their styles are different too! Anna loves smart clothes (especially elegant dresses), while Jo prefers ³c_____ clothes: jeans and T-shirts. The girls look different, but they have similar personalities. They are both ⁴e_____ – they love sport and being active. They are really ⁵s_____ too, and spend a lot of time with their friends. And they are definitely the most ⁶c_____ young people I know – they are never afraid of new situations. The two sisters understand each other really well. They show us that looks don't bring people close, but personality does.

2 Choose three words or expressions from the box for each category.

> adult   Australian   be crazy about   can't stand   bald   enjoy   generous   hat   medium-length   middle-aged   pretty   Portuguese   ~~scarf~~   tall   sense of humour   serious   sunglasses   Swiss   tie   teenager   tracksuit   watch   wavy   well-built

Accessories: _scarf_ , _____ , _____

Age: _____ , _____ , _____

Appearance: _____ , _____ , _____

Clothes: _____ , _____ , _____

Hair: _____ , _____ , _____

Nationalities: _____ , _____ , _____

Likes and dislikes: _____ , _____ , _____

Personality: _____ , _____ , _____

3 Put the words in logical order.

☐1 baby   ☐3 adult   ☐2 child

1 ☐ wavy   ☐ straight   ☐ curly
2 ☐ black   ☐ fair   ☐ brown
3 ☐ middle-aged   ☐ young   ☐ old
4 ☐ long   ☐ short   ☐ medium-length
5 ☐ broken-hearted   ☐ happy   ☐ relaxed

HOME

1 Look at the picture. Read the description and correct five mistakes.

The biggest room in our house is the ~~kitchen~~. When we were young, we rode our bicycles in there. But now there is too much furniture. In the room, there is a cooker and a mirror on the wall. There is a small table behind the sofa. Our mum always puts some beautiful flowers there. There is a big wardrobe next to the table. There are two beds opposite the sofa. Our cats often sleep on them.

living room

1 _____   2 _____   4 _____
            3 _____   5 _____

2 Choose the odd one out.

armchair   beanbag   (lamp)   chair

1 behind   wardrobe   chair   table
2 city   sink   town   village
3 dishwasher   cooker   fridge   beanbag
4 between   over   neighbour   under
5 bedroom   shower   kitchen   bathroom
6 flat   roof   wall   window

3 Complete the diagram with the words from the box.

> armchair   bed   cupboard   shower
> sink   ~~sofa~~   toilet   wardrobe

HOUSE ⋯⋯ living room ⋯⋯⋯ _sofa_
                                    _____
      ⋯ bedroom ⋯⋯⋯ _____
                                    _____
      ⋯ bathroom ⋯⋯⋯ _____
                                    _____
      ⋯ kitchen ⋯⋯⋯ _____

SCHOOL

1 Complete the quiz with the missing words. The first letters are given. Then answer the questions. Count the symbols and read the solution.

What kind of student are you?

1 Tomorrow you are going to take an important exam.
- **a** You s<u>tudy</u> a lot. ■
- **b** You don't do anything because you are sure you will p_____ it. ★
- **c** You don't do anything because you are sure you will f_____ it (or you simply forget about it). ◆

2 In primary school
- **a** you always did your h_____ . ■
- **b** you were always l_____ for school. ◆
- **c** you couldn't t_____ because you were bored. ★

3 What do you like best?
- **a** School e_____ a_____ – a theatre group or a sports club. ◆
- **b** Taking exams and getting good m_____ – you are the happiest when you get an A! ■
- **c** Finding solutions to d_____ problems. ★

4 You think
- **a** you will l_____ school as soon as possible because it is a waste of time. ★
- **b** you will go to u_____ . ■
- **c** s_____ school is enough to be successful. ◆

5 You
- **a** never p_____ a_____ in lessons – they are so boring. ★
- **b** l_____ to teachers and take notes. ◆
- **c** always do your b_____ ! ■

Which symbol appears most often in your answers?

- ■ You are a typical 'A' student. Your notebooks are well organised and you get good marks. But don't forget about your friends and hobbies!

- ◆ You like school because your friends also go there. Sometimes you think lessons aren't very interesting. Remember that you can do well if you are doing something creative!

- ★ Good news! You might be a genius! You are so intelligent that you get bored at school. But remember that even a genius must have a basic education!

2 Look at the extracts of textbooks from different subjects. Write the names of the subjects.

Ethanol: C_2H_5OH is a substance which contains an OH group …
<u>Chemistry</u>

1 Sharks and salmon are fish.
_____

2 We use the Past Simple to talk about actions and states in a finished period of time. _____

3 A triangle is a geometric figure with three sides and three angles, which can be the same or different. _____

4 Christopher Columbus discovered America in 1492.
_____

5 The second driest area in the world is the Atacama Desert in Northern Chile.
_____

6 Use your mouse to click on the 'new folder' button.
_____

WORK

1 Look at the pictures. Guess which people need these objects for their work. The first letters are given.

j<u>ournalist</u>

1 h_____
2 b_____
3 n_____
4 p_____
5 d_____

6 a_____
7 s_____
8 s_____
9 g_____
10 p_____

2 Complete the email with the phrases from the box.

answer phones   earn a high salary   fill in forms
gain experience   learn some practical skills
meet people   speak English   work full time
~~working as~~   work long hours   work abroad

Dear Sarah,
How are you doing?

I'm <u>working as</u> a receptionist in a big hotel in Barcelona.
Receptionists have to ¹_____ and they
often ²_____ at work. Before I got the
job, I had to ³_____ , so I worked in
a small hotel in my town to ⁴_____ .
My job isn't always easy. I ⁵_____ .
I usually ⁶_____ and I sometimes finish
work at 6.00 in the morning. I don't ⁷_____
but I like my job very much. I ⁸_____
every day and ask them to ⁹_____ .
I'd like to ¹⁰_____ one day, perhaps in
a holiday resort in England or Ireland.
Write back soon.
Love,
Beatriz

FAMILY AND SOCIAL LIFE

1 Put the words and expressions in the logical or most typical order.

| ③ in the evening | ① in the morning |
| ④ at night | ② in the afternoon |

1 ☐ be late for work   ☐ get ready for work
   ☐ go back home   ☐ have lunch

2 ☐ get married   ☐ fall in love
   ☐ go on your first date ☐ have a baby

3 ☐ grandmother   ☐ child
   ☐ teenager   ☐ husband

4 ☐ on Monday mornings ☐ on a typical weekend
   ☐ on Tuesdays   ☐ on Friday night

5 ☐ have a shower   ☐ have breakfast
   ☐ drive your children ☐ wake up
      to school

2 Complete the diagrams with the words from the box.

a bath   a good time   a musical instrument
a teenager   busy   ~~chess~~   computer games
homework   late for school   out with friends
the dishes   shopping   somebody a favour
supper   to bed

1 play ······ <u>chess</u>
              _____

2 do ······ _____
              _____
              _____

3 go ······ _____
              _____
              _____

4 be ······ _____
              _____
              _____

5 have ······ _____
              _____

FOOD

1 **Match words 1–8 with a–h to make phrases. Sometimes more than one answer is possible.**

a cup of	(i)	a	potatoes
1 a packet of	⃝	b	tuna
2 a loaf of	⃝	c	honey
3 a jar of	⃝	d	milk
4 a bar of	⃝	e	chocolate
5 a tin of	⃝	f	ketchup
6 a bottle of	⃝	g	bread
7 a bag of	⃝	h	crisps
8 a carton of	⃝	i	tea

2 **Choose the correct word.**

Simple recipes/menus

True ITALIAN STYLE Spaghetti

Ingredients:

- 3 large (tomatoes) / strawberries
- some meat
- some olive ¹*flour / oil*
- ²*pasta / seafood*
- mozzarella cheese
- ³*basil / honey*

Preparation:

⁴*Heat / Chop* some oil in a pan and ⁵*fry / try* the meat.
⁶*Eat / Chop* the tomatoes and ⁷*mix / boil* them with the meat.
⁸*Boil / Heat* the pasta until it's 'al dente'.
⁹*Put / Mix* the meat and tomatoes on the pasta.
¹⁰*Add / Taste* some mozzarella cheese on top.
¹¹*Boil / Serve* with basil.

¹²*Enjoy / Slice* your meal!

SHOPPING AND SERVICES

1 **Complete the table with the words from the box.**

> casual   wear   opening times   discount
> shop assistant   smart dresser   style
> supermarket   service

Shopping	Fashion
	wear

2 **Complete the sentences. The first letters are given.**

Most supermarkets **o**_pen_ at 8.00 in the morning.

1 Good **q**_____ products are expensive.
2 Some shops **c**_____ at 6.00 p.m.
It's much too early for me.
3 When you go shopping, you pay at
the **c**_____ .
4 It's a good idea to **t**_____ your shoes
o_____ before you buy them.
5 Your shopping costs less if you get a **d**_____ .

3 **Match words 1–4 with a–e to make compound nouns. Then use them to complete the email below.**

opening	(e)	
1 shopping	⃝	
2 casual	⃝	
3 smart	⃝	
4 extra large	⃝	

a dresser
b clothes
c size
d basket
e times

● ● ●   New Email

Hi Sandra,

Would you like to go shopping for clothes with me?
I'm not exactly a _smart dresser_ so we could go to
a hypermarket. Their ¹_____ are:
Saturday 9.00 a.m. to 9.00 p.m. and Sunday 10.00 a.m.
to 4.00 p.m. Are you free at 5.00 on Saturday?
It won't take us long. We won't even need
a ²_____ . I just want to buy a casual
sweater and a pair of jeans. You know I love
³_____ and I always get ⁴_____ .

I hope you can come.
Anna

VOCABULARY BANK

TRAVELLING AND TOURISM

1 Complete the postcards with the words from the boxes.

> coach guide guidebook
> interesting seats stay

Dear Tom,

It's lovely here in Italy! We were in Venice on Tuesday, then Florence and today we'll be in Rome. We always <u>stay</u> in very good hotels, but there's
a lot of travelling. The **1**_____ is air-conditioned but the **2**_____ are not very comfortable.
Our **3**_____ is very nice and tells wonderful stories. We've seen a lot of **4**_____ places that I didn't read about in my **5**_____ !

Love,
Granny

Tom Jones
14, Park Lane
London WV1V3gJ
United Kingdom

> bag campsite clothes
> hostel island tent

Hi Tom!

The **1**_____ is beautiful – there's an old, dark forest and a wide stream with clear, mountain water. But probably it's not going to be the holiday of my dreams! The **2**_____ where we are staying is ugly. Today it's cold and it's raining all the time, and we're sitting in our wet **3**_____ . My sleeping **4**_____ is wet too and yesterday somebody stole my **5**_____ , so I think I'll catch a cold if we don't find a youth **6**_____ tomorrow. I hope you are not so unlucky ...

See you soon.
David

Tom Jones
14, Park Lane
London WV1V3gJ
United Kingdom

2 Choose the correct answers A–C.

Which of these <u>don't</u> you find at the airport?
A A check-in desk.   B A plane.
Ⓒ A ferry.

1 You can't go cycling
A on water.   B around Europe.
C in the mountains.

2 You practise kayaking
A in the mountains.   B on water.
C in a museum.

3 What do you do when you are a hitchhiker?
A You drive your own car.   B You travel by coach.
C You get free transport
  from other drivers.

4 You can't spend the night at a
A campsite.   B youth hostel.
C reception desk.

CULTURE

1 Put a tick (✓) by the true sentences and a cross (x) by the false ones. Correct the false information.

A guitar is a musical instrument. ☑

The news is a type of book. ☒
It is a type of TV programme.

1 Actors often take part in auditions. ☐

2 Reggae is a type of film. ☐

3 Fantasy is a type of true life film. ☐

4 Writers draw pictures. ☐

5 Singers often have fantastic voices. ☐

6 Film stars play musical instruments. ☐

7 There are lots of pictures in a comic. ☐

8 You can read the drums. ☐

2 Match nouns 1–5 with phrases a–e.

A film star   [f]   a paints pictures.
1 A singer   ☐   b works for a newspaper or television.
2 A musician   ☐   c takes pictures.
3 A journalist   ☐   d plays an instrument.
4 An artist   ☐   e has a fantastic voice.
5 A photographer   ☐   f is a famous actor or actress.

3 For every noun, choose two verbs from the box.

> draw paint play practise ~~read~~ write

read, _____   vampire stories
_____   the violin
_____   a picture
_____

SPORT

1 Match sports equipment b–d to the appropriate group. Then write the correct names of sports in each group. The first letters are given.

b _aseball_   [a]
- Babe Ruth
- Hank Aaron
- Satchel Page

1 h _ _ _ _ _ _   ◯
- Wayne Gretzky
- Sergei Fedorov
- Alex Ovechkin

2 f _ _ _ _ _ _ _ _   ◯
- Robert Lewandowski
- Pele
- Lionel Messi

3 t _ _ _ _ _ _   ◯
- Novak Djoković
- Roger Federer
- Rafael Nadal

2 Match words 1–5 with a–e.

ride	[f]	a	a goal
1 coach	◯	b	for a team
2 take part	◯	c	fit
3 score	◯	d	a football team
4 get	◯	e	in competitions
5 play	◯	f	a bike

3 Use the words from the box to complete the diagram.

> a bronze medal   a gym   a prize
> a sports centre   a stadium   badminton
> gold   golf   jogging   karate   martial arts
> skiing   swimming   ~~volleyball~~   yoga

play .... _volleyball_ _____

1 go .... _____
_____
_____

2 win .... _____
_____
_____

3 do .... _____
_____
_____

4 go to .... _____
_____
_____

HEALTH

1 Label the picture with parts of the body.

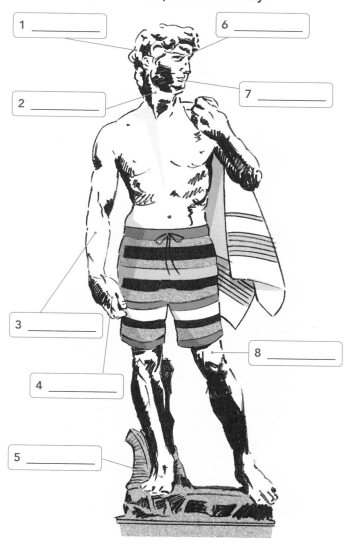

1 _____
2 _____
3 _____
4 _____
5 _____
6 _____
7 _____
8 _____

2 Complete the text with missing words. The first letters are given.

> ### HOW TO HAVE A HEALTHY LIFESTYLE
>
> - Do some **e**_xercise_ after you get up in the morning.
> - Have **1b**_____ before you go to school or work.
> - Spend a lot of time **2o**_____ even when it's cold.
> - Try to **3k**_____ **f**_____ and go to the **4g**_____ twice a week.
> - Get **5e**_____ sleep.
>
> **I hope you'll 6f**_____ **good!**

SCIENCE AND TECHNOLOGY

1 Match words 1–5 with a–e to form names of electronic equipment. Then match them to pictures B–F.

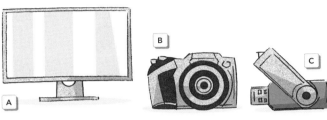

4K	a	player	☐
1 computer	b	stick	☐
2 CD	c	camera	☐
3 digital	d	phone	☐
4 memory	e	game	☐
5 mobile	f	TV	Ⓐ

2 Choose the correct answers A–C.

You use a digital camera
- Ⓐ to take photos.
- B to do photos.
- C to make photos.

1 When you download something to your computer, you
- A move it from your PC to a computer network.
- B print it out.
- C move it from a network to your PC.

2 Marie Curie was a famous
- A writer.
- B scientist.
- C artist.

3 Which of these can't a smartphone do?
- A Download information.
- B Make a film.
- C Cook dinner.

4 Which of these isn't a person?
- A A scientist.
- B A robot.
- C An inventor.

5 Which of these doesn't play music?
- A A memory stick.
- B A tablet.
- C A CD player.

6 Which of these isn't given as a present?
- A A computer game.
- B A tablet.
- C A website.

THE NATURAL WORLD

1 Complete the text with the words and phrases from the box.

> destroy   ~~is in danger~~   plant new trees
> pollute the environment   save animals
> sort rubbish

ECO-FRIENDS

The Earth _is in danger_ !
We must do something!
Big factories ¹_____ !
If we don't do something, the air will be so dirty that we will not be able to breathe!
People ²_____ rainforests!
If we don't stop them, we will live in a world without animals and plants.
Our organisation helps to ³_____ , such as tigers and whales.
We ⁴_____ and produce new materials such as paper and glass.
We also ⁵_____ so that we can save the forests.

BE ECO-FRIENDLY! JOIN US!
The world depends on your decision!

2 Match words 1–10 with a–k to form phrases.

sort	Ⓚ	a	park
1 nuclear	☐	b	station
2 tropical	☐	c	out
3 produce	☐	d	energy
4 national	☐	e	CO₂
5 climate	☐	f	rainforest
6 die	☐	g	transport
7 global	☐	h	change
8 weather	☐	i	warming
9 public	☐	j	forecast
10 power	☐	k	rubbish

STATE AND SOCIETY

1 Match words 1–5 with a–e to make phrases.

Peace   *f*

1 promote
2 government
3 voluntary
4 non-profit
5 poor

a programme
b organisation
c countries
d peace
e work
f Corps

2 Complete the text with the phrases from Exercise 1.

American Peace Corps

President John F. Kennedy started the *Peace Corps* in 1961. His idea was to [1]_____ _____ and friendship between the USA and [2]_____ _____ around the world. The Peace Corps is a [3]_____ _____ . It means Americans go to Africa or Asia for two years and do some [4]_____ _____ . They are not paid but many of them say that taking part in this [5]_____ _____ was the best experience of their lives.

3 Complete the sentences. The first letters are given.

Governments should support **a**_griculture_.
There are too many hungry people in the world.

1 You can't **v**_____ in an election if you are under 18.
2 UNICEF is a **c**_____ which protects children's rights worldwide.
3 Thousands of volunteers **r**_____ money for the RSPCA (Royal Society for the Prevention of Cruelty to Animals).
4 I want to live in the country and **g**_____ my own vegetables.
5 **E**_____ is very important so we need good schools.

CULTURE OF ENGLISH-SPEAKING COUNTRIES

1 Read the information and do the crossword. What's the hidden word?

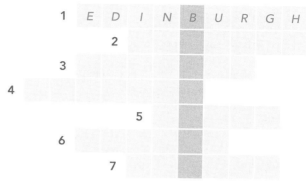

1 E D I N B U R G H

1 the capital of Scotland
2 the capital of Wales
3 the official language in Australia
4 the capital of Northern Ireland
5 one of the four parts of the United Kingdom
6 the capital of Ireland
7 the capital of the United Kingdom

2 Choose the odd one out.

	A	B	C	D
	Lady Gaga	Eminem	Spider-Man (C)	Magic Johnson
1	James Dean	Emma Watson	Johnny Depp	Jennifer Lawrence
2	Leeds	the USA	Australia	Canada
3	the Thames	Scottish Highlands	Cornwall	Niagara Falls
4	Peace Corps	Twitter	YouTube	Google Maps
5	New Year's Day	A-levels	Halloween	Valentine's Day
6	Denali National Park	Alaska	San Francisco	the Farne Islands
7	Kristen Stewart	Stephenie Meyer	Terry Pratchet	William Shakespeare

3 Match names 1–9 with descriptions a–i.

Dublin   *j*

1 Alaska
2 pounds
3 William Shakespeare
4 Kristen Stewart
5 Johnny Depp
6 fish and chips
7 CNN
8 Magic Johnson
9 the Thames

a an actor
b British money
c a writer
d an actress
e a river
f a TV channel
g a sportsperson
h British food
i a state in the USA
j a capital city

1.2 Present Simple

1 Complete the sentences with the correct form of the verbs from the box. Use the Present Simple.

be   drink   have   listen   not drive   not go
practise   say   sleep   study   wake up

1 'What time _____ (she) on weekdays?'
   'At 6 a.m. She gets up and _____
   the guitar before she goes to school.'
2 Ed _____ Spanish and German at school.
3 Sonia _____ to music every day.
4 We _____ to school on Saturday.
5 Edward is a quiet baby. He always _____ all night long.
6 Grannie _____ love is very important.
7 '_____ (you) a lot of tea?' 'Yes, I do.'
8 'What _____ (they) for breakfast?'
   'Milk and cereal.'
9 She _____ jealous when she sees her boyfriend with other girls.
10 My parents _____ me to school every morning.

1.5 Present Simple: *Yes/No* and *Wh-* questions

2 Match questions 1–6 with answers a–f.

1 Does Tim go out a lot every weekend?
2 Are you and your cousin from the USA?
3 What time do you usually get up?
4 Do you often wash the dishes?
5 How many hours does your dad spend on his computer every day?
6 Who is your best friend?

a About six on weekdays and about two at the weekend.
b Yes, I do. I really like it.
c At about 7 a.m.
d No, he doesn't. He often stays at home.
e Yes, we are. Sarah's from Florida and I'm from Kentucky.
f Tim – I think he's awesome!

3 Complete the sentences using *do, does, am, is, are, have got, has got.*

1 What _____ the children want for their birthday?
2 _____ Sue _____ a new dress for the party?
3 When _____ your sister's birthday?
4 A: Where _____ you come from?
    B: I _____ from Glasgow.
5 _____ Mr and Mrs Simpson _____ a Labrador?
6 _____ your brother like the sea?
7 A _____ you hungry?
    B: Yes, I _____ .
8 Excuse me, how _____ that leather jacket?

4 Read the text and choose the correct option.

How important [1]*are friends and family* / *friends and family are*?
Both family and friends play important roles in our [2]*lives* / *lifes*. You [3]*can* / *can't* live without a family or without friends. Why? Because [4]*children* / *child* need family to live and grow. Parents and family form a [5]*child's* / *childs'* first relationships. Friends are important too. Friends are [6]*their* / *our* family outside the closed walls of home. [7]*These* / *This* people make life more fun. So [8]*try to* / *to try* spend a lot of time with your family and friends.

5 Put the words in the correct order to make questions.

1 are / you / both / how
   _____
   _____ ?

2 you / know / how / about / Maria / do / much
   _____
   _____ ?

3 middle name / what / your / is
   _____
   _____ ?

4 you / like / do / English food
   _____
   _____ ?

5 help / sister / in / does / your / garden / the
   _____
   _____ ?

6 singer / who / Adam's / is / favourite
   _____
   _____ ?

7 go out / often / you / together / do
   _____
   _____ ?

8 cousins / how / got / you / many / have
   _____
   _____ ?

6 Complete the sentences with one word in each gap.

1 _____ are five people in the room.
2 _____ is your birthday?
3 This is Maria. _____ favourite singer is Ed Sheeran.
4 _____ tell Jo about the party. It's a surprise for her.
5 A: Can you dance?
   B: No, I _____ .
6 I _____ the guitar really well.
7 A: _____ she play any instruments?
   B: No, she doesn't.
8 He _____ TV on Friday evenings.

2.2 Countable and uncountable nouns; *some* and *any*; *much*, *many* and *a lot of*

1 Match 1–8 with a–h to form sentences.

1 When Joe comes over to my house,
2 There aren't
3 How many tomatoes
4 I know a place
5 The bread my mother makes
6 There are a lot of
7 There is a lot of
8 Have we got any

a with the best food in town.
b milk in the fridge?
c is delicious.
d wind in this area.
e any apples at home.
f he always brings some cakes with him.
g are there?
h windows in our classroom.

2 Find the mistake and correct the sentences.

1 Her parents' furniture are antique.
_____

2 We don't have some strawberries.
_____

3 How many sugar do you need?
_____

4 I need some informations about uncountable nouns.
_____

5 We do a hour of work every day.
_____

2.5 Articles

3 Choose the correct option.

Do you have ¹*many / much / a* time to spend on ²*the / a / –* dinner? Is the answer 'no'? Try these speedy recipes that take just 15 minutes.

Chicken, courgettes, and ham.

³*The / A / –* chicken cooks in ⁴*an / – / the* oven while you fry the ham and the courgettes in a pan.

Easy bruschetta recipe.

Just mix ⁵*some / any / a* ingredients together to make the perfect salad to your taste.
Toast the baguette slices, rub them with garlic, and top them with ⁶*much / any / the* salad dressed in a balsamic vinaigrette.

⁷In *the / a / –* Tahiti people speak ⁸*a / – / the* French.

⁹*The / A / –* President of the United States lives in ¹⁰*a / the / –* White House.

4 Complete the sentences with the words and phrases from the box.

> a lot of   any   aren't   do   does   doesn't
> haven't   many   much   never   often

1 There _____ many Italian restaurants in this part of the town.
2 Megan usually takes _____ photographs when she is on holiday.
3 How _____ money does it cost?
4 How _____ candles are on that birthday cake?
5 How _____ does he go to the cinema?
6 We _____ got much time left.
7 _____ you usually put much sugar in your coffee?
8 She's a vegetarian. She _____ eats meat.
9 _____ she eat _____ fish?
10 Most kids like milk, but Joe _____ .

5 Read the answers and complete the questions.

1 _____ pasta do you want?
Not much, thanks. I don't like pasta.
2 _____ spoons of sugar do you want?
Only two spoons of sugar, please.
3 _____ do you go skiing?
We go skiing only twice a year.
4 _____ he work?
He works in a take-away restaurant.
5 What _____ weekend?
He usually stays at home at the weekend.
6 _____ it? It's only £2.
7 _____ in front of the theatre?
About two hundred people are in front of the theatre.
8 A: _____ like to drink?
B: I'd like an orange juice, please.

6 Complete the text with one word in each gap.

Jamie Oliver's fourteen 'hero' ingredients

How ¹_____ of the 'super foods' ²_____ you eat?

TV chef Jamie Oliver says that eggs, fish and seaweed are among ³_____ foods to eat if you want to live to a hundred. There ⁴_____ also some unusual ingredients like goat's milk, tofu and black beans. Mr Oliver wants to start ⁵_____ new programme to encourage people to make changes to their lifestyle. For the programme Mr Oliver visits a ⁶_____ of places around the world where people ⁷_____ long lives, including Costa Rica, Japan and Ikaria in Greece. He wants to find ⁸_____ food secrets to help people live to a hundred. The TV star also suggests eating meat only twice ⁹_____ week. ¹⁰_____ of the other kinds of food on the list include fresh fruit, garlic, prawns and wild rice.

3.2 Present Continuous

1 Complete the sentences with the correct form of the verbs in brackets.

1 What is that noise? I _____ (try) to study and I can't concentrate on my work.
2 A: Why _____ (you/take) a taxi?
   B: Because I don't want to drive. It _____ (get) dark.
3 Melissa _____ (talk) to her friend on the phone right now.
4 Don't forget to take your umbrella. It _____ (rain).
5 I'm sorry I can't understand what you _____ (say).

3.5 Present Simple and Present Continuous

2 Complete the sentences with the Present Simple or the Present Continuous form of the verbs from the box.

enjoy   forget   go   have   jump   not want

1 Do you think the kids _____ the party?
2 Brenda _____ (always) her purse.
3 She _____ lunch in the school canteen every day. But today she _____ to the new sushi restaurant with Pete.
4 Look! Steve _____ into the water.
5 Jim _____ to go to the theatre tonight.

3 Use the words to write sentences. Use the Present Simple or the Present Continuous.

1 he / usually / work / at the office, but this week he / stay / at home
_____
_____

2 They / not / know / a word of Italian!
_____
_____

3 I / study / Arabic this year. / It / be / very difficult.
_____
_____

4 How often / he / wash / his car?
_____
_____

5 She / speak / three languages. / Right now / she / speak / Chinese / on the phone.
_____
_____

6 The sun / shine. / It / be / a beautiful day!
_____
_____

Summative Practice Unit 3

4 Complete the sentences with the words and phrases from the box.

a   an   are   aren't   doesn't   how many
how much   lot   is   many

1 She _____ know what to say.
2 When _____ you leaving for New York?
3 There _____ any spoons on the table.
4 She needs _____ holiday.
5 _____ vinegar do you usually put in the salad?
6 There are a _____ of policemen in front of the station.
7 _____ people are coming to the party?
8 What _____ happening?
9 Do you have _____ umbrella with you?
10 There aren't _____ dishes left to wash.

5 Read the answers and complete the questions.

1 When _____ ?
   I usually do my homework before dinner.
2 Where _____ ?
   She's taking the dog to the vet's.
3 How often _____ ?
   They have dinner out once or twice a week.
4 Where _____ ?
   I'm studying in the UK this year.
5 How much _____ ?
   Not much. I don't like coffee.
6 How many _____ ?
   I usually drink two cups of tea a day.
7 Who _____ ?
   Jeff and Sam are meeting their friends in the afternoon.

6 Choose the correct option.

The pressure of exams means not [1]*many / much / some* young people [2]*now take / aren't taking / are now taking* on Saturday jobs. Among 16- and 17-year-olds only one in five has [3]*the / a / some* part-time job while studying. It seems that [4]*the / a / –* young people don't like the idea of working while studying. But this is wrong. Millions of young people don't have the experience of the world of work that can help them find [5]*a work / the jobs / jobs* in the future. Annabel, 17, [6]*is now studying / now studying / now studies* to be a secretary and also has a part-time job in a bar. 'It's hard to find jobs at the moment,' she says. But she thinks it's important for people of her age to try to find [7]*much / many / some* employment while they're studying. Tyler, 16, says 'I'm too lazy to study and work at the same time'. He explains he [8]*spends / is spending / spend* most of his spare time doing sport.

4.2 Comparative and superlative adjectives

1 Complete the sentences with the comparative or superlative form of the adjectives in brackets.

1 My sister is _____ (young) than me.
2 Julie is _____ (bad) than Thomas at Maths.
3 Japanese cars are now _____ (expensive) on the market.
4 Those cakes look much _____ (delicious) than they actually taste.
5 Which is _____ (small) country in the world?
6 I don't think money is _____ (important) thing in life.

2 Find and correct one mistake in each sentence.

1 Greg is the slower runner in the race.
   _____

2 This is the most busy restaurant in town.
   _____
   _____

3 Helen is much more sad than Susan.
   _____
   _____

4 Do you know the name of the older building in London?
   _____
   _____

5 Sarah is the more serious than her brother Daniel.
   _____
   _____

6 They are some of funniest people I know.
   _____
   _____

4.5 have to / don't have to

3 Choose the correct answer, A or B.

1 In my country all men __ do military service. It's obligatory.
   A have to
   B don't have to

2 What time __ leave tomorrow?
   A do we have to
   B have we to

3 __ work at the weekend?
   A Does Sonia has to
   B Does Sonia have to

4 Oh no! Our train leaves in half an hour! We __ run!
   A don't have to
   B have to

5 I __ get up early tomorrow. I can stay in bed.
   A have to
   B don't have to

6 Greg __ work on Sunday, so he can't come to the seaside with us.
   A has to
   B doesn't have to

Summative Practice Unit 4

4 Complete the sentences with one word in each gap.

1 Where _____ Harry usually study for his exams?
2 'How _____ do you go swimming?' 'Twice a week.'
3 There aren't _____ chairs left. I'm sorry!
4 Lucy is at home today. She's not _____ very well.
5 These days I'm _____ part-time as a sports instructor.
6 You don't _____ to do it if you don't want to.

5 Choose the correct answers A–C.

1 What __ on New Year's Eve in your country?
   A does people do
   B people do
   C do people do

2 I __ go. The flight to Dubai leaves at 2.30.
   A has to
   B have to
   C haven't to

3 She goes to see her mother __ .
   A all days
   B every day
   C every days

4 He __ late for work.
   A is ever
   B isn't never
   C is never

5 __ tables do we need for the party?
   A How much
   B How many
   C How

6 You __ have a visa to come to Italy.
   A don't have to
   B haven't to
   C have not

7 Is there __ pepper in the soup?
   A many
   B some
   C any

8 Your tablet is __ expensive than my tablet.
   A most
   B more
   C the more

9 What __ about?
   A do you think
   B are you thinking
   C you think

10 It is not free, we __ pay.
   A don't have to
   B have to
   C do we have to

6 Complete the text with the words from the box. There is one extra word.

always   any   biggest   have   many (x2)
more   wants

HOW TO FIND A JOB IN FASHION

These days, it seems like everyone [1]_____ to work in fashion. But it's much [2]_____ difficult than you can imagine. Looking nice on a street-style blog is not enough. Listen to some of the [3]_____ names in the fashion world and you can see what it really takes to get this dream job.
Fern Mallis, Fashion Executive, says that you [4]_____ to know about everything that goes on in the industry and go to as [5]_____ events as possible – especially if you're in NYC, where they are free. It's [6]_____ good to meet someone you'd like to work with face to face. You'd be surprised how [7]_____ people are open about giving their business cards and following up!

5.2 must/mustn't, should/shouldn't

1 Complete the sentences with the verbs and phrases from the box.

> don't have to   must   mustn't   should   shouldn't

1 Plants _____ have light and water to grow.
2 We _____ talk about it. It's top secret.
3 You _____ listen to her because she doesn't know anything about that.
4 The situation is really complicated and I think he _____ ask a lawyer.
5 You _____ come if you don't want to.

2 Complete the sentences with must/mustn't, (don't/doesn't) have to.

1 I can stay in bed tomorrow morning because I _____ work.
2 Whatever you do, you _____ touch that switch. It's very dangerous.
3 My mother is a surgeon. Sometimes she _____ work at weekends.
4 We _____ leave yet. We've got plenty of time.
5 The windows aren't dirty. You _____ clean them.
6 In many countries men _____ do military service.
7 You _____ buy a calculator. You can use this.
8 This train doesn't go to London. You _____ change at Cambridge.

5.5 Past Simple: was/were, could

3 Match questions 1–5 with answers a–e.

1 Could your brother play the piano when he was six? ☐
2 Was your granddad a good student? ☐
3 What were you good at when you were ten? ☐
4 Could you speak English well when you were four? ☐
5 Were Alex and Jo friends at primary school? ☐

a I was really good at languages.
b No, he couldn't.
c Yes, he was.
d No, they weren't.
e Yes, I could.

4 Complete the sentences with was/wasn't, were/weren't or could.

1 At the time, there _____ any traffic lights.
2 At the age of six she _____ much fatter than now. Look how slim she is!
3 _____ you swim when you were a child?
4 Anna _____ very well last night and left the party early.
5 She is twenty now, so last year she _____ nineteen.
6 After the trip we _____ very tired.
7 _____ it difficult to find?
8 My sister _____ ski very well by the age of eleven.

5 Choose the correct option.

1 Where *should they / they should* have the meeting?
2 You *shouldn't / should* make brave decisions now that you are young. Don't wait till you grow *older / the oldest* – people often become more careful and less flexible with age.
3 How *know you / do you know* Jackie is not well? She *were / was* at school yesterday.
4 How *many / much* of you have your projects ready?
5 *Can you / Could you* scuba dive when you were fifteen years old?
6 You *don't have to / mustn't* use a mobile phone in the classroom. You have to switch it off.
7 How often *Sue invites / does Sue invite* her best friend to the cinema?
8 Zoe and Larry *was / were* late for the Art lesson again.
9 Let me give you *some / any* advice: always try to be punctual!
10 We *don't wear / aren't wearing* school uniforms on Fridays. We can wear what we want on this day.
11 *Do / Does* Frank have a good sense of humour?
12 Dad, *is / are* there any milk in the fridge?

6 Complete the sentences with one word in each gap.

1 You _____ forget your homework tomorrow because Mr Ryan will be angry.
2 If you still have a headache, I think you _____ see a doctor.
3 The signs were only in Japanese, so we _____ read them.
4 During the exam you _____ do exactly what the teacher tells you.
5 'Education is the _____ powerful weapon you can use to change the world.' (Nelson Mandela)

7 Choose the correct option.

Schoolchildren in the UK

British schoolchildren are [1]*some / any / the* of the [2]*more / most / very* unhappy and stressed in [3]*the / a / –* Western world, a recent survey shows. Experts say that schoolchildren in the UK spend [4]*a lot of / more / few* time in front of televisions, games consoles and the Internet instead of playing outside. Childcare experts [5]*saying / is saying / say* British children eat more junk food and have poorer diets [6]*but / than / of* kids in other countries.

6.2 Past Simple

1 Complete the email with the Past Simple of the verbs in brackets.

Dear Susie,
I'm having a great time. Last Saturday night we
¹_____ (go) to the new Games Arcade with some
friends. We ²_____ (want) to go by bus but we
³_____ (be) very late so we ⁴_____ (take) a taxi
and ⁵_____ (get) there easily and on time.
We also ⁶_____ (have) dinner there.
We ⁷_____ (find) our seats in the main restaurant
and ⁸_____ (order) some seafood. Then we
⁹_____ (begin) to play. We really ¹⁰_____ (enjoy)
every minute of the evening. Everything ¹¹_____ (be)
so much fun and we ¹²_____ (laugh) a lot! What a night!
Love,
Kris

2 Complete the sentences with the Past Simple form of the verbs in the box.

lose   not catch   not sleep   carry   feel   meet

1 I _____ your brother yesterday. He was with his teammates.
2 He _____ a big bag to the car.
3 The police _____ the thief.
4 She _____ the key to her flat.
5 I _____ very well last night.
6 He _____ exhausted after the show.

6.5 Past Simple negatives and questions

3 Read the answers and ask correct questions.

1 _____?
   I got there at 5 o'clock.
2 _____?
   No, unfortunately they didn't win the match.
3 _____?
   He played football when he was at school.
4 _____?
   Yes, I locked the front door.
5 _____?
   For lunch? Just a sandwich.

4 Complete the sentences with the correct verbs. Use Past Simple negatives of the verbs from the box.

come   eat   like   sleep   write

1 A: George. Where is my apple pie?
   B: Don't look at me like this. I _____ it!
2 A: What's wrong, Kathy? You look tired.
   B: Oh, I _____ all night, but I'll be OK.
3 A: Did you actually meet Sarah at the lecture?
   B: No, I didn't. She _____ .
4 A: Did you see Black Panther? What did you think?
   B: Yes, did. I _____ it.
5 A: Josh, can your read your essay, please?
   B: Sorry, miss, I _____ it.

5 Choose the correct option.

Roger Federer has the highest number of major titles in the history of men's tennis. Federer ¹*begins / is beginning / began* playing tennis at a very early age and quickly showed ²*the / – / a* signs that he had ³*a lot of / many / any* talent. He is one of the ⁴*greatest / greater / great* players of all time and continues to be among the world's ⁵*better / good / best* players. He still ⁶*holds / held / hold* the record for seventeen major singles title wins.
In 2009 Federer ⁷*marry / married / is marrying* Mirka Vavrinec, a former professional tennis player. Do they have ⁸*some / a / any* children? Yes, they ⁹*do / did / have*. They have four children. Federer's family lives in Bottmingen, Switzerland.
In 2003, Federer established the Roger Federer Foundation. It helps ¹⁰*the poor countries / the poor country / poor countries* with high child mortality rates by sponsoring education and sports related projects.

6 Read the text in Exercise 5 again and ask questions for the answers.

1 _____ ? At a very early age.
2 _____ ? Mirka Vavrinec.
3 _____ ? Four.
4 _____ ? In Bottmingen, Switzerland.
5 _____ ? In 2003.

7 Complete the sentences with the correct form of the verbs in brackets: the Present Simple, the Present Continuous or the Past Simple.

1 Mike _____ (talk) to John on the phone last night.
2 Sarah _____ (talk) to Ellen on the phone right now.
3 Ed _____ (talk) to Adam on the phone every day.
4 Sue _____ (write) a letter to her parents yesterday.
5 Alice _____ (write) a letter to her parents every week.
6 Liz is in her room at the moment. She _____ (sit) at her desk. She _____ (write) a letter to her boyfriend.
7 My father _____ (come) home around five every day. Yesterday he _____ (come) home after six.
8 George usually _____ (sit) at the back of the room, but yesterday he _____ (sit) in the front row.
9 Today Alan _____ (be) absent. He _____ (be) absent two days ago too.

7.2 Present Perfect with *ever/never*

1 Complete the sentences with *ever* or *never* and the verbs in brackets.

1 _____ (you/be) to New York?
2 I don't know this story very well because I _____ (see) the film.
3 Do you know Picasso's early paintings? Picasso? I _____ (hear) of him.
4 _____ (Diana/tell) you that she's got a boyfriend?
5 This is the best lunch I _____ (have).
6 John _____ (apologise) to me for what he did.

7.5 Present Perfect + *just/yet/already*

2 Complete the dialogues with *just*, *yet* or *already*.

1 A: Have you been to Canada _____ ?
   B: Yes, I've _____ visited it three times.
2 A: Has Meg read *The Lord of the Rings* for tomorrow?
   B: No, she hasn't even bought it _____ .
3 A: Have you made the reservation _____ ?
   B: No, but I have _____ found a special offer. Just look.
4 A: Have you heard the news about the volcano eruption?
   B: Yes, I've _____ read about it in a newspaper.
5 A: You have wonderful suntan. Where have you been?
   B: Oh, I've _____ come back from Bali.
6 A: Have you booked the tickets for *Mamma Mia* _____ ?
   B: I'm afraid all the tickets for the next two weeks have _____ been sold.

Summative Practice   Unit 7

3 Choose the correct options A–D.

1 Shakespeare __ many plays, such as *Othello* and *Romeo and Juliet*.
   A is writing   C has wrote
   B wrote   D has written
2 Mum __ cooking.
   A did already start   C has already started
   B already started   D was already started
3 __ Thai food?
   A Have you ever tried   C Did you ever tried
   B Do you try   D Have you ever try
4 Frank __ to the mountains last weekend.
   A goes   C has been
   B has gone   D went
5 __ Boston when you were in the USA?
   A Have you visited   C Do you visit
   B Are you visiting   D Did you visit
6 We __ three Maths teachers so far.
   A did have   C are having
   B have had   D have

7 __ your homework yet?
   A Are you done   C Are you doing
   B Did you do   D Have you done
8 When __ ?
   A did John Lennon die   C is John Lennon die
   B has John Lennon died   D has John Lennon die
9 Last year I __ my birthday with a big party.
   A hasn't celebrated   C didn't celebrated
   B celebrated not   D didn't celebrate
10 He __ at least five Christmas cards yesterday.
   A receive   C has received
   B received   D didn't received
11 'Hi, Bob! You are as brown as a berry!'
   'Yes, I __ on a cruise.'
   A have been   C has been
   B went   D have gone

4 Choose the correct option.

Britain's Red Phone Boxes get second life

The United Kingdom's famous red phone boxes are still popular but nobody [1]*used / is using / has used* them for calls for some time now. In 2008, British Telecommunications [2]*began / is beginning / has begun* to sell the boxes for £1. They [3]*are selling / sell / have already sold* more than 2,500. In 2014, two university students [4]*have turned / turned / are turning* one phone box into a place where people [5]*could / should / have to* charge their mobile phone using solar energy in London. It was very successful and the inventors [6]*are often receiving / often receive / has received* letters and emails from people around the world who [7]*want / wants / has wanted* to do the same. But technology isn't the only way these phone boxes are reconnecting with people. Some [8]*became / become / have become* art galleries, coffee shops, defibrillator stations or minilibraries.

5 Complete the text with the correct form of the verbs in brackets.

I [1]_____ (visit) Yosemite last weekend, and I was surprised I [2]_____ (not/can) find any of the famous waterfalls or the mountains reflected in Mirror Lake. The long periods of low rainfall over the last few years [3]_____ (have) an impact on the amount of water in the park. For example, Mirror Lake [4]_____ (now slowly/dry up). During our visit there we [5]_____ (expect) to see some water. But we soon [6]_____ (realise) that it was only a tiny little pond. It [7]_____ (be) impossible to swim in it. This trip really [8]_____ (change) my perspective on water and nature. These days I am [9]_____ (write) and [10]_____ (talk) a lot about this experience. I believe everyone should think about how they [11]_____ (use) water. Everyone, even teenagers and children, can do their part. For example, don't spend a long time taking a shower and don't let the water run while you are [12]_____ (brush) your teeth. Everyone plays a role in saving our planet.

8.2 Future *will*

1 Put the words in the correct order to make sentences.

1 I'm / I will / so / that / a / hungry / have / three-course meal.

_____

_____

2 tomorrow? / the weather / you / what / think / be / do / will / like

_____

_____

3 home / she / arrive / will / late / probably / today.

_____

_____

4 that much / I'm glad / will get / for the house! / you

_____

_____

5 me / with the suitcases? / will / who / help

_____

_____

8.5 *be going to*

2 Complete the sentences with the correct form of *be going to* and the verb in brackets.

1 I'm not very well. I _____ (stay) at home.

2 What _____ (you/do) next summer?

3 I _____ (not/sell) my car. It is still in very good shape.

4 My lawyer _____ (write) a letter of complaint.

5 Sally _____ (not/live) with her parents next year.

3 Complete the sentences with the correct forms of *will* or *be going to*.

1 It's Sandra's birthday next week, so we _____ (buy) her some chocolates.

2 We _____ (have) a barbecue tomorrow. It's all planned, so I hope it _____ (not/rain).

3 A: Nick's starting university tomorrow.
    B: What _____ (study)?

4 Do you think they _____ (like) the books we ordered for them?

5 A: What are your plans for next week?
    B: I _____ (fly) to New York.

6 A: Why are you wearing your best suit?
    B: Because I _____ (have) lunch with an important person.

7 A: Why do you want my suitcase?
    B: Because I _____ (visit) my brother in Ireland next weekend.

Summative Practice   Unit 8

4 Match sentences 1–6 with sentences a–f.

1 They have already made their decision. ⬜
2 My old car has just broken down. ⬜
3 I have just finished work. ⬜
4 My grandpa is going to retire next week. ⬜
5 I haven't read the latest book by Stephen King yet. ⬜
6 Meg's never travelled by plane before. ⬜

a I'm tired and I'm going to go to bed early.
b They are going to move abroad next year.
c He's not going to get up so early in the morning any more.
d She thinks she will fly to Greece this summer.
e I'm going to buy a new one.
f I think I'll do it next week.

5 Choose the correct option.

The University of Georgia's Regenerative Bioscience Center (RBC) [1]*is building / built* a 'frozen zoo'. Scientists hope it [2]*is protecting / will protect* endangered species from extinction. Researchers [3]*used / are using* skin cells from endangered animals, freezing them, and expecting to use them in the future.

Now they [4]*take / are taking* cells from a Sumatran tiger that [5]*died / has died* in 2010. A Florida panther is next. Franklin West, an animal professor leading the project, [6]*has declared / declared* in an interview last month: 'I'm certain that it [7]*works / will work*.' He and the rest of the team [8]*have just decided / just decided* to raise money for the project online. They hope public interest [9]*is coming / will come* as a result.

6 Complete the sentences with the words from the box. There are three extra words.

> every   going   is   most   more
> much   not   than   the   will

How [1]_____ will science change in the future? There are at least four things to say about the next 100 years in science …

⋙ There will be [2]_____ change in the next fifty years of science [3]_____ in the last four hundred years.

⋙ This will be a century of biology. It is [4]_____ area with the most scientists, the [5]_____ new results, the most economic value, the most ethical importance, and the most to learn.

⋙ Computers will keep leading to new ways of science. Information [6]_____ growing by 66 percent per year while physical production by only 7 percent per year.

⋙ New ways of knowing [7]_____ become more popular. 'Wikiscience' is leading to more and more papers with a thousand authors.

WRITING BANK

Accepting suggestions

That sounds fantastic!

I'd love to (go).

Agreeing with an opinion

I (completely) agree that/with …

That's fine with me.

I think so too.

Apologising

Informal phrases

I'm really sorry (that) …

Sorry for any trouble.

Sorry to bother you.

Sorry I didn't write earlier, but I …

Formal phrases

I'm writing to tell you how sorry I am to … (about) …

Closing formulas: emails and letters

Informal phrases

Best wishes

Bye for now/See you!!

Love/Take care!/All the best

Formal phrases

Yours sincerely,

Regards,

Disagreeing with opinions

I disagree that/with … / I don't agree that/with …

I am totally against …

I see your point but …

I'm afraid I can't agree with …

I don't think it's the best solution.

Encouraging participation

Come on, don't be afraid / it's not difficult / it's easy!

Why don't you come and meet some interesting people / see some great things?

Come and tell us what you think.

Come and have fun!

Don't miss it!

Ending emails and letters

Informal phrases

It was good to hear from you.

Email me soon.

Bye for now.

Say hello to …

Give my love/my regards to (everyone at home).

Have a nice (trip).

See you (soon/in the summer).

Write soon.

Keep in touch!

Formal phrases

I look forward to hearing from you/your reply.

I hope to hear from you soon.

Expressing opinions

I believe/think/feel (that) …

I really believe …

In my opinion/view, …

It seems/appears to me (that) …

My opinion is that …

Expressing preferences

I really enjoy/like/love … because …

I prefer … to …

I'd like to … / I hope to …

… is great because …

I don't like… / I can't stand… / I really hate …

It's not really my thing.

Giving advice

You should …

Why don't you …?

Giving good and bad news

Guess what!

I heard that …

Paul has passed his driving test!

Unfortunately, …

I've got some good news.

I'm afraid I've got some bad news.

Inviting

I'd like to invite you to …

I'd like you to come …

Would you like to come to …?

I'm writing to invite you to (Madrid/my party).

I hope you can come/join us/make it.

If you want, you can bring a friend.

Join us today!

Come and meet me …

Why don't you come …?

Maintaining contact

Drop me a line sometime.

I hope to hear from you soon.

Give me a call later.

Let me know if you can make it or not.

I was glad to hear about …

Let me know as soon as possible.

Email or text me and let me know.

WRITING BANK

Making requests and enquiries

Informal phrases

Can you ..., please? / Could you please ...?

Let me know if you can (come).

Could you tell me ...?

Could you do me a favour?

Could you help me?

Do you think you could ...?

Could you also ...?

Formal phrases

Would it be possible for you to ...?

I'd be grateful if you could ...

I'm writing to ask for your help/advice ...

I am writing to inquire about ...

Making suggestions

I think I/you/we should (go to) ...

Perhaps I/you/we could (go to) ...

What do you think about (going to) ...?

What/How about (going to) ...?

How do you feel about ...?

Would you like me to ...?

Why don't we (go) ...?

Let's go to ...

Opening formulas: emails and letters

Informal phrases

Dear Margaret,

Hi Anne,

Formal phrases

Dear Mr and Mrs Edwards,

Dear Ms Brennon,

Refusing suggestions

It doesn't sound very good.

I'm sorry but I can't join you.

I'm not really into ...

Responding to good and bad news

You're joking!

That's good/great/fantastic news!

That's awful/terrible!

I'm really sorry to hear that.

Congratulations!

Starting emails and letters

Informal phrases

It was good to hear from you.

I hope you're doing well/you're fine/you're OK.

How are you (doing)?

How are things? / How's life? / What's your news?

I'm writing to tell you ...

Thank you/Thanks for your letter/email.

I wanted to / I must tell you about ...

I just wanted to ask/remind/thank you ...

Just a quick email to tell you ...

Formal phrases

I am writing to thank you for ...

Telling a story

It all happened some time ago.

It was three years ago.

First, ...

Then, ...

Finally, ...

Suddenly, ...

Unfortunately, ...

Fortunately, ...

It was the best/worst time ever.

We had a great/awful time when we were ...

Thanking

Informal phrases

Thank you for your letter/email.

I'm writing to thank you for ...

Thank you so much.

It was so/really/very kind of you to ...

Thank you for doing me a favour.

Formal phrases

Thank you for sending it back to me.

I am really grateful for your help.

It's very kind of you.

Thank you for your help in this matter.

Unit 1

Exercise 1
1 does she wake up, practises
2 studies
3 listens
4 don't go
5 sleeps
6 says
7 Do you drink
8 do they have
9 is
10 don't drive

Exercise 2
1 d 2 e 3 c 4 b 5 a 6 f

Exercise 3
1 do 2 Has (Sue) got 3 is 4 do, am
5 Have (Mr and Mrs Simpson) got
6 Does 7 Are, am 8 is

Exercise 4
1 are friends and family
2 lives
3 can't
4 children
5 child's
6 their
7 These
8 try to

Exercise 5
1 How are you both?
2 How much do you know about Maria?
3 What is your middle name?
4 Do you like English food?
5 Does your sister help in the garden?
6 Who is Adam's favourite singer?
7 Do you often go out together?
8 How many cousins have you got?

Exercise 6
1 There 2 When 3 Her 4 Don't
5 can't 6 play 7 Does 8 watches

Unit 2

Exercise 1
1f When Joe comes over to my house,
he always brings some cakes with him.
2e There aren't any apples at home.
3g How many tomatoes are there?
4a I know a place with the best food in
town.
5c The bread my mother makes is delicious.
6h There are a lot of windows in our
classroom.
7d There is a lot of wind in this area.
8b Have we got any milk in the fridge?

Exercise 2
1 Her parents' furniture **is** antique.
2 We don't have **any** strawberries.
3 How **much** sugar do you need?
4 I need some **information** about
uncountable nouns.
5 We do **an** hour of work every day.

Exercise 3
1 much 2 a 3 The 4 the 5 some
6 the 7 – 8 – 9 The 10 the

Exercise 4
1 aren't
2 a lot of
3 much
4 many
5 often
6 haven't
7 Do
8 never
9 Does, any
10 doesn't

Exercise 5
1 How much
2 How many
3 How often
4 Where does
5 does he usually do at the
6 How much is
7 How many people are there
8 What would you

Exercise 6
1 many 2 do 3 the 4 are 5 a
6 lot 7 live 8 the 9 a 10 Some

Unit 3

Exercise 1
1 am/'m trying
2 are (you) taking, is/'s getting
3 is/'s talking
4 is/'s raining
5 are/'re saying

Exercise 2
1 are enjoying
2 always forgets
3 has, is going
4 is jumping
5 doesn't want

Exercise 3
1 He usually works at the office, but this
week he is staying at home.
2 They don't know a word of Italian!
3 I'm studying Arabic this year. It is very
difficult.
4 How often does he wash his car?
5 She speaks three languages. Right now,
she's speaking Chinese on the phone.
6 The sun is shining. It's a beautiful day.

Exercise 4
1 doesn't 2 are 3 aren't 4 a 5 How much
6 lot 7 How many 8 is 9 an 10 many

Exercise 5
1 do you usually do your homework
2 is she taking the dog
3 do they have dinner out
4 are you studying (this year)
5 coffee do you drink
6 cups of tea do you usually drink
7 are Jeff and Sam meeting in the
afternoon

Exercise 6
1 many
2 are now taking
3 a
4 –
5 jobs
6 is now studying
7 some
8 spends

Unit 4

Exercise 1
1 younger
2 worse
3 the most expensive
4 more delicious
5 the smallest
6 the most important

Exercise 2
1 Greg is **the slowest** runner in the race.
2 This is **the busiest** restaurant in town.
3 Helen is **much sadder** than Susan.
4 Do you know the name of **the oldest**
building in London?
5 Sarah **is more serious** than her brother
Daniel.
6 They are some of **the funniest** people
I know.

Exercise 3
1 A 2 A 3 B 4 B 5 B 6 A

Exercise 4
1 does
2 often
3 any
4 feeling
5 working
6 have

Exercise 5
1 C 2 B 3 B 4 C 5 B 6 A 7 C
8 B 9 B 10 B

Exercise 6
1 wants
2 more
3 biggest
4 have
5 many
6 always
7 many

Unit 5

Exercise 1
1 must
2 mustn't
3 shouldn't
4 should
5 don't have to

Exercise 2
1 don't have to
2 mustn't
3 has to / must
4 don't have to
5 don't have to
6 have to
7 don't have to
8 have to / must

Exercise 3
1 b 2 c 3 a 4 e 5 d

Exercise 4
1 weren't 2 was 3 Could 4 wasn't
5 was 6 were 7 Was 8 could

Exercise 5
1 should they
2 should, older
3 do you know, was
4 many
5 Could you
6 mustn't
7 does Sue invite
8 were
9 some
10 don't wear
11 Does
12 is

Exercise 6
1 mustn't 2 should 3 couldn't
4 have to / should 5 most

Exercise 7
1 some 2 most 3 the 4 a lot of 5 say
6 than

Unit 6

Exercise 1
1 went
2 wanted
3 were
4 took
5 got
6 had
7 found
8 ordered
9 began
10 enjoyed
11 was
12 laughed

Exercise 2
1 met
2 carried
3 didn't catch
4 lost
5 didn't sleep
6 felt

Exercise 3
1 What time did you get there?
2 Did they win the match?
3 What did he play when he was at school? /
   When did he play football?
4 Did you lock the front door?
5 What did you have/eat for lunch?

Exercise 4
1 didn't eat
2 didn't sleep
3 didn't come
4 didn't like
5 didn't write

Exercise 5
1 began
2 –
3 a lot of
4 greatest
5 best
6 holds
7 married
8 any
9 do
10 poor countries

Exercise 6
1 When did Federer begin playing tennis?
2 Who did he marry (in 2009)?
3 How many children do they have?
4 Where does Federer's family live?
5 When did Federer establish the Roger
   Federer Foundation?

Exercise 7
1 talked
2 is talking
3 talks
4 wrote
5 writes
6 is sitting, is writing
7 comes, came
8 sits, sat
9 is, was

Unit 7

Exercise 1
1 Have you ever been
2 have/'ve never seen
3 have/'ve never heard
4 Has Diana ever told
5 have/'ve ever had
6 has never apologised

Exercise 2
1 yet, already
2 yet
3 yet, already/just
4 just/already
5 just
6 yet, already

Exercise 3
1 B 2 C 3 A 4 D 5 D 6 B 7 D 8 A
9 D 10 B 11 A

Exercise 4
1 has used
2 began
3 have already sold
4 turned
5 could
6 often receive
7 want
8 have become

Exercise 5
1 visited
2 couldn't
3 have had
4 is now slowly drying up
5 expected
6 realised
7 was
8 changed
9 writing
10 talking
11 use
12 brushing

Unit 8

Exercise 1
1 I'm so hungry that I will have a three-
   course meal.
2 What do you think the weather will be
   like tomorrow?
3 She will probably arrive home late today.
4 I'm glad you will get that much for the
   house!
5 Who will help me with the suitcases?

Exercise 2
1 am going to stay
2 are you going to do
3 am not going to sell
4 is going to write
5 is not going to live

Exercise 3
1 are going to buy
2 are going to have, won't rain
3 is he going to study
4 will like
5 'm going to fly
6 'm going to have
7 'm going to visit

Exercise 4
1 b 2 e 3 a 4 c 5 f 6 d

Exercise 5
1 is building
2 will protect
3 are using
4 are taking
5 died
6 declared
7 will work
8 have just decided
9 will come

Exercise 6
1 much
2 more
3 than
4 the
5 most
6 is
7 will

1.9 Self-check

Vocabulary and Grammar

Exercise 1
1 F 2 D 3 B 4 H 5 A

Exercise 2
1 On 2 at 3 on 4 in 5 at

Exercise 3
1 get 2 look 3 go 4 have 5 go

Exercise 4
1 We are always tired after school.
2 My brother doesn't like reading books. He prefers video games.
3 Mike never has lunch at school. He is always hungry by 3.30 p.m.
4 Erin doesn't watch television very often. She thinks it's boring.
5 What kind of music do you listen to when you want to relax?

Exercise 5
1 What sports does your best friend play?
2 What is your cousin's favourite film?
3 What does your father eat for breakfast?
4 What time do your sisters get up on Saturdays?
5 How often do you go to discos?

Exercise 6
1 B 2 A 3 B 4 A 5 C

Use of English

Exercise 7
1 A 2 C 3 C 4 B 5 B

Exercise 8
1 C 2 A 3 B 4 B 5 C

Exercise 9
1 What kind of books do you like?
2 I spend time with my family.
3 I can't stand it!
4 I don't want to get up today.
5 She stays at home and watches TV.

Exercise 10
1 have a good time
2 go for a run
3 looks after
4 get dressed
5 goes to bed/to sleep

2.9 Self-check

Vocabulary and Grammar

Exercise 1
1 can 2 packet 3 onions 4 cheese
5 bar

Exercise 2
1 bag 2 bottle 3 carton 4 jar 5 packet

Exercise 3
1 spicy
2 fry
3 local
4 slice
5 delicious

Exercise 4
Conversation 1: a lot
Conversation 2: a Are there any
               b there is some/ we have some
Conversation 3: a Is there any
               b not much

Exercise 5
1 An 2 the 3 a 4 – 5 the

Exercise 6
1 B 2 A 3 A 4 C 5 A

Use of English

Exercise 7
1 A 2 C 3 A 4 C 5 B

Exercise 8
1 Are you ready to order?
2 Let's get a takeway tonight.
3 I usually make a snack.
4 What would you like to drink?
5 How much is it?

Exercise 9
1 A 2 C 3 A 4 B 5 C

Exercise 10
1 A 2 C 3 A 4 B 5 C

3.9 Self-check

Vocabulary and Grammar

Exercise 1
1 architect
2 journalist
3 mechanic
4 soldier
5 waitress

Exercise 2
1 lawyer
2 receptionist
3 assistant
4 accountant
5 scientist

Exercise 3
1 badly-paid 2 part-time 3 in 4 with 5 why

Exercise 4
Conversation 1: Are you making
Conversation 2: a I'm not working
               b is getting
Conversation 3: a is Seth sitting
               b 's having

Exercise 5
1 He's working 2 He loves
3 He doesn't want 4 He writes
5 I'm dreaming

Exercise 6
1 B 2 C 3 A 4 B 5 A

Use of English

Exercise 7
1 Could you do me a favour?
2 There's a hospital on the right.
3 Would you like to work on a new project?
4 I am sorry to bother you.
5 Grandpa Joe is in the background.

Exercise 8
1 C 2 B 3 A 4 C 5 A

Exercise 9
1 C 2 B 3 A 4 C 5 B

Exercise 10
1 works from home
2 well-paid job
3 are learning French with
4 earns his living
5 works long hours

4.9 Self-check

Vocabulary and Grammar

Exercise 1
1 middle-aged 2 tall 3 quite
4 slim 5 dark

Exercise 2
1 cheerful 2 shy 3 tracksuit
4 scarf 5 socks

Exercise 3 – Sample answers
1 Lionel Messi is more energetic than Serena Williams AND Cristiano Ronaldo is the most energetic.
2 Chris Rock is funnier than Adam Sandler AND Will Ferrell is the funniest.
3 Taylor Swift is more creative than Katy Perry AND Angelina Jolie is the most creative.
4 Queen Elizabeth is more relaxed than Oprah Winfrey AND Madonna is the most relaxed.
5 Daniel Day-Lewis is more unsociable than Hugh Laurie.

Exercise 4
1 more energetic
2 friendlier
3 the cleverest
4 the best
5 less negative

Exercise 5
1 I have to get up
2 my sister has to catch
3 I have to drive
4 You don't have to take
5 does she have to leave

Exercise 6
1 B 2 A 3 A 4 B 5 B

Use of English

Exercise 7
1 C 2 A 3 B 4 A 5 A

Exercise 8
1 C 2 B 3 B 4 C 5 B

Exercise 9
1 B 2 C 3 A 4 B 5 A

Exercise 10
1 don't have to go
2 has got big, brown
3 less funny than
4 has to get/ask
5 are going on

5.9 Self-check

Vocabulary and Grammar

Exercise 1
1 nursery
2 university
3 kindergarten
4 playgroup
5 state

Exercise 2
1 late 2 classes 3 single-sex
4 mixed 5 education

Exercise 3
1 do
2 miss
3 do
4 revised
5 fail

Exercise 4
1 should
2 couldn't
3 don't have to
4 shouldn't
5 have to

Exercise 5
1 were 2 weren't 3 could
4 couldn't 5 wasn't

Exercise 6
1 C 2 A 3 C 4 B 5 A

Use of English

Exercise 7
1 B 2 C 3 A 4 B 5 C

Exercise 8
1 are having a meeting/discussion
2 write because
3 can you leave school
4 is giving a speech
5 do a course

Exercise 9
1 She's ten and she goes to primary school. secondary
2 Can you take part in lots of activities? have
3 I can't put up this tent. take
4 I want to improve my skills in Spanish. from
5 You can find him in the staff room. hall

Exercise 10
1 A 2 B 3 C 4 B 5 B

6.9 Self-check

Vocabulary and Grammar

Exercise 1
1 do 2 go 3 take 4 play
5 keep (stay / be)

Exercise 2
1 cycling
2 skiers
3 joggers
4 sailor
5 swam

Exercise 3
1 ran 2 played 3 had 4 went 5 ate

Exercise 4
1 a What did you do last night?
  b I met my friends.
  c We saw a film, ate burgers and had a good time.
2 a Did you play any sports at school last week?
  b No, I (we) didn't. We had exams all week.

Exercise 5
1 enjoy 2 stand 3 into 4 really 5 care

Exercise 6
1 A 2 B 3 C 4 B 5 C

Use of English

Exercise 7
1 C 2 A 3 B 4 A 5 C

Exercise 8
1 can't stand 2 Make sure you see / Be sure to see 3 I'm not into
4 don't care about 5 go skiing

Exercise 9
1 I like surfing in Hawaii. going
2 Do you play for a team? at
3 Do you want to join a class with me? match
4 He won a judo competition. lost
5 I went ice skating in the park. did

Exercise 10
1 C 2 B 3 C 4 A 5 B

7.9 Self-check

Vocabulary and Grammar

Exercise 1
1 with by 2 signs sights 3 arrangements excursions 4 fly flight 5 young youth

Exercise 2
1 flight 2 guesthouse 3 ferry
4 youth hostel 5 backpacking

Exercise 3
1 platform
2 passengers
3 campsite
4 underground
5 luggage

Exercise 4
1 Have you looked at the departure board yet
2 hasn't left Spain yet
3 She's just given
4 I haven't had breakfast yet
5 We've already booked

Exercise 5
1 I have 2 did you go 3 We went
4 Did you enjoy 5 We slept

Exercise 6
1 to 2 ever 3 yet 4 already 5 bought

Use of English

Exercise 7
1 B 2 A 3 B 4 C 5 A

Exercise 8
1 Have you ever been to France? in
2 I have already bought them. yet
3 Did you travel to Germany by car? in
4 I want to go on a package tour. trip
5 I want to visit the museums. go

Exercise 9
1 B 2 C 3 A 4 C 5 A

Exercise 10
1 A 2 C 3 A 4 B 5 C

8.9 Self-check

Vocabulary and Grammar

Exercise 1
1 elephants 2 river 3 island
4 sharks 5 continent

Exercise 2
1 cloud 2 dolphins 3 whales
4 foggy 5 dangerous

Exercise 3
1 G 2 A 3 E 4 F 5 C

Exercise 4
1 I'm not going to travel by plane this summer.
2 Is Miranda going to get a job next year?
3 Will it be sunny this weekend?
4 We're going to finish our project tonight.
5 There won't be any cars in 2049.

Exercise 5
1 will they live
2 m going to join
3 aren't going to join
4 isn't going to drive
5 are you going to do

Exercise 6
1 attack
2 evolution
3 poisonous
4 dangerous
5 attackers

Use of English

Exercise 7
1 B 2 C 3 A 4 B 5 C

Exercise 8
1 I hope we will have clear skies tomorrow. clouds
2 I think so too. to
3 Some people don't believe that climate change is a problem. weather
4 What's the weather forecast for the weekend? how's
5 To be honest, I don't think so. right

Exercise 9
1 western
2 dangerous
3 foggy
4 poisonous
5 intelligence

Exercise 10
1 A 2 B 3 B 4 A 5 C

Pearson Education Limited
KAO Two
KAO Park
Hockham Way,
Harlow, Essex,
CM17 9SR England
and Associated Companies throughout the world.

www.english.com/focus

Focus 1 Second Edition Workbook

First published 2020
Sixteenth impression 2025

ISBN: 978-1-292-23384-0

Set in Avenir LT Pro
Printed in Slovakia by Neografia

Acknowledgements

The publishers and authors would like to thank the following
people and institutions for their feedback and comments during
the development of the material:

Humberto Santos Duran
Anna Maria Grochowska
Beata Gruszczyńska
Inga Lande
Magdalena Loska
Barbara Madej
Rosa Maria Maldonado
Juliana Queiroz Pereira
Tomasz Siuta
Elżbieta Śliwa
Katarzyna Ślusarczyk
Katarzyna Tobolska
Renata Tomaka-Pasternak
Beata Trapnell
Aleksandra Zakrzewska
Beata Zygadlewicz-Kocuś

Images

Illustrations